Survivors:
An Oral History
of the
Armenian Genocide

Donald E. Miller
Lorna Touryan Miller

University of California Press
Berkeley • Los Angeles • London

University of California Press
Berkeley and Los Angeles, California

University of California Press, Ltd.
London, England

First Paperback Printing 1999

Library of Congress Cataloging-in-Publication Data

Miller, Donald E. (Donald Earl), 1946–
    Survivors : an oral history of the Armenian genocide / Donald E.
Miller, Lorna Touryan Miller.
      p. cm.
    Includes bibliographical references and index.
    ISBN-13 978-0-520-21956-4 (pbk : alk. paper)
    1. Armenian massacres, 1915–1923—Personal narratives.   2. Oral
history.   I. Miller, Lorna Touryan.   II. Title.
DS195.5.M53   1993
956.6'2015—dc20   92-18439
                                            CIP

Printed in the United States of America

08   07   06
11   10   9 8 7 6

The paper used in this publication meets the minimum requirements of
ANSI/NISO Z39.48-1992 (R 1997) (*Permanence of Paper*). ∞

Survivors

To Vahram and Adelina Touryan

and the one hundred survivors
who shared their stories with us

Contents

PART III: ANALYSIS

Illustrations

Acknowledgments

During the years that we have been working on this project we have incurred many debts of gratitude. From the beginning of our research, Professor Richard Hovannisian has been highly supportive of the project. Not only did Lorna profit from the two courses she took with him, but he has also invited us to present papers and to particpate in panels at a number of conferences, including several annual meetings of the Middle East Studies Association and a rather remarkable conference in Yerevan, Armenia, in 1990. In these meetings and other scholarly settings, we have met a number of people whose friendships and insights we value, including Robert Melson, Roger W. Smith, Ronald Suny, Vahakn N. Dadrian, Israel Charny, Salpi Ghazarian, Vigen Guroian, Christopher J. Walker, Gerard J. Libaridian, Frank Chalk, Richard Dekmejian, Leo Kuper, Eliz Sanasarian, and Kevork B. Bardakjian, to name only a few. We are also grateful for the critiques and thorough reading of earlier drafts of the manuscript by Roger W. Smith, Rainer Baum, Barry Jay Seltser, and Richard Hovannisian. Lynne Withey, Assistant Director of the University of California Press, offered formative advice after reading the first draft of the manuscript, and she has been a wonderful source of continuing support and editorial assistance. We are also extremely appreciative of the financial support of both the A.G.B.U. Alex Manoogian Cultural Fund and The Mildred A. Richardson Trust, whose assistance came at a critical period in our research and enabled Lorna to complete the time-consuming task of translation and transcription. Also, we are grateful for a grant from the USC

Faculty Research and Innovation Fund, which supplied us with a computer, thus greatly facilitating the transcriptions. In addition, I appreciate the strong support offered by my colleagues in the School of Religion, and especially John Orr, who commented on an earlier draft of chapter 5. Our greatest debt of gratitude, however, is to the one hundred survivors who invited us into their homes. In small part, we hope that this book repays the trust that they expressed to us by sharing the often painful details of their lives.

Donald E. Miller

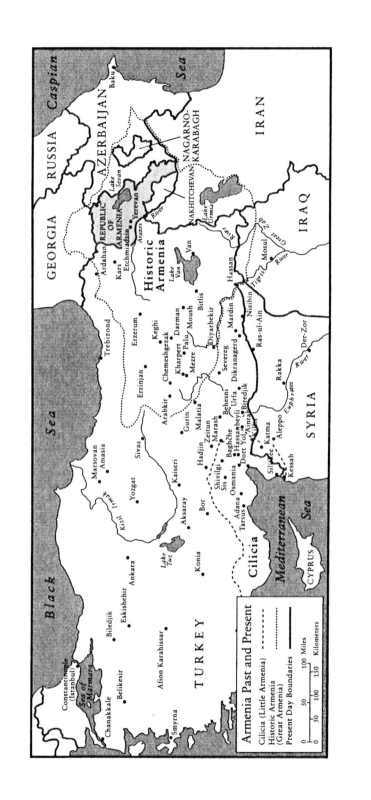

Armenia Past and Present

Cilicia (Little Armenia) – – – – –

Historic Armenia (Great Armenia) ·············

Present Day Boundaries ———

0   50   100 Miles

0   50   100   150 Kilometers

Introduction

In 1974, when our first child, Shont, was a year old, his Armenian grandfather lay ill in the hospital. We feared that our son might never hear the stories of "Medz Hairig," especially about his childhood in Turkey and how he and a sister had survived a genocide that claimed the lives of seven family members and over one million fellow Armenians. So when Medz Hairig returned from the hospital, we invited both grandparents to our home for coffee and dessert, and once a week, for a period of seven weeks, he told his story while our tape recorder sat unobtrusively on the table. Many of the humorous incidents he recounted had already been shared during the "Sunday feast," a weekly ritual that Medz Mama presided over during the early years of our marriage. But neither of us had ever heard a sequential rendering of his life story.

Before meeting Lorna as an undergraduate in college, I, like many Americans, had little knowledge of Armenians. From my childhood I remembered references to the "starving Armenians," but I knew nothing of the genocide of 1915, nor could I have located Armenia at the crossroads between Turkey and what, until recently, was the Soviet Union. Hence, although it was disconcerting at the time, in retrospect I cannot blame Medz Hairig for raising serious objections to his daughter's marrying this blond "odar" (non-Armenian).

However, once Lorna and I were engaged, the real "seduction" began; namely, Medz Hairig started his educational campaign. He was not going to have a son-in-law who did not know his daughter's heritage. And Medz Mama joined the effort by introducing me to eggplant cooked in olive oil, sarma, dolma, pilaf, keufté, and a host of other Armenian delicacies. Perhaps it is unfair to say that my father-in-law engaged in an *intentional* program of education. Actually, I think he could not help talking about his childhood. The genocide had left an irrepressible memory on him as a young boy of seven or eight in 1915 (like many survivors who had lost their parents, he did not know his exact birth date). And so we spent Sunday afternoons listening to fragments of his story, learning the names of great Armenian political figures, and hearing his outrage against the Turks for denying that a genocide had occurred.

Medz Mama was always in the background during these Sunday luncheon feasts. Her role appeared to be one of keeping the table overflowing with food. Hence, it had never occurred to me that she, too, might have a story to tell. But when we got out the tape recorder again one day in 1977, Adelina told us about the deaths of several of her family members and how she had survived by living in the home of a Turkish family, where her mother had placed her for safekeeping while the rest of the family was deported. When she finished talking, I wondered how she had kept all of these memories hidden from view. My father-in-law obviously dealt with his childhood by talking about his sufferings, but how did Medz Mama cope with a childhood that had left equally deep scars?

A few months after our interview with Medz Mama, we interviewed a family friend who told a deeply moving story of the genocide. That was the turning point, and we launched a project that eventually led to interviewing more than one hundred people, mostly survivors living in the greater Los Angeles area. At the time, we did not realize the immensity of the task. Although I am a sociologist of religion by professional training, I had never been involved in an oral history project. All I knew of oral history was gained from reading Studs Terkel's popular books. I was unaware that there were professional journals and societies, such as the Oral History Association. I was also unprepared for the amount of work that would be involved in translating and transcribing tapes—a task that Lorna heroically undertook while raising our two small children.

Indeed, I think that in the early years, Lorna's commitment to the project was stronger than mine. Later, she would talk about it as the "blood call": an irresistible force demanding that she confront the history of her people. Documenting the experience of survivors was her way of coping with the injustice of the genocide. But there were also more subtle motives, largely unarticulated at the time. It was a way of understanding her father: a man of deep moral commitment and a man whose tears flowed very easily.

Only in retrospect have I begun to understand my own commitment to the project. At the most fundamental level, I think it helped me to break through the superficiality of much in contemporary American life. Every one of our interviews has jolted my moral and spiritual sensitivities. The struggle of survivors with death—and the meaning of life in the face of death—provided a model for pondering the meaning of my own life. Also, in ways that I am still attempting to articulate, this research project has started to realign my thinking about many of the crucial questions that lie at the heart of the humanities.

And I also had a purely personal motive: just as Lorna was trying to understand her father through this project, I was trying to understand my Armenian wife. She is a second-generation survivor, bearing in many subtle ways the burden of her parents' tragic childhoods. Except for the genocide, she would not have been born in Haifa, Israel, nor would she have spent a childhood in Beirut, nor would her family have gone through a wrenching cultural shift by moving to the United States when she was eleven.

But at the time of our initial interviews, neither of us had really examined our interest in this project, beyond the realization that the survivors were growing old and that it was urgent to preserve their stories before they died. In 1978 we began interviewing in earnest, as well as familiarizing ourselves with oral history methodology and other oral history projects on Armenian survivors. I did some of the original interviews, but it soon became clear that survivors felt more comfortable talking about their experiences in their mother tongue. Thus, Lorna conducted the majority of the one hundred interviews, most of which were in Armenian. In preparing for this task, she took two courses at UCLA under Professor Richard Hovannisian: one in oral history methodology and one in Armenian history. Locating survivors to interview proved to be a relatively easy task. Using a "snowball" sampling technique, we started with people in our own neighborhood, and these survivors in turn told us about friends who had survived the genocide, and so the referrals developed.

By 1980, Lorna had done thirty interviews. Meanwhile, I had passed through the tenure and promotion process at the University of Southern California, and we set off for a sabbatical year in Cambridge, England. While Lorna translated and transcribed interviews, I spent my days at the Cambridge University Library reading histories of the genocide and accounts of missionaries, and my evenings analyzing the many pages of transcripts that were emerging from Lorna's portable typewriter. Also, I discovered a major archive of original documents in London and devoted part of my time to reading through the correspondence of British consuls and foreign officers who had been stationed in Turkey at the time of the genocide. With the added pleasures of punting on the Cam River, having dinner at "high table" at Trinity College, and walking our children to school each morning, it was a wonderful year of research and creative reflection.

At the end of this sabbatical, we submitted an article to the *Oral History Review*[1] and returned home with the goal of doing one hundred interviews. This required that we go beyond Pasadena, where we lived, and so Lorna began interviewing in an Armenian home for the elderly as well as venturing into the greater Los Angeles area. Amidst the activity of raising two energetic youngsters, Lorna persisted in the rather lonely task of interviewing. On the days she had done interviews, she spent the dinner hour recounting the survivors' stories she had gathered.

While the accounts of survivors were, for me, the source of despairing questions about the human potential for evil, they were, for Lorna, variations on the recurring theme of the fate of her people. I noticed that she began listening to Mozart's Requiem, over and over again. For her, this project was not an exercise in comparative genocide; it was a form of mourning for her people—her parents' families, her nation. And the more I learned about this first genocide of the twentieth century, the more convinced I became that the story of the Armenian Genocide should be told through the experience of survivors.

This has not been an easy book to write. We continually imagined our own children in the place of the survivor-children we interviewed. And perhaps equally painful is the realization that there are currently many children in the world who are orphaned or who have been discarded by their parents or an uncaring society. They, like the survivors who told us their stories, are wandering in search of a piece of bread and a little human warmth. During this project our emotions have ranged from melancholy to anger, from feeling guilty about our own privileged status to being overwhelmed by the continuing suffering in our world. Working with these interviews over a period of years has led to a permanent loss of innocence about the human capacity for evil—and to a recognition of the need to combat such evil.

Despite this pessimistic assessment of human nature, it is important to state that the survival of many of the subjects we interviewed turned on a single act or two of human kindness. There were "good Turks"— equivalent to the "righteous Gentiles" cited in Holocaust literature—

who hid Armenian children to save them from deportation and who fed, clothed, and sheltered starving urchins they encountered on the deportation routes. There were also heroic parents who, by giving away their food and water, sacrificed their lives so that their children might live. And there were thousands of people in the United States and Europe who gave money to establish orphanages after the war—and more than a few who gave their lives in running these institutions.

We acknowledge that the discovery of something redeeming in these tales of human tragedy has been our defense against despair. We refuse, however, to allow these examples of good to turn our attention from the awful reality of the genocide itself. There is a universal tendency to avoid seeing, as well as remembering, the human capacity for evil. Adolf Hitler understood this well when, on August 22, 1939, he said to his military commanders regarding his plans for Poland: "Who, after all, speaks today of the annihilation of the Armenians?"[2]

We increasingly believe that there is considerable truth in the statement that to deny genocide is to repeat it. Indeed, we would add that to shield ourselves from suffering in this world is to perpetuate it. We need to keep our consciences soft and vulnerable; only then will we rise up to challenge the suffering that surrounds us. Denial of evil is a defense mechanism that a just world simply cannot afford.

The Armenian Genocide was the first major genocide of the twentieth century, but it was certainly not the last. It has been estimated that 60 million people have died in this century alone of state-orchestrated violence.[3] In the public imagination, the Jewish Holocaust is often remembered as the only genocide of the modern age and, therefore, considered to be something of an anomaly. But since World War II, genocide has occurred repeatedly in Africa, Latin America, and Asia.[4] The one way in which the Jewish Holocaust *is* anomalous is that it has not been denied, except by a few revisionists. The same cannot be said of of the Armenian Genocide.

Given the amount of world press coverage of the massacres of Armenians at the time of the deportations, it is difficult to believe that fifty years later the same newspapers, under the pressure of lobbying by the Turkish government, would refer to the genocide of the Armenians as "alleged."[5] But denial seems to be the final stage of most genocides.[6] Denial is motivated, in part, by our own fear of suffering and death, but beyond that, genocide is a moral embarrassment that the perpetrator, as well as the observing world community, often seeks to repress. It is only the victims who struggle with the problem of forgetting.

It is through the eyes of survivors that we tell the story of the Armenian Genocide in the following pages. The first chapter recounts the story of Lorna's father, Vahram. His account is prototypical of the survivors' reminiscences. The second chapter provides historical background on the Armenian people and places the genocide within the political context of the Ottoman Empire. This chapter is intended for those not familiar with Armenian history or the pattern of the genocide. The next four chapters draw directly on our interviews to tell the story of the genocide: the culture that was destroyed (chapter 3), the deportation marches (chapter 4), the experience of women and children (chapter 5), and life in the orphanages (chapter 6). Chapter 7 traces the diaspora of Armenians out of Turkey, focusing on the experience of survivors who settled in the United States. The final two chapters are interpretive rather than descriptive, examining, first, the adult responses of survivors to the trauma of their childhood experience and, ultimately, some moral issues related to the genocide.

PART I

Historical Background

CHAPTER 1

Remembrances of a Forgotten Genocide

Although Vahram was in his middle sixties when we interviewed him, he recalled his childhood in the village of Darman in the district of Keghi in eastern Turkey with the surprising clarity and great fondness characteristic of the one hundred survivors we interviewed. Indeed, many survivors remembered the period before the deportations in nearly idyllic terms. Families were stable, and children were surrounded by an extended family network of grandparents, aunts, uncles, and cousins. Fathers went daily to their shops or fields to work, and mothers spent long hours tending the home and making sarma, dolma, keufté, and bread. In the evenings, the entire famly sat around the *tonir* (a covered fire), with their feet tucked under a communal blanket that drew them into a tight circle of warmth. Survivors remembered going to church and attending festive weddings where they danced and ate, as well as many anecdotes about their schools and family life. They also remembered vines heavy with grapes, apricot trees in their yards, and walking from house to house across adjoining roofs.

Vahram's father was a merchant who traded goods between the Armenians and the neighboring Kurds. The Kurds wanted items from the larger cities, and Vahram's father bartered with them for their goats, sheep, oil, and butter, which he sold to the Armenians in turn. Vahram remembered his father being a rich and influential man in the village who would often travel to Keghi and pay forty gold coins to Turkish officials in order to exempt young Armenian men from military service.

On one of these trips in the spring of 1915, Vahram's father was arrested for no cause other than being a leader in the community. Vahram never saw him again. The family heard that he had been killed, along with other Armenian men who had been arrested at the same time. Coincident with these arrests, the Turks ordered all Armenians to bring their guns to government headquarters. The Armenians presumed that these weapons were to be used in the war effort against the Russians, British, and French. Instead, soon after collecting these weapons, the Turks displayed them publicly and accused the Armenians of treasonous intentions.

Vahram recalled that Turkish soldiers came through his village on their way to the Russian front and that Armenians housed these troops in their churches and homes. But in the midst of this activity came an announcement that all the Armenians of Darman were to be deported. The rationale was that they were too close to the battlefront and would therefore be temporarily relocated. With a week to prepare for the journey, Vahram's mother and other women baked bread, sold disposable goods to secure money for their journey, and packed a few household items to take with them. Because Vahram's family was relatively affluent, they hired several mules to carry their belongings. Vahram's task was to herd two cows so that the family would have a ready supply of milk. At this point, the Armenians of Darman had no idea that deportation was simply another word for annihilation. They believed that they would be temporarily relocated and, in a short time, allowed to return home.

The appointed day arrived and, with the exception of Vahram's father, who had been imprisoned and killed, the family gathered in the street with other Armenians. Vahram recalled mothers with newborn infants, including his own mother, who held little Kenell tightly to her breast, while his three-year-old brother, Papken, attempted to clutch his mother's hand. His older brother's wife nestled baby Zaven in her arms. Side by side, the family walked in a long processional caravan. Even the elderly had been ordered to leave Darman, and Vahram recalled them leaning heavily on their canes as they walked. Escorted by gendarmes, the villagers of Darman spent their first night camped at the outskirts of the village.

On the third day of the journey, Ibosh, the Turkish soldier who led this caravan, told the villagers that they were in danger of being attacked by Kurds and that they should leave all of their possessions behind as an appeasement. They followed his instructions, depositing many of their household articles, and then proceeded into a valley. Suddenly from behind, the Kurds—whom their gifts were to have pacified—attacked them. Vahram remembered everyone in the caravan running in a futile attempt to escape. Only seven or eight years old, Vahram became separated from his family. He fell down, and people were running all around him to avoid the bullets. He finally got up and ran until he found cover next to a large rock. Vahram described what happened next: "Before I could catch my breath, a hefty Kurd appeared before me. He ordered me to take off my clothes and shoes and hand them over to him. I had no choice but to comply. I sat there dazed and shaken, but grateful that my life had been spared."

A few yards away, a group of Kurdish women was playing drums and chanting, apparently cheering on their husbands' plundering of the Armenian caravan. While he sat there, Vahram witnessed a middle-aged Armenian man appear from behind the rock where he had taken cover. Several Kurds rushed toward him, pinned him to the ground, and stabbed him repeatedly. Somehow this large and powerful man managed to break free and, bleeding heavily, started to run. But another Kurd noticed him, took aim with his rifle, and with a single shot, knocked him to the ground.

Bewildered, Vahram looked around for someone he knew and spotted his classmate Armenag. This young boy told him that his whole family had been killed, including his grandfather, who had been protecting him. Uncertain what to do, Vahram suggested that they kneel down and pray, so they said the Lord's Prayer together. Feeling somewhat strengthened, they then got to their feet, and Vahram began searching for his family. On a rock in the middle of a shallow river, he saw an abandoned infant crying. In retrospect, he wondered if the baby had been placed there in an act of mercy or left in a moment of desperation as the child's mother fled the shots of the Kurds.

Vahram finally found the remnants of his family: his mother, who was still clutching baby Kenell to her breast, and his older sister Siroun, who had been wounded in a struggle with two men. The two had attacked her and even though one had stabbed her in the back, she had managed to throw herself off a cliff and into the river below. And an elderly Armenian woman told the family about the fate of Papken: he had been abducted by a Kurd while standing over his grandfather's fallen body. Vahram also saw his uncle, whose right arm had been severed and was hanging loosely against his body.

Reflecting on what had occurred, Vahram said that he felt highly fortunate, since many children had lost their entire family or had been abducted. For example, Vahram had observed a baby being snatched from his mother's arms and a young girl being pulled from the grasp of her mother; he also saw a three-year-old child knocked away from his mother's skirts as she was forcibly taken for what was surely sexual assault. After the Kurdish attack, Vahram and the remnant from Darman regrouped. Reduced in number, the caravan once again moved forward under the "protection" of the supervising gendarmes.

As they walked, the villagers' hopes that the attack would be an isolated occurrence were soon dashed. Vahram said that they began to observe an increasing number of corpses on the roadway and, over the next few days, he witnessed scenes that he would ponder for the rest of his life. For example, he recalled an aunt giving birth to her first child out in the open, without a bed or midwife. The next day the women of the caravan urged her to abandon the infant. Vahram watched her wrap the child in rags, place him in a cave, and walk away. But she had taken only a few steps when she returned to fetch her child.

All the survivors we interviewed had a story to tell of how their lives were spared, and Vahram was no exception. The circumstances of his survival were almost like the plot of a novel: Ibosh, the very gendarme who had orchestrated the Kurdish attack on the caravan was also, ironically, the instrument of his salvation.

It happened that Ibosh was attracted to Siroun, Vahram's older sister, even though she was engaged to be married. In this one-sided love affair, he planned to abduct her to his father's house. So once the caravan was reconstituted, Ibosh placed Siroun—who apparently was very attractive—on his horse. She, in turn, let Vahram and another younger brother, Mardiros, ride with her. In an effort to win Siroun's favor, Ibosh gave special treatment to her whole family. This was fortunate, because by the time the caravan reached Palu, many more deportees had perished: the sick and elderly were left to die along the road, children and attractive women were abducted, and the caravan continued to be plundered, with many survivors left with only the shirts on their backs.

As the caravan entered a fork in the road near Ibosh's home, both Mardiros and Vahram were riding on the horse with their sister, one in front of her and the other behind. The gendarme holding the reins of the horse took Mardiros down and directed him to take the road with his family and the rest of the deportees. At this point, Siroun violently protested and held on to Vahram, refusing to let him go. The gendarme acquiesced and Vahram remained. Thus, Vahram and Siroun were taken in the direction of Ibosh's house, while their mother and the remaining children went down the opposite fork in the road, presumably to their deaths, for they were never seen again.

Ibosh was the son of a wealthy Turkish landowner who lived in the mountains outside of Kharpert. Abandoning the caravan to another gendarme, he took Vahram and Siroun toward his father's house in the mountains. Once they arrived, a local official took Ibosh aside and advised him to get rid of Vahram, as had been done with the other Armenian boys who had passed through the area. But, perhaps out of fear of further alienating his abducted bride, Ibosh appealed to a higher official in the town, explaining that as the son of a noble family and an officer in the Turkish army, he had the right to take Vahram as a servant for his father's household. His request was granted, and so Vahram survived another threat to his life.

When the three arrived at the palace of Bey Haji Rashid, Ibosh was greeted with a warm smile and an embrace from his father. He had been away in the army a long time, and his father welcomed his return. Vahram also remembered his introduction to the bey: "Father, I would like you to meet a maidservant and her brother, a new grandson for you." Surprised by the hospitality implied in this greeting, Siroun and Vahram were taken to the women's quarters of the harem, where they were accepted as part of the family by Ibosh's four sisters and other members of the household. And to his delight, Vahram found his new "grandfather" to be a kind and gentle man:

> The bey followed Islamic law to the letter and was a devout believer. He prayed five times a day and fasted one month out of the year. I used to join him in these [observances]. He had also made a pilgrimage to Mecca and was thus called "Haji." He was a principled and just man. He felt genuine sorrow for the Armenian massacre and considered it a sin to bring any confiscated Armenian possessions into his home. He used to condemn the Turkish government, saying, "The Armenians are a hardy, intelligent, and industrious people. If there are any guilty among them, the government can arrest and punish them instead of slaughtering a helpless and innocent people."

Vahram lived in his "grandfather's" house for more than two years. Conversion to Islam was a prerequisite for being a family member, so Siroun reluctantly recited several times a day: "There is only one God and His prophet is Mohammed." Vahram was circumcised by a religious leader and given the name Abdallah, meaning "the servant of God."

Vahram and Siroun quickly learned Turkish. Food was plentiful in the house, and a genuine human bond developed, especially between Vahram and his Turkish sisters. He became a star pupil in his Turkish school; in fact, his teachers would call on him to recite when visitors came to school. Siroun was less happy. Being older, she felt more keenly her Armenian identity; she also pondered the fate of her mother and siblings and, from a vantage point on the mountain, would watch numerous caravans of deported Armenians below.

However, several incidents that occurred while Vahram lived in this Turkish home continued to ignite his conscience, even in his adult years. One event was the brutal killing of Nevrieh, a young Armenian girl. His Turkish sisters had adopted this beautiful young girl, who had been abducted from one of the Armenian caravans. She had contracted a serious case of dysentery during the deportation journey, and Siroun became her nurse. But Nevrieh got progressively worse until the eldest Turkish sister finally decided that she would not recover and therefore should be killed. A servant was instructed to perform the task. Vahram recalled the servant taking Nevrieh a short distance from the house and then hearing what he described as a "heartrending wail" as the servant clubbed her on the head. This memory festered like an open wound even when we interviewed Vahram sixty years later. Perhaps the memory remained unresolved not simply because of the brutality of Nevrieh's death but also because of Vahram's inability to reconcile his adopted sister's behavior with his respect for her.

Vahram also recounted another event that haunted him as an adult. Two cousins of his Turkish sisters amused themselves by robbing Armenian caravans that passed through the valley below. One of these young boys—perhaps not knowing Vahram was an Armenian orphan— returned from a foray into the valley and described how they had found an Armenian mother with an infant in her arms. The elder cousin, along with some Kurdish friends, killed the mother and then asked the younger Turkish boy if he wanted to kill the baby. This lad told Vahram how he kept striking the infant, but hit as he might, the baby continued to cry and moan, refusing to fall silent.

Vahram also encountered orphans from the caravans who had somehow made their way to his town. Specifically, he recalled a small band of very emaciated Armenian children crying in front of his house. He asked them what was wrong, and they said that they had spent the day gathering a bundle of sticks to sell for a loaf of bread. But an older Turkish boy had stolen the sticks, and now they would go hungry for the day. This greatly angered Vahram, obviously arousing latent feelings of his own Armenian heritage, and he rushed after the thief, gave him a resounding slap, and returned the orphans' bundle to them.

After the defeat of the Turks in October 1918, the widely publicized plight of the "starving Armenians" brought millions of dollars of aid, as well as relief workers and medical personnel, to Turkey from the United States and Europe. Hearing of these developments, Vahram's sister began to plan their escape to a recently established orphanage nearby. The only problem was that Vahram did not want to leave; having lost one family by violence, he was not inclined to voluntarily part from his surrogate family. He had become a Muslim, was the grandson of a wealthy bey, and, furthermore, was first in his class. Why should he leave his comfortable home? More important, Vahram had grown genuinely attached to his Turkish grandfather. He had spent many hours visiting various villages with him and observing him settle accounts with tenant farmers. He had also passed many evenings with him learning the Koran, as well as praying and fasting. Even if he was an Armenian, not a Turk, how could he disappoint his grandfather by running away?

His sister finally resorted to deception, telling Vahram that their mother was still alive and was waiting for him at the orphanage. And so, reluctantly, one night he slipped away with Siroun from the Turkish home to a German orphanage that now was run by Americans. All that Vahram took with him was a Koran clutched in his hand. After they waited at the bolted gate of the orphanage for a while, the night guard finally opened the door to admit two more orphan children to the ranks. Vahram went to the boys' ward, and Siroun to the girls'. The next day, Vahram was quickly nicknamed "the Turk" because he had forgotten his native Armenian tongue and could speak only Turkish.

Several weeks later, a black-veiled woman timidly approached the orphanage. It was Tahireh, one of his older Turkish sisters. Vahram, eavesdropping in a corner, heard her tell Siroun that since they had left, their adoptive home had become a house of mourning. She pleaded with Siroun to return with Vahram. Vahram would have gone gladly, but his sister was firm: she and Vahram would remain with their people.

Some time later, while Vahram was still in the orphanage, he heard the news that his Turkish grandfather had died. He was very saddened and decided to visit his grave, where he fulfilled his duty as a "son," reciting the Yā Sīn—a Turkish rite for the dead. He performed this ritual act not only out of gratitude to a man who had meant much to him but also to "lighten the burden," he said. The years in the Turkish home had been good, in spite of the treatment he had observed of other Armenians. After all, he owed his life to this grandfather, and he felt deeply ambivalent about having abandoned him.

In the orphanage, Vahram relearned Armenian. He also began to read the Bible and eventually rediscovered his own faith. Much of the day was spent in academic or vocational instruction. He remembered food being scarce and monotonous. For breakfast the orphans had lentil soup, at noon only a piece of bread, and in the evening soup again—a soup they all detested, made with dried apricots and cracked wheat. Sunday was special, however, for they had rice pilaf and often some meat. And there was time for romance or, at least, romantic thoughts. The boys were separated from the girls, and with fantasy more powerful than reality, they had endless arguments over whom they would marry.

In 1922, Vahram and his fellow orphans were transported out of Turkey to Syria, under pressure from the Turkish government. From Syria, Vahram was sent to Greece and lived for some time in Corfu, where he continued his education and worked in the orphanage dispensary as a pharmacist. In 1925, he went to Beirut, where he rejoined Siroun, who had become a nurse. But as if life had not been cruel enough, their re-union was tragically short-lived. While working in an orphanage in Antelias, Siroun contracted a severe cold, which turned to pneumonia, and she died a few weeks later. Vahram was heartbroken. Indeed, in our interview he could scarcely talk about this moment in his life, for he was now completely alone in the world, save for a religious faith that was becoming increasingly important to him.

Shortly after our interview with Vahram, he decided to write his story—the text from which we have quoted above. He began writing his reflections on a yellow tablet during a family vacation. At first, the writing seemed to flow easily, and every time we saw him in subsequent months, we would ask, "How is the book coming?" He would tell us that he was still writing. Months later, he was rewriting, and the rewriting seemed to go on and on. Gradually, we realized that he was doing more than writing a life story; he was coming to grips with events that were unresolved.

In some ways, Vahram's experiences were not typical of those under-gone by some other survivors whom we interviewed, because he had been deported for only a few weeks. Many other survivors witnessed hundred of deaths from brutality, dehydration, exposure, starvation, and disease. Nevertheless, Vahram, who had been a very sensitive and bright lad, described a number of events that we heard echoed in other interviews. For example, his father had been imprisoned and ex-ecuted without cause before the deportation marches. The Turks de-manded that the Armenians turn in their weapons, which were then used as evidence of treasonous activity. Armenians were deported from Darman without distinction, including women, children, and old people. The gendarmes conspired with Kurds, who did much of the robbing and massacring.

In addition, Vahram, like many survivor-children, temporarily lost his cultural heritage: he forgot his native language and assumed a new religious identity. For him, as for many other survivors we interviewed, the orphanage was a place to rediscover his cultural roots and to begin healing some of the emotional wounds caused by the genocide. Like thousands of other orphans, Vahram was the beneficiary of aid sent from the United States and various European nations. Thousands of other orphans, however, remained in Turkish homes and were assimilated.

Vahram also shared another characteristic with the others we interviewed. Because of the genocide, he became a person without a country and lived in a number of locations. Born in Turkey in the Ottoman Empire, he was transported as an orphan to Syria, to Greece, and eventually to Beirut. Then, as a young married man, he moved to Palestine. But during the 1948 war, he was forced to leave Jerusalem, and he returned with his family to Beirut. For six months, Vahram, Adelina, and seven children lived with another family in a two-bedroom dwelling in Beirut until they could find more permanent housing. Finally, in 1956, seeking better conditions for his children, Vahram brought the entire family to Pasadena, California, to begin life once again. Altogether, Vahram lived in six different countries, which is not exceptional for many of the survivors we encountered.

Also like many other survivors, Vahram struggled all of his adult life with unreconciled feelings about his childhood experiences. Certain images haunted him inescapably. In particular, he could not forget the Armenian baby being beaten to death for sport by his young Turkish acquaintance. Nor could he rid his mind of the screams of the orphan girl who was ordered to be killed because of her dysentery. And he felt the pain of having left his adoptive Turkish grandfather, whom he loved.

As much as Vahram attempted to reconcile his Christian spirit with the violence he had witnessed in childhood, his anger and outrage simmered just beneath the surface. And he could never adjust to losing his mother, father, and siblings. Yet the Vahram we knew as an adult was a cheerful, tender-hearted, life-affirming man. It was principally at night that the demons visited him. Until the age of eighty-two, when he became too weak from leukemia to get out of bed, he could be found every night, at two or three in the morning, sitting in the living room thinking, praying, and reading his Bible. He would then go back to sleep for a few hours and greet the new day with a strength that belied the struggles of the darkness.

DOCUMENTATION OF THE GENOCIDE

Vahram told us his story more than sixty years after the events he described. Thus, one might legitimately ask whether his memory was accurate. Had he inflated the magnitude of the genocide? Are contemporary representatives of the Republic of Turkey correct when they deny that a genocide occurred? Or is denial by the perpetrator simply the last stage of genocide?

One approach to answering these questions is to examine eyewitness testimony that was collected very close to the time of the events and to compare it with the accounts given by Vahram and the other one hundred survivors we interviewed. In the rest of this chapter, we will cite from several different types of documents: first, reports and letters from the U.S. State Department files, including memoranda from various American consuls; second, a blue book of eyewitness accounts presented in 1916 by Viscount Bryce to the Secretary of State for Foreign Affairs in Great Britain; and, third, other reports and firsthand accounts of the genocide, including German sources such as those collected by Dr. Johannes Lepsius, head of the Deutsche Orient-Mission.

U.S. STATE DEPARTMENT FILES

The archives of a number of countries contain documents describing the genocide of the Armenians, and an extremely useful bibliography of these sources has been compiled by Professor Richard Hovannisian at the University of California, Los Angeles.[1] We will quote from a few of the entries to be found in the United States National Archives, specifically, a file entitled "Internal Affairs of Turkey, 1910–1929," and a subcategory within this file entitled "Race Problems."[2] This latter record group, comprising 520 entries, includes documents from American missionaries, consuls in different parts of Turkey, relief workers, and survivors. Although we will quote from only a few of these sources, they document recurring themes that vary principally in the details of occurrences in particular areas.

Consul J. B. Jackson was stationed in Aleppo, Syria, during the period of the deportations, and in that setting he witnessed thousands of

Armenian refugees arriving from the interior of Turkey. The State Department files contain many statements that he sent to Ambassador Henry Morgenthau in Constantinople (Istanbul) regarding the plight of these deportees. The following is an excerpt from a report he completed on March 4, 1918, after his return to Washington, D.C.:

> Late in July, 1915, when the thermometer registered from 105 to 115 degrees, as a group of more than 1,000 women and children from Harput [Kharpert] was being conducted southward near Veren Chiher, East of Diarbekir, they were turned over to a band of savage Kurds who rode among them, selecting the best looking women, girls and children. Terrified by the fears of their fate should they fall into the hands of such ferocious brutes, the women resisted as best they could, thereby enraging the Kurds, who killed a number of their intended victims. Before carrying off those finally selected and subdued, they stripped most of the remaining women of their clothes, thereby forcing them to continue the rest of their journey in a nude condition. I was told by eye-witnesses to this outrage that over 300 women arrived at Ras-el-Ain, at that time the most easterly station to which the German-Baghdad railway was completed, entirely naked, their hair flowing in the air like wild beasts, and after travelling six days afoot in the burning sun. Most of these persons arrived in Aleppo a few days afterwards, and some of them personally came to the Consulate and exhibited their bodies to me, burned to the color of a green olive, the skin peeling off in great blotches, and many of them carrying gashes on the head and wounds on the body as a result of the terrible beatings inflicted by the Kurds.
>
> One of the most terrible sights ever seen in Aleppo was the arrival early in August, 1915, of some 5,000 terribly emaciated, dirty, ragged and sick women and children, 3,000 on one day and 2,000 the following day. These people were the only survivors of the thrifty and well to do Armenian population of the province of Sivas, carefully estimated to have originally been over 300,000 souls! And what had become of the balance? From the most intelligent of those that miraculously reached Aleppo it was learned that in early Spring the men and the boys over 14 years old had been called to the police stations in the province on different mornings stretching over a period of several weeks, and had been sent off in groups of from 1,000 to 2,000 each, tied together with ropes, and that nothing had ever been heard of them thereafter. Their fate has been recorded by more than one eyewitness, so it is needless to dwell thereon here.[3]

Consul Jackson continues his summary report with numerous accounts of the plight of refugees who arrived in Aleppo, as well as stories recounted to him by eyewitnesses. He tells, for example, of the typhus epidemic that broke out in Aleppo because of the miserable conditions of the deportees:

> The number that succumbed in the city was so great that the sanitary authorities could not cope with the situation, and the military authorities

provided huge ox-carts into which the dead bodies were thrown, 10 or 12 in
each cart, and the procession of 7 or 8 carts would proceed to the nearby
cemetery with their gruesome loads of ghastly uncovered corpses, usually
nude, with the heads, legs and arms dangling from the sides and ends of the
open carts.[4]

Jackson also reports the scenes his relief workers encountered in outlying cities: "At Meskéné they died in such numbers that one of my em-
ployees who was sent there to distribute relief to the sufferers late in
1916 said that he had seen more than 150 long mounds where the dead
had been buried in trenches (dug by the victims themselves) wherein
from 100 to 300 bodies had been buried."[5] The same relief worker also
said that he had "seen many hundreds of skeletons lying strewn along
the highways between Aleppo and Deir-el-Zor [Der-Zor] and Ourfa
[Urfa] at which no effort whatever had been made to bury."[6]

Consul Jackson stated that even the survivors who made it as far as
Aleppo were still not safe. Many deportees were then sent further into
the deserts of Syria. In Der-Zor, for example, Armenian refugees were
attacked "by bands of Turkish, Circassian and Kurdish ex-convicts that
had been liberated from prisons and taken there for that purpose."[7]
Jackson continues: "Aside from less than a hundred that escaped, and
about 250 small children that were left running in the streets of Deir like
dogs, the entire 60,000 Armenians were wiped out within a week."[8]
Jackson's report continues at some length, detailing relief efforts in
which he was involved.

In addition to Jackson's report, this State Department file also contains copies of earlier correspondence between Consul Jackson and Ambassador Morgenthau in Constantinople, as well as correspondence sent
directly to the Secretary of State in Washington, D.C. From these materials Jackson drafted his report. Typical of the entries is the following
account given by a deportee from Kharpert.

On the 52nd day they arrived at another village, here the Kurds took from
them everything that they had, even their shirts and drawers and for five days
the whole caravan walked *all naked* under the scorching sun. For another five
days they did not have a morsel of bread, neither a drop of water. They were
scorched to death by thirst. Hundreds over hundreds fell dead on the way,
their tongues were turned to charcoal and when at the end of the fifth day
they reached a fountain, the whole caravan, naturally, rushed on it, but the
policemen stood in front of them and forbade them to take even a drop of
water, for they wanted to sell the water, from one to three liras the cup, and
sometimes not giving the water, after getting the money. At another place,
where there were some wells, some women threw themselves into it, as there

was no rope and pail to draw water but these were drowned and in spite of that the rest of the people drank from that well, the dead bodies still staying and stinking in it. Sometimes, in other shallow wells, when the women could enter and come out, the other people would rush and lick and such [sic] the wet dirty clothes, to quench their thirst.[9]

This source said that by the seventieth day, only 35 women and children remained from the original group of 3,000 exiles from Kharpert, and only 150 women and children survived from the entire caravan that arrived at Aleppo.

Rev. F. H. Leslie, an American missionary in Urfa, also corresponded with Jackson:

For six weeks we have witnessed the most terrible cruelties inflicted upon the thousands of Christian exiles who have been daily passing through our city from the northern cities. All tell the same story and bear the same scars: their men were all killed on the first days march from their cities, after which the women and girls were constantly robbed of their money, bedding, clothing, and beaten, criminally abused and abducted along the way. Their guards forced them to pay even for drinking from the springs along the way and were their worst abusers but also allowed the baser element in every village through which they passed to abduct the girls and women and abuse them. We not only were told these things but the same things occurred right here in our own city before our very eyes and openly on the streets.[10]

Rev. Leslie closes his letter with a plea for money to help him care for the deportees.

From Kharpert, Consul Leslie A. Davis wrote to Ambassador Morgenthau in Constantinople describing conditions he observed in the camps of Armenians deported from Erzerum and Erzinjan:

A more pitiable sight cannot be imagined. They are almost without exception ragged, filthy, hungry and sick. That is not surprising in view of the fact that they have been on the road for nearly two months with no change of clothing, no chance to wash, no shelter and little to eat. . . .

As one walks through the camp mothers offer their children and beg one to take them. In fact, the Turks have been taking their choice of these children and girls for slaves, or worse. In fact, they have even had their doctors there to examine the most likely girls and thus secure the best ones.

There are very few men among them, as most of them have been killed on the road. All tell the same story of having been attacked and robbed by the Kurds. Most of them were attacked over and over again and a great many of them, especially the men, were killed. . . .

The system that is being followed seems to be to have bands of Kurds awaiting them on the road to kill the men especially and incidentally some of the others. The entire movement seems to be the most thoroughly organized and effective massacre this country has ever seen.[11]

Davis also described specific events, such as this massacre on July 7, 1915, for which there were eyewitness accounts.

> On Monday many men were arrested both at Harput and Mezreh and put in prison. At daybreak Tuesday morning they were taken out and made to march towards an almost uninhabited mountain. There were about eight hundred in all and they were tied together in groups of fourteen each. That afternoon they arrived in a small Kurdish village where they were kept over night in the mosque and other buildings. During all this time they were without food or water. All their money and much of their clothing had been taken from them. On Wednesday morning they were taken to a valley a few hours' distance where they were all made to sit down. Then the gendarmes began shooting them until they had killed nearly all of them. Some who had not been killed by bullets were then disposed of with knives and bayonets.[12]

The State Department files also contain correspondence from other consuls, such as Oscar S. Heizer in Trebizond, Edward I. Nathan in Mersina, and others, and their accounts are similar to those we have quoted.

THE BRYCE/TOYNBEE REPORT

Shortly after reports of the spring 1915 deportations began to appear in the Western press, Viscount James Bryce, a member of the British Parliament and former ambassador to the United States, secured the services of a young historian, Arnold Toynbee, to collect and organize eyewitness accounts by missionaries, doctors and nurses, travelers, and Armenian survivors themselves.[13] Toynbee organized 149 separate statements by region so that it was possible to compare accounts from one city or village with another.[14]

One of the accounts was written by Rev. Haroutioun Essayan, the Vicar of the Apostolic Church at Aleppo, and was smuggled out in the sole of a shoe by a refugee who gave it to the Armenian Apostolic Bishop of Cairo, who then had the handwriting authenticated. In his letter, Father Essayan describes a group of ten thousand deported women and children that he had observed:

> They had been on the road for from three to five months; they have been plundered several times over, and have marched along naked and starving; the Government gave them on one single occasion a morsel of bread—a few had it twice. It is said that the number of these deported widows will reach 60,000; they are so exhausted that they cannot stand upright; the majority have great sores on their feet, through having to march barefoot.[15]

In this group, Father Essayan saw no men or boys over eleven years old, the latter having all been slaughtered on the way. His letter also states, "one does not see a single pretty face among the survivors," implying that all such women had been abducted. In addition, Father Essayan offered estimates of survivors from the various caravans. For example, he said that one thousand Armenians were deported from one city, and only four hundred arrived in Aleppo. Of these survivors, he estimated that 60 percent were sick, and all were suffering from serious malnutrition.

Lest one assume that Father Essayan's report is biased because it was written by an Armenian, we can also cite similar evidence from a German missionary's account. Because Germany and Turkey were allies during the war, this document was particularly incriminating, and the German censor immediately moved to confiscate the publication:

> Between the 10th and the 30th May [1915], 1,200 of the most prominent Armenians and other Christians, without distinction of confession, were arrested in the Vilayets of Diyarbekir and Mamouret-ul-Aziz [Kharpert]. . . . On the 30th May, 674 of them were embarked on thirteen Tigris barges, under the pretext that they were to be taken to Mosul. The Vali's aide-de-camp, assisted by fifty gendarmes, was in charge of the convoy. Half the gendarmes started off on the barges, while the other half rode along the bank. A short time after the start the prisoners were stripped of all their money (about £6,000 Turkish) and then of their clothes; after that they were thrown into the river. The gendarmes on the bank were ordered to let none of them escape.[16]

Continuing his account, the author describes other atrocities he had observed or heard of:

> For a whole month corpses were observed floating down the River Euphrates nearly every day, often in batches of from two to six corpses bound together. The male corpses are in many cases hideously mutilated (sexual organs cut off, and so on), the female corpses are ripped open. . . . The corpses stranded on the bank are devoured by dogs and vultures. To this fact there are many German eyewitnesses. An employee of the Baghdad Railway has brought the information that the prisons of Biredjik are filled regularly every day and emptied every night—into the Euphrates. Between Diyarbekir and Ourfa a German cavalry captain saw innumerable corpses lying unburied all along the road.[17]

In addition to reporting incidents of mass slaughter, this statement also gives examples of individual suffering. For example, a woman who gave birth to twins while being deported was allowed no time for recovery and was forced to start walking the next day. In despair, she placed the newborns under a bush and collapsed herself a short time later.[18]

Among the 149 documents contained in the Bryce/Toynbee volume, it is possible to find, almost at random, equally graphic passages detailing

the deportations. Two final examples will suffice, both describing events
in the city of Moush:

> The leading Armenians of the town and the headmen of the villages were sub-
> jected to revolting tortures. Their finger nails and then their toenails were
> forcibly extracted; their teeth were knocked out, and in some cases their
> noses were whittled down. . . . The female relatives of the victims who came
> to the rescue were outraged in public before the very eyes of their mutilated
> husbands and brothers. . . .[19]
>
> The shortest method for disposing of the women and children concen-
> trated in the various camps was to burn them. Fire was set to large wooden
> sheds in Alidjan, Megrakom, Khaskegh, and other Armenian villages, and
> these absolutely helpless women and children were roasted to death.[20]

The above account, offered by an Armenian, is substantiated by Alma
Johannsen, a German missionary eyewitness to events in Moush: "When
there was no one left in Bitlis to massacre, their attention was diverted
to Moush. Cruelties had already been committed, but so far not too
publicly; now, however, they started to shoot people down without any
cause, and to beat them to death simply for the pleasure of doing so."[21]
She then describes how Moush was burned:

> We all had to take refuge in the cellar for fear of our orphanage catching fire.
> It was heartrending to hear the cries of the people and children who were
> being burned to death in their houses. The soldiers took great delight in hear-
> ing them, and when people who were out in the street during the bombard-
> ment fell dead, the soldiers merely laughed at them. . . .
>
> I went to the Mutessarif and begged him to have mercy on the children
> at least, but in vain. He replied that the Armenian children must perish
> with their nation. All our people were taken from our hospital and orphan-
> age; they left us three female servants. Under these atrocious circumstances,
> Moush was burned to the ground.[22]

This German missionary left Moush for Kharpert, where, she reported,
conditions were no better: "In Harpout and Mezré the people have had
to endure terrible tortures. They have had their eyebrows plucked out,
their breasts cut off, their nails torn off; their torturers hew off their feet
or else hammer nails into them just as they do in shoeing horses."[23]

These selected accounts are representative of the statements contained in the Bryce/Toynbee volume presented to the British Parliament.
Because they are arranged by city, it is possible to corroborate statements
by witnesses who did not know one another and could not have collaborated in concocting a story. This volume is extremely important not

only because it provides detailed information but also because it was published within months of the time eyewitnesses wrote their accounts. Additionally, the report concludes with a summary of the genocide written by Arnold Toynbee, which continues to be a valuable overview of the events that occurred in 1915 and 1916.

OTHER SOURCES

U.S. State Department files and the blue book compiled by Bryce and Toynbee are but two examples of eyewitness testimony on the Armenian Genocide. In subsequent chapters we will quote from the autobiography of Henry Morganthau,[24] the American ambassador to Turkey from 1913 to 1916. He had regular contact with the Young Turk leaders and kept the State Department informed of the atrocities that were reported to him by eyewitnesses to the deportations. Morgenthau's autobiography includes passages from his diary, in which he reflects on conversations with Enver Pasha (Minister of War), Talaat Pasha (Minister of the Interior), and other Young Turk leaders, as well as with the German ambassador to Turkey, Hans von Wangenheim, to gain insight into the centralized nature of the Armenian Genocide.

Other informants include Dr. Johannes Lepsius, who as head of the Deutsche Orient-Mission until 1917, was an important German advocate for addressing the plight of the Armenians. He became interested in the Armenians during the 1894–96 massacres and published a compilation of eyewitness accounts of the slaughter of more than one hundred thousand Armenians. In response to the deportations, he published a report in 1916 that once again cited extensively from eyewitnesses to those events.[25] It was printed in an expanded form in 1919 and included an interview that he had with Enver Bey in August 1915.[26] The document went into multiple printings, but not without difficulty. Copies were confiscated by the Berlin police, and Lepsius was considered politically subversive for documenting the atrocities of Germany's Turkish ally.[27] A third important publication by Lepsius was *Deutschland und Armenien 1914–1918,* which reprinted 444 documents, many of them reports by German consuls in provincial capitals such as Adana, Aleppo, Erzerum, and elsewhere.[28]

In addition to these compilations, many individual accounts of the genocide have also been printed. For example, Dr. Martin Niepage, a German teacher in Aleppo, wrote a compelling account of what he and other German acquaintances witnessed. A few sentences from his book, *The Horrors of Aleppo*, illustrate the conditions of the deportees as they arrived in this city:

> Opposite the German Technical School at Aleppo, in which we are engaged in teaching, a mass of about four hundred emaciated forms, the remnant of such convoys, is lying in one of the hans. There are about a hundred children (boys and girls) among them, from five to seven years old. Most of them are suffering from typhoid and dysentery. When one enters the yard, one has the impression of entering a mad-house. If one brings them food, one notices that they have forgotten how to eat. Their stomach, weakened by months of starvation, can no longer assimilate nourishment. If one gives them bread, they put it aside indifferently. They just lie their quietly, waiting for death.[29]

Dr. Niepage also summarizes accounts told to him by other Germans whom he trusted, especially engineers working on the Baghdad Railway:

> One of them, Herr Greif, of Aleppo, reported corpses of violated women lying about naked in heaps on the railway embankment at Tell-Abiad and Ras-el-Ain. Another, Herr Spiecker, of Aleppo, had seen Turks tie Armenian men together, fire several volleys of small shot with fowling-pieces into the human mass, and go off laughing while their victims slowly perished in frightful convulsions. Other men had their hands tied behind their back and were rolled down steep cliffs. Women were standing below, who slashed those who had rolled down with knives until they were dead. . . . The German Consul from Mosul related, in my presence, at the German club at Aleppo that, in many places on the road from Mosul to Aleppo, he had seen children's hands lying hacked off in such numbers that one could have paved the road with them.[30]

Niepage's report does not stand alone. There were other Germans, who as allies of the Turks, had firsthand access to events. Dr. Armin T. Wegner, who worked for the German-Ottoman Health Mission team, for example, took photographs of deported Armenians in Meskene and Aleppo and published a report of what he observed.[31]

News of the atrocities against the Armenians began to be published in the world press in the spring of 1915. Marjorie Housepian Dobkin reports that by December 1915, the *New York Times* had published more than one hundred articles on the genocide, the majority of which were featured in the first six pages of the newspaper.[32] Articles in the *Times* carried such headlines as: "Turks Depopulate Towns of Armenia; Traveler Reports Christians of Great Territory Have Been Driven from Homes; 600,000 Starving on Road" (August 27, 1915); "1,500,000 Armenians Starve; Relief Committee Asks Aid for Victims of Turkish Decrees" (September 5, 1915); "Mission Board Told of Turkish Horrors; Correspondents Confirm the Reports of the Wiping Out of Armenians"

(September 17, 1915).[33] Similar reports appeared in newspapers in Britain, Australia, and other countries as well as the United States.[34]

Since the conclusion of World War I, there has been a steady trickle of autobiographical accounts published by survivors and observers of the genocide. Some of the most interesting of these are written by missionaries and relief workers. For example, Clarence Ussher, who served as a physician in both Kharpert and Van, offers a fascinating description of the attack on Van in 1915 and the defense of the Armenians.[35] Jacob Kuenzler and his daughter have both written of "Papa Kuenzler's" efforts to aid thousands of orphans after the war, including the successful attempt to remove them from Turkey to safer environments.[36] Also, Stanley Kerr, who served with Near East Relief in Marash and later witnessed the burning of the city in 1920, has written an autobiography of his experience with Armenian refugees.[37] These firsthand records, together with various secondary works on relief efforts, illuminate the condition of survivors after the war's end.[38]

In addition, survivors themselves have written about their experiences. A compelling account is provided by Abraham Hartunian, a Protestant minister who witnessed the massacres of 1894–96 and 1909 as well as the deportations of 1915.[39] At least one hundred books have been written by survivors; it is difficult to single out particular works among them, for each has its own poignancy.[40] Some survivors focus on orphanage experiences, others emphasize the process of emigration, while still others give vivid accounts of life before 1915 or the horror of the deportations and massacres that they witnessed.

Finally, since the fiftieth anniversary of the genocide, there has been a renewed interest in collecting survivors' testimonies.[41] From a survey of oral history projects in the United States and abroad, we estimate that approximately 2,500 formal interviews have been done with survivors since the late 1960s,[42] and another 850 interviews have been done for documentary films or as part of research projects that deal indirectly with the genocide.[43] Of the 2,500 formal interviews, approximately 1,700 are on audiotape,[44] while the remaining 800 are part of videotape projects.[45] Our project is unique in that the one hundred interviews have all been translated into English and transcribed. Summaries of interviews have been made for some of the other collections, but very few interviews have actually been transcribed. Moreover, only a very few studies based on oral history interviews have been published.[46] The Armenian community thus faces a substantial challenge to fund the translation and transcription of survivor testimony and to create a centralized archive that would make accessible to researchers this important documentation of Armenian history and culture.

AUTHENTICITY OF SURVIVOR TESTIMONY

The formidable body of firsthand documentation—contemporaneous with the events described—by consuls from foreign governments, missionaries, relief workers, and other observers provides a credible basis for evaluating the survivor testimony that we gathered some sixty to seventy years later. Such independent corroboration is important because of the perception, especially among those with a stake in denying the genocide, that survivors fabricate their stories. This sentiment is encapsulated in the following statement from the pamphlet of an American-Turkish organization:

> The most recent Armenian propaganda activity has involved the recording of stories related by aged Armenians regarding the so-called massacres during World War I. Carefully coached by their Armenian nationalist interviewers, these aged Armenians relate tales of horror which supposedly took place some 66 years ago in such detail as to astonish the imagination, considering that most of them already are aged eighty or more. Subjected to years of Armenian nationalist propaganda as well as the coaching of their interviewers, there is little doubt that their statements are of no use whatsoever for historical research.[47]

Clearly, the author of this statement believes that Armenian oral history is a propaganda ploy: survivors are manipulated by interviewers, and therefore their testimony has no historical value.

We actually have some sympathy with the charge that survivors remember "tales of horror . . . in such detail as to astonish the imagination." Indeed, we ourselves have often been amazed by the specificity of survivor recall. However, rather than discrediting the testimony because of its detailed nature, we have been drawn to ask a different question: namely, what accounts for the remarkable quality of survivor memory?

We believe the answer to this question lies in the exceptional nature of the events described: fathers being shot or tortured, mothers and siblings being sexually abused, children being abducted, and a litany of other horrors. Such memories are not easily forgotten. Indeed, they seem to be burned irrevocably into the consciousness of survivors. They dream about them at night. They have an incessant, even obsessive, need to talk about these events.

Also contrary to the statement quoted above, interviewers do not manipulate survivors to answer in a way that fits nationalistic propaganda.

In our interviews, and those with which we are most familiar, survivors are allowed to tell *their* stories. Although we always entered interviews with a list of questions, organized by specific categories (see Appendix B), there was no coaching or other indication of what constituted the "right" answer. Typically, we began the interview by asking survivors about their family life and Armenian culture before 1915. We then asked about their memories, if any, of the deportations. At this point, the interview often unfolded on its own, without much questioning except to ask for clarification or more detail. The conversation usually turned to the survivor's admission to an orphanage or reunion with family members—if any had survived. After that we always asked about patterns of emigration, marriage, employment, the birth of children and their education. Finally, we asked survivors about their interpretation of the genocide and what they had experienced.

In upholding the authenticity of survivor interviews, we do not wish to defend a simplistic view that survivors' stories are photographic snapshots of events, devoid of interpretation. To argue such a position would be to ignore the entire weight of humanistic research of the last hundred years and more. Life stories are complex narratives that situate particular events within a larger context of meaning.[48] With sufficient analysis, it is possible to identify specific themes that structure life history narratives. Indeed, interpretation is the very essence of our humanity. But there is a decided difference between interpretation and falsification, and those who wish to discredit survivor testimony imply that survivors concoct the stories they tell. Our experience of interviewing survivors leads us to disagree with this assessment.

The validity of survivor testimony can be evaluated in a number of ways, one of which is comparing statements by survivors who offered testimony close to the time of the events they described with statements from survivors who were interviewed years later. In doing this, we have found striking similarity between our interview transcripts and accounts in the Bryce/Toynbee Blue Book as well as in the U.S. State Department documents. Given the relatively large number of interviews found in various oral history collections, it should be increasingly possible to compare testimony of survivors from the same locale.

One of the most important measures of authenticity, however, rests on a subjective assessment of the truth of survivor testimony. In our "snowball" sampling technique, individuals did not *volunteer* to tell us their story, which conceivably could have led to a highly skewed sample. Instead, we sought them out, one by one (see Appendix A for a fuller statement of methodology). On the one hand, some survivors were hesitant, and some even refused, to be interviewed. Those who declined said that it was simply too painful to reopen this wound from their childhood, for after telling their stories, they frequently had difficulty sleeping and once again became preoccupied with the deaths of parents and siblings. We, of course, accepted their refusal. On the other hand, almost all of the survivors we interviewed appeared to find their hours with us to be cathartic. The most common response we received, in fact, was gratitude that someone cared about their "insignificant" story. Quite a few of the survivors had never told their life history to anyone, not even their children.

Given our selection process, the most important test of validity for us was the emotion that surrounded the stories survivors told us, for example, when elderly men wept as they talked about the deaths of mothers, fathers, and siblings. These were not accounts they had been coached to tell by their "nationalist propagandists"; they were events that had troubled survivors at the very deepest levels of their conscience and consciousness for decades.

We did not walk away from our interviews quickly. Survivors had opened their hearts to strangers, and so we lingered for "Armenian coffee," dessert, and small talk. Quite often, we received phone calls after an interview, with more details that survivors had remembered. Clearly, our questions had stimulated reflection. And on some occasions we returned for a second or third interview, during which we usually heard the same stories repeated, but often with added details. Also, in a handful of cases, we reinterviewed survivors several years later; interestingly, when we compared accounts, we found that stories were often told in nearly the same words as the original interview.

CONCLUSION

What does survivor testimony contribute to documentation of the Armenian Genocide? In answering this question, we must first state the limitations of oral history research. Most oral history studies, and certainly our research, deal with the experience of common people rather than the political or cultural elite. Oral history tends to reveal the underside of politics and social change. While much written history focuses on the actions of kings, presidents, and people of distinction, oral history often captures the local experience of individuals who do not wield power and whose lives are entirely ordinary.

Although some of the survivors in our sample were born into rather affluent homes in Turkey, the genocide had a great leveling effect on the socioeconomic status of Armenian children who survived. All had their education interrupted during the period of the deportations, and many never received schooling beyond what they had in the orphanages. The social class of survivors at the time we met them was varied, with some leading comfortable middle-class lives, while others lived in very humble circumstances, occupying one- or two-room apartments or rental houses.

The survivors we interviewed were, on average, eleven to twelve years old in 1915. Only a quarter of our sample was older than sixteen when the deportations commenced. Thus, in this book, genocide is seen through the eyes of children, and this youthful perspective is somewhat different from that offered by most historical interpretations of events. But rather than seeing it as a liability, we believe that this point of view offers a unique opportunity to understand human tragedy as it affects those who are typically voiceless in society. Survivors' descriptions of relationships between parents and siblings during the genocide are extremely poignant, as are the perceptions of loss and loneliness that followed the death of parents or separation from family members during the deportations.

In the following chapter, we will temporarily turn our attention from survivor experience in order to place the Armenian Genocide within the larger context of Armenian history and theories about genocide. The summary of the deportations in this chapter is drawn directly from the pattern of these events as represented in our interviews, but the rest of the historical information is based more generally on surveys of Armenian history. In subsequent chapters we will return to survivor experiences as the basis for describing the genocide and analyzing survivor responses to this event.

CHAPTER 2

The Historical and Political Context of the Genocide

Armenians are mentioned in Persian and Greek sources from 600 B.C., but they trace their historic origins to the Indo-European migration of the third and second millennia B.C.[1] Mount Ararat, the reputed resting place of Noah's ark, is located in northeastern Turkey and is often viewed as the spiritual center of the Armenian soul. Historical Armenia, or what is sometimes called "Great Armenia," covered an area of about 100,000 square miles,[2] including parts of what are now the republics of Armenia, Azerbaijan, and Georgia. It also extended south to the northern borders of Iran and Iraq, and west to include most of what is currently northeastern Turkey. Between 1080 and 1375 there was also an Armenian kingdom (Little Armenia) in the Cilicia region of Turkey on the Mediterranean, in the area surrounding the city of Adana.[3]

The ancestors of the Armenian people lived in a harsh climate on the plateaus surrounding the base of 17,000-foot Mount Ararat. Although the snow-covered mountain is breathtakingly beautiful, much of the land at its base is rocky until one reaches the fertile valley of the Araxes River and Lake Van. Adding to the difficult conditions is the incidence of earthquakes; historic records document the destruction of entire villages and cities. As recently as 1988, an earthquake near Leninakan (currently Gumairi) left 530,000 Armenians homeless and killed at least 25,000, as well as maiming many thousands more.

Before the genocide of 1915, more than 2 million Armenians lived in Turkey; today, only about 60,000 live there. Not only was the population decimated, but thousands of Armenian churches, monasteries, and monuments were also destroyed in eastern Turkey.[4] Across the border the Republic of Armenia, about one-tenth the size of historical Armenia, fights for its economic life, being landlocked and isolated from natural resources to support its industry. Three million Armenians currently live in the Republic of Armenia, while 3.5 million more are dispersed around the world, including six hundred thousand who live in the United States. This chapter will provide a brief history of the Armenian people, focusing particularly on the genocide of 1915.

LANGUAGE, RELIGION, AND CULTURE

Armenian is an Indo-European language distinct from Turkish or Arabic, and it has played an important role in enabling Armenians to maintain their cultural integrity despite repeated invasions and occupations.[5] In the fifth century A.D., Saint Mesrop Mashtots invented an alphabet with thirty-eight characters to translate the Bible into Armenian; consequently, it also led to an outpouring of national literature. Krapar (classical Armenian) functioned as the literary language into the nineteenth century, and it continues to be used in liturgies of the Apostolic Church. The Armenian language remains an important source of social cohesion for the Armenian community throughout the world.[6] In modern times, two dialects have evolved, with Armenians in Iran, the Republic of Armenia, and the former Soviet Union speaking Eastern Armenian, while in the Middle East, Europe, and America, Western Armenian is spoken.

Religion has also played a crucial role in maintaining a distinctive national and ethnic consciousness. Armenians take considerable pride in having been the first nation to accept Christianity. The apostles Thaddeus and Bartholomew brought the Christian gospel to the Armenians as early as A.D. 43, and this event is commemorated in the name of the mother church, the Armenian *Apostolic* Church. The Armenian Church is sometimes also called the *Gregorian* Church, in honor of Saint Gregory the Illuminator, who converted the Armenian sovereign Trdat III to Christianity in about A.D. 301. In A.D. 506 the Armenian Church reaffirmed its independence from both Constantinople and Rome and has remained separate to the present. Currently, there are two rival branches of the Armenian Church: the Mother See in Etchmiadzin, Armenia, and the Cilician (Sis) See in Antelias, Lebanon, each of which appeals to Armenians of somewhat different political inclinations.

In 1915, 95 percent of Armenians were members of the Apostolic Church.[7] The various saints' days and feast days played an important role in structuring the Armenian year, with Easter (rather than Christmas) being the high point; Armenian women often spent weeks preparing food for the festive celebration. In addition to the Apostolic Church, there were also about two hundred thousand Eastern-rite Armeno-Catholic Christians, stemming from missionary activity in the eighteenth century.[8] There were also some fifty thousand Protestant Armenians at the time of the genocide.[9] Armenian missions were established in 1831, primarily by Americans, and by 1844 the Protestant Armenians were recognized as an official *millet* (community) within the Ottoman Empire as were the Catholic Armenians.[10] However, the Patriarch of the Armenian Apostolic Church functioned as the principal political representative of Armenians living in Ottoman Turkey.

Except for brief periods, Armenians have been a subjugated people. It was both their fortune and misfortune to live at the crossroads between the East and West. This strategic location provided a rich cultural life with Persian, Hellenistic, and Byzantine influences, as well as plentiful opportunities for trade and commerce. However, it also invited frequent plundering and invasions. If it were not for their language and religion, Armenians would have vanished from Turkey long before the attempted extermination in 1915. Central prohibitions against intermarriage with Muslims, as well as the preservation of Armenian culture through language, contributed significantly to maintaining a separate Armenian identity.

From the sixteenth century, Armenians were ruled by the Ottoman Turks and existed as a semiautonomous *millet* in a multinational empire.[11] Armenians were relatively free to practice their religion, and they had considerable autonomy in civil matters, as did other *millets* within the empire, such as the Greeks and Jews. But they were also considered to be second-class citizens in Ottoman Turkey: they did not have the same legal rights as Turks, and they were subject to special taxes, which were often extortionary. Equally important, Armenians were viewed as *gâvurs* (infidels) which, particularly at a local level, meant that they were often thought to have less human worth than Muslims.

The single largest element of the Armenian population in the nineteenth and early twentieth centuries consisted of peasants who worked as sharecroppers or tenant farmers within a semifeudal social structure. However, similar to the situation of Jews in Germany at the start of

World War II, there were significant numbers of Armenians in banking, finance, business, and trade. Armenians responded to capitalistic forces of the industrialized world at a faster rate than did the majority population, and they achieved a major economic presence in Turkey, disproportionate to their actual numbers.[12] Wealthy Armenians who had moved to Constantinople and other parts of western Turkey to escape persecution in Eastern Anatolia often sent their children to Italy and other European countries for education, and this positioned Armenians to function as an economic bridge for trade and commerce with the Western world.

Although they were well integrated into the economy of the Ottoman Empire, Armenians were culturally distinct. They lived in their own separate quarters. It was unthinkable that their sons or daughters would marry Turks. The church was the center of their cultural life, and the seasons of the year were marked by religious holidays. Armenians lived in extended families—as many as five generations under the same roof—with the grandmother exercising considerable authority over the household.

As a minority in the Ottoman Empire, Armenians were in a precarious situation. Looting by Kurdish tribes and attack by neighboring Turks were common events, especially in the eastern provinces.[13] Armenians who lived east of Sivas were, in a sense, subject to two rulers: the Kurdish tribal princes as well as the Turkish government.[14] In addition to an annual head tax that Armenians paid for the right to live in the empire, there were local taxes extorted by Turkish and Kurdish officials, along with special levies, fines, and bribes.[15] Armenian stores for the winter also seemed to be available for plunder whenever it suited the whim of Kurdish or Turkish bandits.[16] Legal recourse was impossible, or at least very difficult, in Turkish courts. Consequently, relations between Armenians and Turks, as well as Kurds,[17] were frequently cautious or fearful, although it is important to note there were both Turks and Kurds who intervened to save Armenians during the deportations.[18]

THE NINETEENTH CENTURY

In the nineteenth century, Armenians began to awaken to ideas of human rights and self-determination that were current in Europe and the United States.[19] Increasing numbers of affluent Armenian students went to study in France, Germany, Italy, and the United States, where they absorbed liberal ideas of political governance. Also, American missionaries imported and modeled modern understandings of human rights and representative government. Turkish leaders recognized the potential danger of modernization and directed some of the blame toward the westernizing influence of the missionaries. Thus, in 1892, for example, a missionary's house was burned, and Ottoman police also set fire to a building being constructed at Anatolia College, with the intention of driving Protestant missionaries out of the region.[20] In addition, Kurds also felt threatened by the growing Armenian awareness of political rights, because the semifeudal servitude of the Armenians had worked greatly to their advantage.[21]

The nineteenth century was a period of cultural, as well as political, awakening among Armenians. This renaissance was manifested in many ways, including building schools and libraries, publishing books and newspapers, and developing literature in the vernacular. Higher education became more widely available, with colleges being established in Constantinople, Marsovan, Aintab, Tarsus, and Kharpert. In addition to schools sponsored by the Apostolic Church, by 1914 there were 20,000 students in four hundred elementary schools, 4,500 pupils in high schools, and 2,500 in colleges—all of which were sponsored by Americans.[22] Traditional ideas of subjugation were challenged as this younger generation absorbed American and European notions of romanticism and revolt.

Simultaneously, Armenians were increasingly oppressed. In 1891, Sultan Abdul-Hamid created the *Hamidiye,* armed bands of Kurds that were to protect the Russian border but instead devoted much of their time to plundering Armenian households. In response to these attacks and the government's failure to honor its promises for reform, several political parties had formed by the latter part of the nineteenth century: the Armenakans of Van (1885), the Hunchakian Party in Geneva (1887), and the Dashnaktsutiun in Tiflis (1890), all of which opposed the continuing exploitation of Armenians and also articulated political ideas regarding the right of self-determination.[23] Only the Hunchakian Party, however, advocated separatism. Despite some ideological differences, these groups shared the common goal of obtaining for Armenians the same rights already guaranteed to Muslims.[24]

Armenian revolutionary groups, known as *fedayee,* also arose in response to the looting, plunder, and extortion experienced by the Armenians, especially in the eastern provinces.[25] The *fedayee* developed into small but well-armed units capable of countering attacks by Turks or Kurds, giving Armenians a limited capacity for self-defense for the first time in centuries. The *fedayee* were both a reflection of the broader cultural awakening Armenians experienced and a stimulus to a new sense of pride and nationalism.

It is important to note, however, that the Armenians were known as the "faithful *millet*." Unlike the Balkan peoples who had declared independence, the majority of Armenians sought to achieve greater civil rights under Ottoman rule rather than to establish a separate state. Independence was not politically viable. The 2 million and more members of the Armenian community in Turkey were concentrated in Eastern Anatolia but also were scattered throughout Turkey; and, except in a few areas such as Van and Erzerum, they did not constitute a majority.[26] Another 1 million Armenians lived across the border in the Russian Caucasus, and approximately 2 million lived elsewhere in the Russian Empire. Under such conditions, seceding from the Ottoman Empire—as Bulgaria, Romania, Serbia, and Montenegro had done— was not possible.

The San Stefano Treaty of 1878, which granted independence to various Balkan states as a result of the Russo-Turkish War (1877–78), contained Article 16 that required reforms in Turkish Armenia. The Russians were to guarantee the sultan's observance of these reforms, but the sultan had no intention of giving further independence to any of the minorities within the empire. His strategy, states Arnold Toynbee, was to set the various minorities at each other's throats.[27] And unfortunately for the Armenians, the British failed to see that their own interests were served by this treaty and called for a congress to be convened a few months later in Berlin.

Article 61 of the Treaty of Berlin supplanted Article 16 of the San Stefano Treaty, and although it required the sultan to implement reforms, Russian troops were forced to withdraw from the eastern provinces. As a result, there was no one to guarantee that the required reforms were carried out. And, in fact, they were not. As soon as the Russian troops left, Kurds started plundering Armenian villages. Foreign diplomats were powerless to do anything beyond file reports to their home offices. These abuses inspired the Armenians to take matters into their own hands.[28]

In 1894, Armenians in Sassun refused to continue paying an extortionary protection tax to Kurdish chieftains. In response, Turkish soldiers were sent to the region and, together with Kurdish calvary units, they ravaged Sassun. Estimates of the number of dead range between nine hundred and sixteen thousand, and some twenty-six to forty villages were destroyed.[29] Missionaries reported these atrocities to the

American and European press, and the British, French, and Russians demanded that abuses against the Christian population cease. Sultan Abdul-Hamid agreed to a plan of reform in 1895, but diplomatic agreement was merely the cover for engaging in continued pogroms.

From 1894 to 1896, more than one hundred thousand Armenians were killed. These massacres were often carried out by irregular Kurdish troops (*Hamidiye*) who had been armed by the government with sophisticated repeating rifles.[30] They were encouraged to loot and kill Armenians, while regular Turkish troops stood by and observed. Those who perpetrated the violence at a local level were motivated by greed as much as by politics. The sultan, however, intended the massacres to teach the Armenians a lesson that liberty and equality were not to be pursued by infidels living within the empire.

On occasion, acts against Armenians during this period were particularly sadistic. For example, in Urfa, Turks set fire to an Armenian cathedral in which three thousand men, women, and children had gathered for protection. However, as atrocious as these acts were, they did not approach the attempt at total extermination that followed in 1915. The acts of violence against Armenians in the late nineteenth century were usually confined to a few days of bloodletting before life returned to normal. The goal of the 1894–96 massacres was not extermination; rather, it was to keep the Armenian *millet* in its subservient political position.

Armenian outrage against these pogroms mounted, and in August 1896 a group of Dashnak Party members took hostages as they entered the Ottoman Bank in Constantinople and threatened to blow it up unless their demands for reform were met. This bold attempt to obtain guarantees from the sultan failed, although the Armenians who seized the bank were allowed free exit out of the country. But in retaliation, the local population in Constantinople was massacred, with most of the victims being poor Armenians involved in menial jobs in the city.[31] Foreign diplomats were not spared this sight, and news of atrocities against the Armenians continued to spread to the Christian world.

THE RISE OF THE YOUNG TURKS

Although Abdul-Hamid was successful in quelling the Armenian quest for civil liberties, there were groups within the Turkish population itself that also sought to modernize the Ottoman government.[32] By the turn of the century, Turkey was referred to as the "sick man of Europe." It was deeply in debt to creditors; the empire was coming unglued from secession movements; and frustration with the sultan's autocratic rule ran deep. In 1908 Abdul-Hamid was overthrown, and the Committee of Union and Progress (Ittihad ve Terakki Teshkilati) came to power.[33] Abdul-Hamid represented a traditionalist style of despotic governance, and Turks as well as Armenians were looking for change. Armenians supported the Young Turk revolution, seeing it as potentially ushering in a new era of reform. In fact, Turks and Armenians embraced each other in the streets.

Unfortunately, concurrent with ideas of reform, an ideology of pan-Turkism developed, with theorists such as Ziya Gökalp playing a key role in fashioning an intellectual rationale for the creation of a homogeneous nation.[34] In the midst of economic and structural collapse, the vision of a renewed empire was born—an empire that would unite all Turkic peoples and stretch from Constantinople to central Asia. This vision, however, excluded non-Muslim minorities, such as the Armenians. In 1913 an extremely nationalistic element among the Young Turks came to power, led by the three individuals who, two years later, were responsible for the deaths of half the Armenian population in Turkey: namely, the triumvirate of Enver (Minister of War), Talaat (Minister of Internal Affairs), and Jemal (Minister of the Navy).[35] These three constituted a virtual dictatorship—a requisite of most genocides.

During the early years of Young Turk rule, Armenians suffered yet another series of massacres. In the district of Cilicia, Armenians became increasingly bold in expressing their hopes for reform,[36] and in response some fifteen thousand to twenty thousand Armenians were killed in pogroms in 1909 that were ascribed to agents of Abdul-Hamid during a brief counterrevolution by the sultan against the Young Turks.[37] As a part of the pogroms, fifty churches were destroyed along with five thousand Armenian homes and shops.[38] The Young Turk government later apologized for these massacres and destruction of property; however, in light of the events yet to come, it is possible that the nationalist element of the Young Turk government might have been sympathetic to what occurred, especially since some of the soldiers sent to quell the pogroms appeared to have participated in them. Meanwhile, in the eastern provinces of Turkey, a state of anarchy continued, in which Armenians were regularly subjected to looting and violence.

World War I began in August 1914. On November 2, Turkey formally declared war, joining forces with Germany and the Central Powers against the Triple Entente of Great Britain, France, and Russia. The

Armenians wished to remain neutral in the conflict. Some months earlier, in July, a Young Turk delegation had come to the annual congress of the Dashnak Party in Erzerum and offered them a deal: if Armenians would organize subversive operations in Transcaucasia, they would be rewarded after the victory over Russia with additional territory. The Dashnaks refused, arguing instead for neutrality, which greatly angered the Young Turks.

The Armenians felt that they were being put in an untenable position: how could they agitate against Russia, where more than a million Armenians lived? From the Armenian perspective, the boundary between Turkey and Russia was artificial—their historic homeland for twenty-five hundred years had spanned this border at the foot of Mount Ararat. But the Young Turks viewed the Armenian response as treasonous, proclaiming that the Armenians would side with the Russian army if it advanced onto Turkish soil.

Nevertheless, on August 3, 1914, Turks and Armenians alike were mobilized for the war effort. At first, only young Armenian men were drafted; but later even older Armenians who were physically fit were inducted. It was no longer possible to pay a tax to gain exemption from the army. Altogether, a quarter of a million Armenian men were conscripted.

THE PATTERN OF EXTERMINATION

As the events of 1915 unfolded, most Armenians were unaware that a centralized plan of genocide was in process. Communication from one area to another was slow and difficult. And how could they have imagined that the Young Turks, who came to power on the platform of liberty, equality, and fraternity, would attempt to obliterate a people that had resided within the borders of Turkey for over two thousand years? But by the end of the decade, a mere handful of Armenians remained. The rest had been massacred; had died of starvation, dehydration, or illness; or had fled Turkey, leaving behind the corpses, often unburied, of their family members. Although Turks continue to deny that there was a systematic plan to exterminate the Armenians in fulfillment of a pan-Turkic ideology, the evidence contradicting this view is formidable.[39]

Three related actions by the Young Turk government diminished the possibility of Armenian resistance. First, as already mentioned, those most capable of defending their towns and villages had been drafted and were serving as loyal soldiers of the Ottoman army. But early in 1915, the Armenians were disarmed. Many were put into labor battalions to build roads, while others served as pack animals to carry war supplies. They were poorly fed and clothed, and the goal of working them until they dropped from hunger and exhaustion soon became evident. With few exceptions, those who did not die in this manner were taken in groups of fifty or one hundred and shot, often after having been forced to dig their own graves.

A second step to ensure lack of resistance was the Turkish requisition of all guns possessed by Armenians. In some areas, Armenians were given quotas, and if they did not produce enough weapons, they had to buy them from their Turkish neighbors. These confiscated guns were then photographed and presented as evidence of Armenian insurrection. Such propaganda created a political climate that legitimized inhumane treatment of Armenians. But disarming the Armenians also served to eliminate any opportunity for resistance.

A small number of Armenian revolutionaries had hidden weapons in their homes or had buried them. Members of Armenian political groups were tortured until they revealed the location of these weapons, and if they did not confess, their wives or other family members were tortured. Once again, any evidence of revolutionary activity, even if it involved only a handful of the total population, was used to dramatize the "treason" of the Armenians and to incite the local Muslim population against them.

A third action by the Turks robbed Armenians of their indigenous leadership. Armenian leaders were instructed to report to local government headquarters, and they did so, with no suspicion that this was merely a ruse, part of a coordinated effort to kill the local leaders of the Armenian population. As soon as they reported, they were imprisoned without trial. Many men were tortured, and others were simply shot. There was surprisingly little resistance; poor communications kept Armenians unaware of the occurrence of such events throughout Turkey.

On April 8, 1915, the Armenians of Zeitun were deported. On April 24—now commemorated annually by Armenians worldwide as a day to remember the genocide—several hundred Armenian intellectuals and religious and political leaders living in Constantinople were arrested. Within a few days, more than six hundred Armenians were deported from Constantinople, including such individuals as the famous musician Gomidas, who survived the march but reportedly suffered a total mental breakdown as a result. The stage was now set for the deportation of the local populations, the method of extermination that was to characterize this first genocide of the twentieth century.

During the closing days of May 1915, an emergency order called the Temporary Law of Deportation was enacted. This order authorized deportation of persons who might be guilty of treason or espionage or who could be justifiably removed for military purposes. Armenians were not specifically cited in this order, but the target was obvious.[40] Suspicion—not guilt—of treasonous activity was all that was required. This cleared the way for deporting the entire Armenian population: men, women, children, and the elderly.

Only a few groups of Armenians escaped deportation. Those living in Constantinople and Smyrna (Izmir) were not deported because of the many foreign officials present in these areas of western Turkey. Additionally, a handful of Armenians were sometimes left behind because they possessed specific skills, especially those important to the military. Occasionally, Armenians elected the option—which was sometimes, but not always, offered—of converting to Islam, and by symbolically abandoning their national identity were spared from deportation. Finally, a small number of Armenians were not deported because Turks, Kurds, and Greeks, at considerable personal risk, hid Armenian children, or sometimes even whole families, when deportation orders were given.[41]

In addition, some Armenians avoided deportation by flight or resistance. For example, Armenians living near the Russian border were able to escape into Russia. And in a few places, such as Musa Dagh, Armenians fled to the mountains and resisted the Turks. In this famous case, later dramatized in a novel by Franz Werfel, the resisters escaped down the backside of a mountain and were rescued by French ships.[42]

If Armenians had been deported only from the areas of conflict with the Russian army, then the deportation might have had some political legitimacy (especially if Armenian sedition had actually been demonstrated). But Armenians were deported from areas extremely remote from the battlefront. Furthermore, what rationale could have been offered for deporting women and children or the elderly?

When a deportation was to occur, orders were posted as well as announced by town criers. The more fortunate Armenians had a week or so to prepare for the journey. Others had only a day or two to gather their belongings. Women scrambled to prepare food. Valuable possessions were sold to Turks or Kurds at a fraction of their worth in order to secure money. Because many of the men were either in the army or in prison, these arrangements often fell to the women.

Officially, Armenian homes and possessions were safeguarded by government orders. In some towns, in fact, doorways were sealed. But this was simply a manipulative sham to deceive Armenians about the real purpose of deportation, for the homes were looted as soon as they were evacuated or, in some instances, were used as housing for immigrant Turks. When survivors returned after the war, not only were their possessions gone, but many of the houses that were not occupied had even been stripped of wood from the doorways, windows, and staircases, to warm the homes of Turks during the winter months.

On the appointed day of departure, gendarmes (police) came through the streets of the Armenian village or city quarter and ordered the people to assemble. Wealthy Armenians sometimes hired carts to transport their possessions, while poor Armenians carried their food and clothes in bundles. It was a dismal sight: elderly men and women, mothers with babies in their arms, young children (and men if they had not already been imprisoned). Escorted by only a few gendarmes, the caravan members set off walking, with whatever provisions and possessions they could carry.

When the caravans reached the city limits, the men were often separated from the group; gendarmes tied their hands and escorted them away from their families. Wives and children heard shots ring out, and then the gendarmes returned alone, forcing the remnant to resume their journey. (This was a typical scenario, although in some deportation groups the men were allowed to remain with the caravan.)

The remaining deportees were marched in circuitous routes, through mountain passes and away from Turkish population centers. The destination for many caravans was Aleppo and, beyond that, the deserts of Syria—especially towns such as Der-Zor. But the more fundamental goal of the deportations appeared to be death through attrition. Turks were not allowed to assist deportees, on pain of imprisonment. And gendarmes were often sadistic, for example, refusing deportees access to water.

The actual butchering of deportees was often left to members of the "Special Organization." Created by an order of the Ministries of Justice and the Interior, these units were made up of criminals and murderers who had been released from prison in the Ottoman Empire. Morally suited to their task, they were led by officers from the Ottoman War Academy. Two nationalistic physicians, Drs. Nazim and Shakir, played a key role in organizing these killer units of *chété*, as they were called. Although these units at first fought against the Russians in the Caucasus, the Turks found a better use for them in massacring caravans of Armenian deportees. These men were heartless, butchering deportees in ravines and on narrow mountain passes, raping women, and stealing what few possessions they still carried. Kurdish tribal groups were similarly encouraged to raid caravans. The gendarmes who were supposed to "protect" the caravans either disappeared during these attacks or joined in the assault.

In addition to Drs. Nazim and Shakir, other physicians were involved in the genocide. For example, Dr. Ali Saib was accused in postwar trials of having poisoned and gassed infants and children. Numan Pasha, also a physician, was accused of having poisoned sick Armenians in Erzerum, Sivas, and Erzinjan. Tevfik Rushdu, a brother-in-law of Dr. Nazim, had been responsible for disposing of bodies by putting them in wells and covering them with lime and soil.[43]

As deportees continued on their forced march, they began to encounter the remnants of earlier caravans—the rotting bodies of deportees who had died from exhaustion were now littering the roadways. By this time, some caravan members were naked as a result of continual raids; others were walking skeletons. Survivors ate grass that grew along the roadside or picked grains out of animal manure. Many had dysentery or typhus. Their hair was filled with lice and they scarcely appeared human.

Caravans that had started out with thousands arrived in Aleppo with hundreds, or even less. Deportation was a very effective method of genocide, although there is great controversy about how many died.[44] Armenians calculate that 1.5 million perished between 1915 and 1923. Some scholars believe the number was lower, perhaps as few as eight hundred thousand. Much of the discussion centers on the size of the Armenian population in Turkey at the time and whether to consider the period from 1894 to 1923 or the narrower time frame of 1915–16. An accurate generalization, however, is that approximately half of the Armenian population of Turkey died as a direct result of the genocide. Worldwide, one-third of the total population of Armenians died.[45] Surviving Armenians included the several hundred thousand who were living in Constantinople and Smyrna who were not deported, children who were adopted into Turkish or Kurdish homes, perhaps three hundred thousand Armenians who escaped across the Russian border, and the pathetic remnant that survived months of deportation.

WAS IT A GENOCIDE?

Because the Turkish government denies that a genocide occurred—and the Western press sometimes uses the term "alleged genocide"—it is important to consider whether the events just described fit the definition of genocide, as the term is commonly used.[46] The definition in the United Nations' Convention on the Prevention and Punishment of the Crime of Genocide, which the United States finally ratified in 1988, offers a useful standard for judgment.[47] Article II of the convention states:

> In the present Convention, genocide means any of the following acts committed with intent to destroy, in whole or in part, a nation, ethnical, racial or religious group, as such: (a) killing members of the group; (b) causing serious bodily or mental harm to members of the group; (c) deliberately inflicting on the group conditions of life calculated to bring about its physical destruction in whole or in part; (d) imposing measures intended to prevent births within the group; (e) forcibly transferring children of the group to another group.[48]

On the basis of this definition, the events of 1915 clearly constitute a genocide of the Armenians. Because of their national, racial, and religious characteristics, the Armenians were singled out for death and deportation. They were judged guilty not on the grounds of individual culpability but solely because they were Armenian. Conditions "a" and "b" were met by outright massacre and also by the more indirect means of killing through starvation, dehydration, and exposure. Condition "c" was met by the method of deportation, the goal of which was not to transport deportees but rather to create conditions that would cause extremely high attrition rates. Conditions "d" and "e" were a direct result of the deportations: the male population was greatly reduced in size, making procreation difficult, and children were abducted in considerable numbers from the caravans, were abandoned by their mothers, or were sold or given to passing Turks or Kurds on the calculated risk that their chance of survival would be increased.[49]

Several aspects of the above definition bear elaboration, as they relate to the broader literature on genocide. First, most definitions of genocide stress the intentional identification of a particular group for destruction. Thus, victims may include members of a specific ethnic, racial, or religious group; those who are clearly identified with a particular nationality; and individuals who are in some other way different from the majority population. According to the perpetrators of genocide, these individuals or groups represent a threat, lack characteristics that fulfill dominant group goals and values, or are perceived to fall short of being fully human. It is only when the victim group is dehumanized through such labeling that genocide can occur.

Second, genocide requires a legitimating principle or ideology to justify mass human destruction. Genocide is not simply a reflection of human depravity; rather, it is associated with a quest for group meaning, however extreme the means. In short, *individual* acts of violence may be committed by madmen, but *collective* acts of violence inevitably involve a myth or theory that asserts the moral rationale for killing those who fit a particular category.

Third, mass violence often emerges out of unstable political conditions that threaten the social order: the economy is failing, political boundaries are changing, or previously disenfranchised minority groups are progressing economically. The dominant group needs a scapegoat; for the actual forces of change, such as modernization, are too abstract to discharge the group's accumulated frustrations. A victim group is needed, whose destruction promises a return to the old social order or, alternatively, a new utopian order. Under these circumstances, political leaders create the legitimating ideology, while collaborators at the local level respond, often more primitively, to perceived threats to their economic position and established way of life.

Fourth, war and revolution are frequently occasions for genocide. During war, even the most secure nations often feel vulnerable. Hence, suspicions are easily aroused about potential enemies, particularly minority populations perceived to have connections with the actual enemy. Revolutionary leaders are also subject to paranoid fantasies; having themselves displaced an established authority, they are aware of the fragility of political regimes.

Finally, because the perpetrator's justification for genocide is seldom acceptable to the broader human community, mass violence is often carried out in conditions that discourage intervention by outside parties. Hence, many genocides occur during wartime, or they are committed covertly and immediately covered up, with denial of genocide being the predictable final stage of mass human destruction. Killing fellow human beings, however noble the ideal, is in hindsight a moral embarrassment. Thus, the perpetrating group later minimizes the number of victims, blames victims for their own deaths, or stonewalls in the face of overwhelming evidence of guilt.

CAUSES OF THE GENOCIDE

All of the elements just discussed were exemplified in the case of the Armenian Genocide, and in retrospect, we can see that conditions were ripe for genocide. The Armenian Genocide was not the result of any single factor; rather, it was the simultaneous coalescence of a number of different dynamics that, given the stimulus of wartime conditions, led to the attempted extermination of the Armenian population.

As stated in the previous section, radical solutions tend to be sought in conditions of social upheaval, and that, indeed, characterizes the Ottoman Empire at the turn of the century, including the period of Young Turk rule. Robert Melson summarizes the political climate as follows:

> ... on October 5, 1908, some three months after the Young Turk revolution, Bulgaria proclaimed her complete independence, and on October 6, 1908, Austria annexed Bosnia and Herzegovina, which she had occupied since 1878. Due to the rapaciousness of the Great Powers and the weakness of Turkish arms, the empire was to experience still greater losses: in 1911, the Italians captured Libya, and the next year the Balkan states effectively eliminated Turkey from Europe.
>
> Out of a total area of approximately 1,153,000 square miles and from a population of about 24 million, by 1911 the Turks had lost about 424,000 square miles and 5 million people. By 1913, when Talaat and Enver were already in power, the Ottoman government had lost all of its European territory except for a strip to protect the straits of Istanbul itself.[50]

Given the precarious state of the empire, it is not surprising that in January 1913 there was a coup d'état, in which a much more conservative and ultranationalist agenda replaced the more liberal platform on which the Committee of Union and Progress had come to power; pluralism does not fare well when things are falling apart.

The triumvirate of Enver, Talaat, and Jemal who took over the leadership of the Unionists redefined Ottomanism in a way that was disastrous for the Armenians. Under Ottoman policy, as well as the relatively liberal viewpoint of the Young Turks who overthrew the sultan, Armenians were a legitimate *millet* within Ottoman Turkey. However, when the ideology of Turkish nationalism supplanted Ottoman multinationalism, Armenians were suddenly defined as a potential hostile threat. As Robert Melson so aptly describes the new situation, "[Armenians] ceased being perceived in religious terms as a *millet* and came to be viewed as a rival nationality occupying the same land claimed by the Turks."[51] Armenian political ambitions had not changed appreciably, but the perception of them as non-Turkic people who were an impediment to the vision of pan-Turkism had changed.[52]

Political instability and insecurity frequently breed delusionary visions as compensation for actual power. It is within this soil that the xenophobic nationalist ideology of Ziya Gökalp, one of the principal ideologists for the Young Turks, took root. He asserted nationalism, rather than Ottomanism, as the modern religion and viewed pluralism as a threat to the social solidarity of the state. Thus, Armenians, with their different religion, customs, and language, were a threat to pan-Turkism. Distorting the theory of social cohesion expressed by the French sociologist Emile Durkheim, Gökalp argued for a homogeneous Turkey in which allegiance to the nation replaced obedience to God. Cultural homogeneity became an end in itself, giving the Young Turks the justification for eliminating what they perceived to be a troublesome element of their population.

In addition to the ideology propounded by the leadership, a genocide requires massive participation at the local level by those who are willing to follow orders and who may also be expressing their personal frustrations and hostilities. In the case of the Armenian Genocide, animosity was created by unequal patterns of modernization between the Armenians and their Turkish and Kurdish neighbors. For a variety of reasons—including the influence of Protestant missionaries, the education of Armenians in Europe and America, and the multilingual ability of many Armenians—Armenians had much greater social mobility than did their Muslim neighbors.[53] Although 70 percent of the Ottoman Armenians were peasants or relatively impoverished,[54] Armenians in the empire controlled 60 percent of imports, 40 percent of exports, and 80 percent of commerce.[55] Ronald Suny summarizes the imbalance as follows: "Of the 42 printing plants in the empire, 26 were owned by non-Muslims, only 11 by Muslims; of metal-working plants, 20 were owned by non-Muslims, only 1 by a Muslim; of the famous Bursa raw silk manufactories, 6 were owned by Muslims, 2 by the government, and 33 by minorities."[56] (Although in these instances, most of the "non-Muslims" were Armenian, the term also encompassed Greeks and Jews.) At the local level, too, Armenians had made great progress compared to the Turks. For example, Stephan Astourian cites sources indicating that in Cilicia 70 percent of the Turkish newborn babies died at birth in contrast to only 10 percent of the Armenian babies. In addition, he states that Armenians in Cilicia were modernizing by importing machine technology which, in turn, was putting Turkish laborers out of work.[57] Such differences created jealousy and hostility and help to explain the participation of local Turks and Kurds in the Armenian Genocide and, especially, their sadism and brutality expressed against Armenians. The Young Turk leadership mobilized the Turks and Kurds by preying on their feelings of threat and jealousy toward Armenian modernization. In short, a minority group such as the Armenians is tolerated as long as it remains powerless and serves the interests of the dominant class or population; but if it achieves equality or threatens actual superiority, then the likelihood of repression is increased.[58]

The issue of modernization is also a helpful matrix for understanding the events that preceded the genocide, and especially the massacres of 1894–96. Armenians were caught between two opposing ideological forces: liberal, modern, and democratic views of human rights and older feudal notions regarding the rule of minorities.[59] Sultan Abdul-Hamid clearly represented the older order and viewed the Armenians as a threat to that highly paternalistic pattern of intergroup relations. Extortion, plunder of minorities by the dominant group, and limitation of civil rights are fully consonant with premodern societies. The "Armenian question" would never have arisen if the Armenians had not experienced an intellectual renaissance in the nineteenth century that made them increasingly intolerant of their subjugation under the sultans.

Although conflicts related to unequal rates of modernization by Turks and Armenians are an important element in contributing to the genocide, it is doubtful that a genocide—as opposed to localized pogroms and persecutions—would have occurred except in the context of Turkey's entry into World War I.

First, the possibility of genocide is always increased when a modernizing minority is linked politically to an enemy of the state in which they reside, and unfortunately, such was the case for the Armenians. As discussed previously, during the nineteenth and early twentieth centuries, the massacres and exploitation of Armenians by the sultan had brought cries of outrage and attempted intervention by Great Britain, France, and Russia. Now that Turkey was at war with these countries, suspicion of disloyalty was cast on the Armenians, regardless of their actions.

Second, historic fate had placed Armenians on both sides of the Turkish-Russian border, where they had lived for almost three thousand years. Thus, this artificial dividing line created the appearance of treason when Armenians refused to fight against their fellow Armenians who lived across the Russian border.

Third, the paranoia of wartime was inflamed when a few revolutionary Armenians joined with advancing Russian troops; their action was seized as proof of insurrection, which justified labeling *all* Armenians as dangerous.[60]

And, finally, the Turks' disastrous losses in a foolish engagement against the Russians in the first winter after their entry into the war might have contributed to their need for a symbolic victory. The Armenians were an easy target on which to displace Turkish frustrations, especially given the previous identification of the Russians, British, and French with the plight of the Armenians.

In considering the conditions that led to the genocide, it is important to discard two theories that are sometimes offered to explain the events. First, the Armenian Genocide was not inspired by religion. The ideology that drove the Young Turks was nationalism, not Islam. The most important role religion played in the genocide was at the local level, where Armenians were often referred to as *gâvurs* (infidels). This label dehumanized Armenians, making them more acceptable victims of brutality. A second misconception is attributing the genocide to racism. Unlike the Nazis, the Young Turks were *ultranationalists* rather than *racists*. Their goal was to establish a Turkic empire. Had race been the reason for exterminating the Armenians, Turks would not have abducted Armenian women into their harems, nor would they have adopted Armenian children with the goal of Turkifying them.

ORPHANAGE LIFE

When the war ended, Armenians attempted to regroup. Many children were living in the homes of Kurds, Turks, or Arabs. They had been kidnapped, left behind on deportation routes, or given away by their mothers in hopes of effecting their survival. Many of the children were in pitiful condition: malnourished, ill, and plagued with lice.

Throughout the war, stories about the treatment of Armenians had filtered out through American and European missionaries, as well as various travelers in Turkey, and these reports had appeared on the front page of newspapers throughout the Western world.[61] When relief workers could enter Turkey after the war, reference to "starving Armenians" became a common topic of household conversation in Europe and America. Relief money was collected by major charities, such as Near East Relief, and even Sunday school classes sponsored orphan children. Medical personnel in the United States and Europe volunteered to go to Turkey, and millions of dollars in relief supplies went with them.

After the war, a heroic effort was made to locate Armenian orphans who were living in the homes of Turks and Kurds. These children were brought to orphanages, bathed and deloused, given clean clothes, and placed under the charge of surrogate Armenian mothers. Education was renewed for these children, some of whom had even forgotten the Armenian language. Remaining Armenian political leaders from abroad gave inspiring talks about their heritage, helping survivor-children reclaim a connection with their Armenian identity.

Orphanages also attempted to locate the parents of the children in their care, through both word of mouth and advertisements in Armenian newspapers. Many of the younger children did not know their date of birth, and some did not even know their family name. But when reunions occurred, they were joyful occasions, filled with tears and embraces and stories of the fate of other relatives.

By 1922, orphanage leaders responded to Turkish pressures to remove Armenian children, so they transported all of their charges to Lebanon, Greece, and Egypt. As the children grew older, they were taught skills that would enable them to live independently. Also, orphans fell in love with each other, and suitors came from as far away as America to marry an "orphan girl" as a way of repairing a shattered moral order.

THE REPUBLIC OF ARMENIA

Russia was the scene of another attempt at resurrection. Following the collapse of czarist Russia, on May 28, 1918, a ragged group of Armenians declared an independent state, the Republic of Armenia. This new nation included some three hundred thousand destitute refugees from across the border in Turkey as well as Armenians who had lived in the region for thousands of years. But the odds against the survival of this fledgling nation were insuperable: the economy was shattered, thousands of refugees were homeless, and there was little but empty promises from the Allied Powers who had proclaimed at the Paris Peace Conference that the Armenians should have a homeland.[62]

President Woodrow Wilson, for example, had proposed generous boundaries for an independent Armenian state, but he faced an isolationist Congress that was hostile to further foreign intervention. And in Great Britain, Lloyd George declared to Parliament his support for an independent Armenia, as did various French leaders, but war-weary Europe was unwilling to extend support beyond eloquent words. Meanwhile, the Turks had undergone a remarkable recovery from the war under Kemal Ataturk and were once again threatening the Armenians.

In August 1920, representatives of the sultan signed the Treaty of Sevres, which recognized Armenia's independence and also renounced Turkey's rights over Van, Bitlis, Erzerum, and Trebizond. Nevertheless, in September Mustafa Kemal invaded Armenia. The Armenians were forced to give up their historic territories in the eastern provinces of Turkey, as well as Kars, Ardahan, Surmalu, and Mount Ararat. No foreign powers were willing to protect a decimated Armenia.

After two disastrous winters in which thousands of Armenians died of starvation and cold, the Dashnak government decided that it was in no position to repel the continuing attacks of the Turks,[63] and in the latter part of 1920 it accepted the protection of the Bolsheviks, which eventually spelled the end of Armenian independence. The Lausanne treaties of 1923 represented the abandonment of the Armenian cause by failing to even mention the Armenians. Hence, the chapter on the first genocide of the twentieth century was complete: Armenians had been deported from nearly everywhere but Smyrna and Constantinople; in 1920, the Armenians who had returned to their homes in Marash and elsewhere were driven out by Turkish nationalists; in 1922, relief workers removed their Armenian orphans from Turkey; and that same year, Smyrna was burned and Armenians fled.[64] The Armenian question had been settled.

Lorna Miller's parents: Vahram Sarkis Touryan, born in Darman in 1907, and Adelina Touryan, born in Marash in 1907.

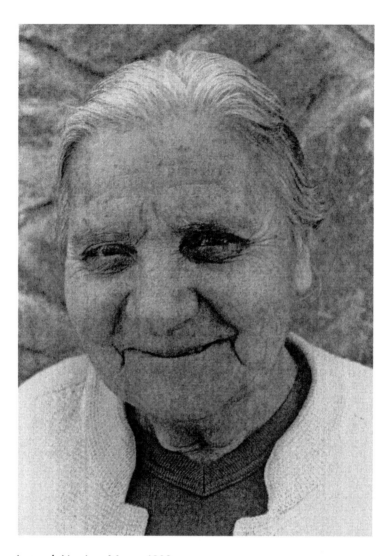

Anaguel Ajemian, Mezre, 1909.

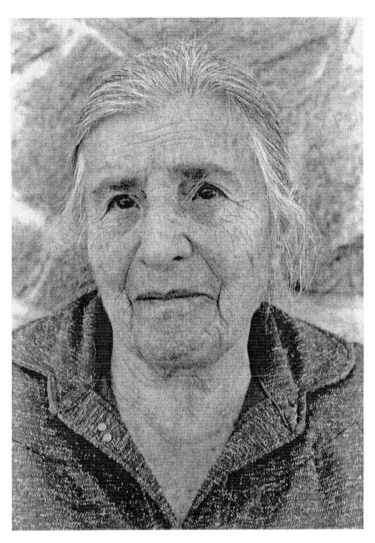

Mary Apkarian Almoyan, Aintab, 1903.

Albert Ailanjian, Yozgat, 1906.

Khatoun Marashlian, Tarsus, 1908.

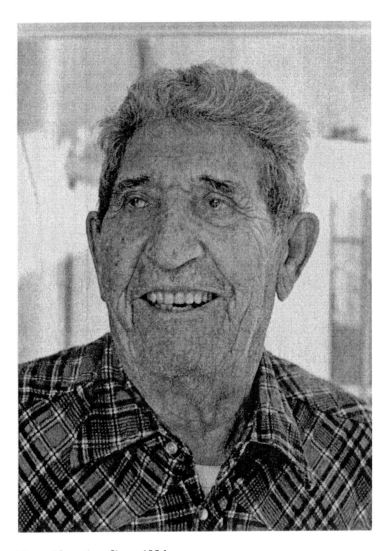

Hagop Elmassian, Sivas, 1896.

Simon Piranian, Aksaray, 1903.

Henry Vartanian, Sivas, 1906.

Mary Dulgerian, Amasia, 1893.

Satenig Marashlian, Belikesir, 1902.

Dikran Paloulian, Bor, 1910.

PART II

Survivor Accounts

Life and Politics
Before the Deportations

The genocide of 1915 destroyed a culture that had evolved for three thousand years. The initial questions of our interviews with survivors focused on this culture, asking them to recall memories of their village or town, their house, the school they attended, their father's profession, the preparation of food, and religious practices. Our goals in beginning our interviews this way were, first, to invite survivors to place their stories of the genocide within a cultural context and, second, to elicit ethnographic information about everyday life before the genocide.[1]

HOME AND FAMILY LIFE

Armenians often lived in extended family units that included grandparents as well as aunts and uncles. The family was patriarchal in structure, with the bride living with her husband's family. Great respect was given to older members of the family clan. In fact, the new bride was often forbidden to speak to her elders—unless spoken to—until the birth of her first child.[2] The eldest man played an important role in representing the family in social and political interactions; the eldest woman, however, ruled domestic matters. Marriage within the family clan was forbidden up to the fourth degree (second cousins could not marry).[3] Family clans aggressively protected each other against insult or threat and banded together to defend themselves when challenged.

Houses varied in construction from place to place depending on available building materials, severity of the climate, and threat of attack by outsiders. Many houses were made of mud bricks, although stone and wood were also used,[4] and roofs were often tile. Very frequently there was a wall at the street that formed a courtyard, containing fruit trees and sometimes a well or fireplace for heating water during the summers. Because of the need to preserve heat, windows were scarce, and the typical house often had only two or three rooms. If the house had several stories, domestic animals might live on the lower level, with the family on the upper story. Many houses were linked by roofs that joined each other, allowing access between houses by the rooftops as well as the streets.

The centerpiece of the house was the living room, which contained a *tonir*, or circular fireplace. Sunken in the floor several feet deep, the *tonir* was often kept burning continuously, at least during the long winter months. In areas where wood was scarce, the principal fuel was dried animal dung. By day, the *tonir* was used to bake bread and cook food. By night, it was the hub of family life: the whole family gathered around the circular *tonir*, sometimes tucking their feet under a blanket spread over it to capture the warmth. On the top of the *tonir*, raisins and other food were often spread as family members told stories, knitted, or played cards and games.

In villages in particular, furniture was scarce. Everyone had his or her own woolen mattress and comforter that were spread on the floor at night—only wealthy families had separate sleeping rooms. There were no chairs; instead, there were cushions (or *minders*) to sit on. The floor was usually covered with rugs and straw matting. The only furnishings were a loom, a spinning wheel, chests that held the dowries of female members of the household, and earthenware jugs for water. Dinner was usually served on the *tonir*, or else on a separate tray that was placed on a stool about two feet high. Those who were dining sat on the floor around the tray, either using bread or their personal spoon to scoop up food; forks were rare except in Constantinople. Every house had a pantry that was stocked with food during the summer to ensure an adequate winter supply.[5]

Mary Ely, one of the founders of the Mount Holyoke Seminary in Bitlis, describes a typical mealtime setting of her students:

> They sit on the floor around a low table or bench on which is spread the native bread, baked in round thin loaves about a quarter-inch thick and one-and-a-half-feet in diameter, looking like a gigantic pancake. On the center of the table is a large earthen bowl, with soup, pilaf, or other native food in it. No plates, knives, forks, or tumblers—simply a few wooden spoons. Little

ceremony is possible at such a plain board. Soon seated in order around the bench, the one whose turn it is asks the blessing and the meal is opened by each tearing off a bit of bread and dipping it in the soup—the process repeated until the bread—their only substitute for plates—is eaten up.[6]

In western Turkey, Armenians were much more likely to reflect European culture in dress and eating habits.

Only the wealthy could afford meat, except on special occasions such as holidays, weddings, and funerals. Otherwise, the typical daily fare consisted of grains, vegetables, fruits, and dairy products. The short growing season did not allow Armenians to waste their agricultural products feeding animals, except insofar as they were necessary for milk, wool, and other by-products. Although they engaged in limited trading Armenians were relatively self-sufficient.

The typical breakfast consisted of tea, bread, *madzoon* (yogurt), and cheese. Lunch was similar to breakfast, but pilaf, eggs, olives, beans, onions, and/or greens might also be available. Dinner was based on the same staples, but might also include small quantities of fish or meat if the family could afford them.[7]

Villa and Matossian offer the following description of clothing worn by villagers:

> Small children of both sexes were dressed in long shifts. Men and some women wore baggy trousers that reached the ankle, a matter of convenience, especially in cold weather, to people who often sat on the floor. Both sexes also covered their heads, thereby providing insulation against both heat and cold. Wool was the most common fiber, but many could afford to buy cotton, linen, or silk cloth for undergarments and summer wear.[8]

Women frequently wore jewelry and, particularly in western Armenia, often wore much of their family savings on their person.[9]

Details elicited in our interviews further illustrate some of the generalizations above, but they also demonstrate differences based on conditions in various areas in Turkey. For example, a survivor from Kharpert said that his family rented their house from a Kurd (rather than an Armenian). On the bottom floor they kept a cow and some horses, and the family occupied three rooms above the stable. In addition to a central living area, there was a bedroom, but it had no separate heating source. The family members slept on the floor and rolled up their bedding during the day. Above their living quarters was an additional area where they could hang clothes to dry. He recalled that the women did their wash in a nearby river, taking with them big pots and wood to burn. After washing the clothes, they would hang them on rocks to dry.

Simpler houses might consist of a single room. For example, a survivor from Hassanbeyli said that they actually shared living quarters with their animals. Only a partition separated them, and it is clear that economy of heat as well as space was afforded by this arrangement. Other survivors described more elaborate houses. A women from Konia, for example, took delight in telling us about her family's kitchen, which was separate from the rest of the house. She said that often the neighbors would get together and roll sarma, make dolma and bread, and other foods. She also reiterated what others had told us: namely, that they had no beds and slept on the floor; they did all their entertaining in a central living area where they ate; and they sat in a circle on the floor to eat.

A survivor from Mezre painted a vivid picture of family life during the cold winter months:

> You know what a *tonir* is? It's a place where you prepare the fire until it is hot and, then in a container, put it in a spot underneath, with ashes on top of it. Then you spread a large comforterlike blanket on top of it so that whoever wanted to would go and place his or her feet under the blanket and get warm. I remember, I'd place my feet under and lie down and sleep in the winter. Also, when guests would come, they'd each go around and find a spot to put their feet under, with the comforter pulled over them, sometimes all the way up to their waist. Then my mother would place all the winter goodies, like the raisins and dried food, on top of the blanket, and we would eat. In the winter, we then slept in the same room.

The cold winter nights provided long hours for visiting, whether with relatives or smaller family units. A survivor from Baghche (near Adana) recalled: "Someone would tell stories and all the rest would sit around listening, sometimes until one o'clock in the morning. The younger children, of course, would go to sleep early, like eight o'clock, just as they do now. It was the older ones who stayed up late, and they would bring out all the food, too, like raisins. Lots and lots. It was so nice."

A survivor from Konia recalled a very similar pattern of family interaction: "We spent wonderful days in the winters together. We never were alone. Either others came to visit us, or we visited them. We told jokes, we played games, cards. We would play cards for apples and things like that. We had wonderful days. This was done with relatives, mostly, because we had a lot of them."

Sophisticated techniques of food preparation had evolved to preserve goods for the winter months. For example, a survivor from Jibin recalled: "My grandmother used to feed us grapes in the winter. They used to put molasses made from grapes in big earthen jars and, in this, place clumps of fresh grapes. The molasses would preserve them until Easter-time, when we would take them out, rinse them with water once, and drink that water as punch, and then rinse a second time and eat the grapes fresh."

This same survivor remembered that his grandmother preserved tomatoes and peppers by digging a hole in the ground, which was protected from rain: "She would place a layer of tomatoes and cover them up with dirt; then she would place several more layers of tomatoes, each time with dirt on it. The tomatoes were preserved until winter, as long as no water got to them." Survivors provided details about other types of prepared foods, as well, including fruit rolls made from dried grape juice, and *rojig* made by dipping walnuts threaded on a string into a thick grape syrup.

The people we interviewed also recounted the religious practice of their families. In some regions, families that belonged to the Apostolic Church actually purchased places for themselves to sit in the church. There were no chairs, so everyone brought his or her own *minder,* or cushion, to sit on. Typically, the women and children sat on one side of the church (or upstairs), while the men sat on the other side. The liturgy was in Armenian, but in areas where Armenians spoke only Turkish, the sermon would be in the Turkish language.

The church was the central gathering place for the Armenian population. Survivors often recalled the deep piety of their parents and grandparents. For example, a survivor from Darman said about his grandmother: "I remember very well. Three times a day, she had a rug which she used to put in the middle of the house and kneel down, three times a day, and pray and pray." Other survivors recalled that their fathers read the Bible at night and prayed before going to work and that their mothers crossed themselves while making bread. Furthermore, Christmas and especially Easter, as well as various saints' days, were occasions of great ritual significance for the Armenian community. Survivors told us, for example, how their mothers baked piles of *kata* (a sweet bread) on Easter to give to friends and neighbors, and they would also dye eggs for the children.

Many survivors also recalled their school days with considerable fondness. Attendance was not mandatory, and because tuition was charged, poor children were less likely to attend. Schools were sponsored either by churches—Apostolic, Protestant, and Catholic—or political parties. Boys and girls were typically segregated by seating or building. It was not unusual for students to take a stick of wood to school with them along with their books to help keep the furnace going during the winter. Students living in Turkish-speaking regions learned Armenian, as well as the three R's, at school. Religious and/or political indoctrination was also a part of their education, depending on the particular school. Because of their age at the time of the genocide, most of our interviewees had their education interrupted, and it was only in the orphanages that their education resumed.

The fathers of the survivors we interviewed held a broad range of jobs prior to the deportations. At the professional level were dentists, pharmacists, doctors, lawyers, and ministers. But more common were shopkeepers, merchants, bakers, goldsmiths, tailors, cobblers, and stonemasons. A number of fathers were also common laborers who tended vineyards, chopped wood, and trapped animals. The vast majority of Armenians were peasants, not professionals. Although relatively few women were employed, some survivors told of mothers or grandmothers who worked as a result of the death of their husband or to supplement the family income. There was a weaver, a seamstress, and a maid, and several did needlework. One mother cleaned the homes of wealthy Armenians, washed their clothes, and ground wheat for them.[10]

ATTITUDES TOWARD TURKS

The relationship between Armenians and Turks before the deportations of 1915 was complex, according to survivors we interviewed. In some locations, Armenian and Turkish houses were intermingled; other areas had a separate Armenian quarter; and in still other places, the entire village or city was Armenian.

A number of the survivors stated that they had had good family friends who were Turks or even that their fathers had been in business with Turks. Several survivors told us that their parents had been invited to the weddings of Turkish friends. Interviews also included stories of Turks who attempted to hide Armenians at the time of the deportations. Typical of the positive comments is this statement:

> The Turks in Konia were very good. One of our Turkish neighbors used to roll dough for paklava for all the Armenians. She used to also make bread on the *tonir* and would often give my mom bread for us kids. We got along very well. When they eventually deported all the Armenians and then brought other Turks in their place, apparently the [local] Turks were heard to have said, "What was the fault or guilt of our Armenians that they took them away and brought these people?"

Another survivor from Konia, commenting on the deportations in 1915, stated: "Our Turkish neighbors were very good people. They cried so much at our departure. We had no problem getting along with them. We were peaceful and friendly with each other. We had no fear of Turks. We visited each other and played with their children. When the orders came for us to leave, our Turkish neighbors could not face us, they felt so ashamed."

In Kaiseri, too, the local Turks could not comprehend the rationale for deporting Armenians: "Many . . . were against these hostilities against the Armenians. They were heard to say, 'What have these people done to us? They are helping us. Please don't hurt them.' A judge used to live near us, and apparently he had said repeatedly for the Turks not to do this to the Armenians, stating that we live side by side."

However, relations between Armenians and Turks differed from town to town and region to region. For many Armenians, the memories of the 1894–96 and 1909 massacres were too vivid to allow them to feel at peace with Turks. Several hundred thousand women and children were without husbands, fathers, or grandfathers because of atrocities previously committed by the Turks. Moreover, many Armenians resented a legal and taxation system that they felt was unfair to non-Muslim minorities within the empire. Thus, a survivor from Marash described the precarious nature of Armenian-Turkish relations:

> The Armenians were careful not to get into any arguments with the Turks. When political events were not favorable toward the Armenians, they would stand across from the mosque and watch the Turks come out to see if they were in a good mood or looked gloomy or angry. If happy, the Armenians would assume that positive things were said about the Armenians in the mosque. If they came out looking bitter, then the Armenians would avoid them that day. Watching the Turks in front of the mosque was the way that the Armenians would understand the political affairs concerning themselves.

THE 1894–96 MASSACRES

Among the survivors we interviewed, the massacres of 1894–96 were the most important event conditioning their attitude toward the Turks prior to the genocide. Very few of the survivors we interviewed were born before 1895, so their knowledge of the massacres came from parents and grandparents. Yet memories of the pogroms of this period were deeply etched in the consciousness of our respondents. Survivors from the following towns said that at least one of their relatives had been killed in 1894–96: Marash, Severeg, Aintab, Kaiseri, Kharpert, Mezre, Van, Sivas, and Urfa.

Typical of these memories is the statement of a survivor from Marash, whose grandfather had been killed in 1895:

> Apparently, Sultan Hamid gave orders that there should be a massacre in Marash for one day. They started in the morning and it lasted all day. In the evening, the government gave orders to stop. Just in our city, about one to two thousand people were killed that day. Many of our relatives were killed, including my grandfather Topalian. He was one of the first to have been killed, apparently. They killed him on his horse as he was returning from the vineyards. Turks had announced that they had killed the "leader of the *gâvurs*." Apparently, they cut off his face to show their leaders who this Garabed Amiralian was. When his daughters went to find his body, the priest told them that he had no face. They did not kill the women. They kidnapped and destroyed houses, but, in general, they did not kill the women or children.

This survivor's uncle and cousin were also killed at this time: they had attempted to protect themselves against attack by fleeing from their workplace to their home, but soldiers surrounded their house and burned it. "I remember that house with its burned walls which still stood while we lived in Marash. It was left to us, so we used to go and play there, since it had turned into a field."

An even more vivid image was related by several survivors from Urfa, who said that Armenians there had sought refuge in the church, only to be burned alive when it was set on fire. One of these survivors said that her mother went to the church after the ashes had cooled and found her father's shawl, which had been tied around his waist. A survivor from Aintab also said that Turks had burned one of their churches, and her grandmother had related to her how she saw a young couple burned to charcoal, still embracing each other.

A survivor from Mezre stated that Armenians were killed with extremely crude weapons in the massacres of 1895. His mother told him that she had seen her father hit in the chest with a hatchet and that he had struggled for breath for three days before dying. A woman from Aintab said that her grandfather had been beheaded while reading the Bible (her grandmother had shown her the blood-stained Bible). Among the instruments that survivors said were used to kill Armenians in these massacres were knives, hoes, axes, and hatchets.

Some Armenians who were on good terms with Turks in 1895 did not heed the warnings that massacres were occurring in other villages, assuming that they were immune from attack. For example, a survivor from Kaiseri recounted that her uncle had refused to hide in the basement with his sons when he heard that the Turks were massacring. After three days, his sons came out of hiding to discover their father dead and their house robbed and virtually empty. Not even their clothes remained.

Another survivor said that her father had gone to investigate a store next to his own place of business, where the owner was being beaten by Turks. A friendly Turk grabbed her father, shoved him back into his own store, and shut the door, writing on it: "[her father's name] blood I already drank." Others told us how individual family members avoided the slaughter. For example, one survivor said that her baby brother escaped death by being hidden in a box where his mother stored cracked wheat. And a survivor from Marash said her family was saved by going to the home of an aunt, whose husband happened to be a contractor for the Turkish army. According to a survivor from Misis, Turkish neighbors hid Armenians during the 1894–96 massacres. In Keghi, the neighboring Turks actually armed themselves and blocked the roads in order to protect the local Armenians from attack.

THE 1909 ADANA MASSACRES

In 1909 a series of massacres occurred in the region of Cilicia, claiming the lives of about twenty thousand Armenians. The massacres were centered on Adana, but we also interviewed survivors from Tarsus, Kessab, Baghche, and Dort Yol whose family or friends were killed. In fact, we heard accounts of incidents that had occurred as far away as Marash, Hadjin, and Gurin. Some of the most graphic images from the 1909 massacres involved attempts to kill Armenians by burning them to death.

Mardiros, a survivor from Osmanie was staying with relatives when news came that the Armenians might be massacred. Turkish soldiers came and closed all the shops, telling everyone to go home. This was about Easter time, he said, and sensing that they might not be safe in their homes, all the people gathered in the church. Mardiros said that between four and five hundred people were waiting in the church, without arms to defend themselves: "All of a sudden, we noticed the ceiling of the church was burning and was falling down and burning people like 'kebab.' People were running around like bees. Those who ran outside were shot by soldiers. Those inside were burning."

Finally, Mardiros decided that he would rather die by being shot than by being burned, so he bolted for the door of the church. Just as he was exiting, his aunt thrust a six-month-old baby in his arms. He ran outside to a hail of bullets but, miraculously, was not hit, even though there were bullet holes in his pants. To his surprise, he received a letter years later from a woman who said that she was the baby he had saved. Everyone else in the church, however, died in the fire.

One of the older survivors we interviewed was seven at the time of the 1909 massacres. Both her father and uncle were killed in Adana. She remembered fleeing to the church for refuge with about five to six hundred other Armenians, but the Turks poured gasoline on the roof and it started burning. The Turks were shooting outside to keep the Armenians in the church, but this survivor said that her family decided to "make a run for it." So they opened the metal gates on the front of the church and rushed outside into the bullets. Her father was shot and killed; her mother was hit in the arm; but our informant escaped unscathed, as did a twelve-year-old brother who was dressed like a girl. When they returned to their house, however, they found it had been burned, and she stayed in an orphanage until after the deportations and the end of World War I. Reflecting on the events of 1909, she stated: "I remember that the Turks during this massacre were really after the men and boys. They did not do too much to the women or to the children." Illustrating her point, she offered this example: "I remember one man who was dressed like a woman, with his head covered. The Turks, I guess, suspected [the deception] and made 'her' walk and decided that he did not walk like a woman, but like a man. They pulled off his head cover and saw that, indeed, he was a man with a mustache. So they threw him in a well nearby."

Another survivor recalled having gone from Adana to his uncle's house in Khaser Bazar when the threat of violence erupted. During this absence, his family's home was robbed. He remembered returning and seeing his schoolbooks thrown on the floor. A prized handwritten church songbook was stolen, and most of their household items were also gone.

In Dort Yol, on the Mediterranean coast not far from Adana, a survivor recalled that the Turks had burned many of the homes of Armenians. And in Baghche, a survivor recalled the Turks murdering Armenian men with axes for fifteen days. Some of their acts were particularly sadistic:

> My uncle was very old at the time that we were in our village. The uncle apparently said that the Turks would not do anything to him because he was too old. He sat in front of our house instead. My mother told him not to sit there because the Turks would come and kill him, and suggested that he

should go to the caves in the mountains and hide. Sure enough, soon four or five armed Turks came and asked my mother where the rest of the men were. My mother replied, "Did you leave any around for them to be here?" Upon this, they told her to shut up and that they would kill her, too. Then they asked what this old man was doing in front of the house, and proceeded to say that they haven't seen an old man dance in a long time. My poor uncle said that there were many others they could play with, but the Turk *mukhtar* said that he would show him how he, too, could dance. So they tied his hands and began to cut him up with a knife so that he would jump around. I saw this with my own eyes, standing with my mother. I cannot forget that scene from my eyes, ever.

In the 1909 massacres, this survivor also lost both his father and nineteen-year-old brother.

A woman from Tarsus told of the killing of her father. The family was forced out of the town with other Armenians, and the men were separated from the women and children. The Turks took the men a short distance away, axed them to death, and burned the bodies. She recalled the women going to the site later and searching through the ashes for some means of identifying their husbands, looking for buttons and other objects that were not flammable. Her mother identified their father in this manner.

Threats of violence also occurred in areas farther from Adana, such as Kessab and Marash, but the Armenians there banded together and attempted to defend themselves. A survivor from Kessab recalled that they had only enough ammunition to last them for a brief period, and then they had to flee to the Mediterranean Sea. When they returned, they found all of their household goods looted, and many of their houses burned. Of note, however, is the fact that the Young Turk government compensated the victims for some of their losses, according to this survivor.

In Marash, we were told, about one hundred Armenians were massacred in the market place, but the government issued orders condemning the killings. A survivor from Hadjin, farther to the north, said that Armenians fought with some of the Turkish villagers after they had burned their summer homes. After ten to twelve days, a truce was declared, and the Turks raised a white flag. An elderly Armenian woman volunteered to go inquire what the flag meant, saying that she did not want a young person to be killed but that she was willing to die for her nation.

These events did not go unnoticed by the world press. Once again, Armenians were the focus of international attention, as they had been during the 1894–96 massacres. Yet the widespread publicity could do nothing to reduce the incalculable impact of these massacres on individual Armenians. For example, a survivor from Misis, whose mother had lost her father in 1909, said that she never remembered her mother laughing. Perhaps the strongest effect of these massacres on surviving Armenians was the overarching sense that many developed about the precariousness of life.

IMPRISONMENT AND TORTURE

In the weeks and months prior to the deportations of 1915, the leaders of Armenian towns and villages were imprisoned in many parts of Turkey. At the time, the motive underlying the imprisonments was not apparent to many Armenians, and in fact men reported without protest to the police when solicited. Our information regarding the torture and imprisonment of leaders comes from children who observed actions against their fathers, uncles, and friends.[11]

A survivor from Sivas described some of the methods of torture: "They would take them to jail and beat them up, and such torturous acts as *bastinado,* as they called it, were done—they would raise the feet above the body, tie them and beat under the foot until it bled. They also used to boil eggs and put them in their armpits." Other techniques included pulling out fingernails (mentioned by a survivor from Chemeshgezak, who said this happened to their mailman who was accused of transporting secret letters); pulling out teeth (stated by a survivor from Zeitun); pulling out beards (reported by a survivor who said that this was done to their priest in Marash); branding on the chest with a hot horseshoe (reportedly done to a survivor's uncle from Kharpert); and hanging prisoners upside down by one foot and beating them back and forth (stated by a survivor from Mezre).

After the men were tortured, many were killed, as we were told repeatedly in our interviews. Perhaps this account by a survivor from a village near Kharpert can—because of its poignancy—represent the other examples of the atrocities that followed imprisonment: "First they handcuffed my father and took him to jail. They had beaten him so much there that he looked pathetic. When my mother realized that my father could not escape imprisonment, she took lots of gold pieces, a whole handful, and took it to a high official and brought him [the father] home. For a month, we kept him in cotton to lighten the pain of his wounds." Then a month later, reported this survivor, his father was taken away again:

My younger brother, Boghos, who was only three years old, was yelling after him, saying, "Daddy, let me come with you." [But he did not return.] They took him [his father and other prisoners] near the River Euphrates, made them sit down as though to eat. The person who had seen this said that my father first bowed his head to pray, and when he was done, the Turks attacked them. I cannot even tell you what brutalities they committed. It's unbelievable and almost cannot be repeated. They used whatever they could [to kill them], from bottles on. He died there and was thrown in the river along with everyone else.

On the basis of survivor testimony, it appears that many men were arrested without any advance warning—they believed that they were going to the police station or government building to answer a few questions. Clearly, most of them were unaware of the underlying plan of annihilation; otherwise, they might have resisted arrest, rather than being compliant citizens.

CONFISCATION OF WEAPONS

As mentioned earlier, before deportation orders were given in 1915, Turkish officials demanded that all guns and weapons owned by Armenians be brought to government offices and relinquished.[12] In some instances, specific quotas were given, and Armenians had to buy weapons if they did not own enough within their community. Guns of all kinds were seized, from sporting arms to those that some of the Armenian political groups had stockpiled for defense of their communities.

When the demand for weapons was issued, memories of the 1894–96 and 1909 massacres were still fresh. Although Armenians could not know of the upcoming genocide, some were nevertheless hesitant to relinquish their only means of self-defense and, instead, buried guns in the ground, stored them in dry wells, or hid them in their houses or barns.[13] This led to house-to-house searches in some communities, with Armenians being tortured until they revealed whether they possessed weapons. A survivor from Mezre described the situation in her town: "So they gathered up all the guns and took them away. And there had been so many beatings while collecting the guns. If a man did not have a gun, he would have to go and buy one so that he wouldn't get beaten up. What beatings! I have seen it with my own eyes." Similar events took place in Yozgat:

Now they searched all the houses for guns. If they didn't find one, then they would take the men of that family and imprison them. Now some had them

[guns], but others did not. My uncle apparently was beaten and tortured badly; they did not take my father. They placed my uncle on the floor and put nails through his toenails. So finally my father bought guns [presumably from Turks or Kurds] and took them in so they would release my uncle. He brought him home, killed a goat, and placed his tortured body in that skin; this used to help the sores.

DEPORTATION ORDERS

On May 27, 1915, an official Edict of Deportation was issued. For most Armenians, the deportation orders that followed were a complete surprise. The experience of Sarkis, a survivor from Chemeshgezak, is typical of the stories told in our interviews.

Sarkis said that he was in school having physical education when the wife of his coach came and told her husband that Pastor Arshag, the principal, had just been arrested:

> You see, they [Turks] first took the educated, the intellectuals. They took these people to a home, which they had converted into a prison, and tortured them in order to get them to talk. So upon the news that Pastor Arshag was arrested, we were dismissed from school and asked to go home. We went home. My father was not there. My uncle had run away. They had put a dress on my uncle's son, even though he was not young, to disguise him. My father's uncle was also in prison, for after taking the younger educated men, they also took the elderly.

Because Sarkis was so young that there was little danger he would be imprisoned, his family would send him to take food to his uncle in prison. It was in prison that Sarkis first suspected something disastrous would happen to the Armenians:

> I would go and sit with him [the uncle in prison]. One day when I was taking him food, I met a lot of police who were saying that on that day we could not deliver food, that all the prisoners were going to leave. I saw them in twos, all chained together. I could not take the food, so I returned home and gave the news. I told them that they were chained and that they were coming this way and would pass by our house, there being no other way to leave town toward Kharpert. By now, all the families had heard, so they were all on the streets to see their loved ones. I got on the top of the roof and was yelling, "Uncle."
> There was a doctor in this procession, and when his wife saw him, she ran out to greet him, but with the butt of the rifle the police pushed her away, even though he was an elderly man. So the men marched on, leaving all the women and families crying and grieving. There was a place about twenty minutes outside of town with trees and water. There they took their names to see if

anyone was missing. They marched them to the edge of the Euphrates and killed them.

Sarkis continued his account by saying that after all the men were gone, deportation orders were issued for the women and children. His town was deported in two groups, fifteen days apart. He was in the second group to leave, but lamented, "I wish we had been in the first group, because they made it all the way to Aleppo." Just before leaving, Sarkis's family gave their bedding and other belongings to their Turkish landlord for safekeeping and gave their rugs to people at the public bath next door to their house. "We said that we would get them when we returned, but we are yet to return."

Several survivors indicated that Turkish neighbors used physical coercion for economic gain before the deportations began. For example, a survivor from Jibin reported the following:

> The next day they gathered up other influential men in the church, including my father and his brothers, and began beating them in the churchyard. We were young; I was only about six years old. We used to go and see our fathers get beaten, and we would cry. One of my father's best [Turkish] friends, who used to come to our house several times a week, was now beating my dad and saying to him that he wanted all of his belongings. My poor father, being exhausted, said that he would do that. So right there in the courtyard, this man brought the papers, and my father signed, saying that he had indeed sold all his belongings to Ismail Beg.

Women whose husbands were in prison or had already been killed took the full responsibility of preparing their families for the deportation. They had to pack whatever family belongings could be carried, prepare food for the journey, and arrange for carts or other transportation. Often, these preparations were hampered by complications. For example, a survivor from Sivas recalled that his mother wanted to kill one of their five hundred sheep to take as food, but the Turks had already stolen them. Another survivor said that her mother had to bribe a soldier with five gold pieces in order to get her daughter a good pair of shoes. Other mothers sold household goods to obtain money for the journey. But survivors from both Kharpert and Kaiseri recalled that Armenians were not allowed to sell *any* of their possessions, perhaps because their belongings were destined to end up in the hands of Turks, anyway. Many told us that their mothers buried possessions before being deported in the hope that they could recover them on their return. Indeed, several survivors commented that if they were to go to their village today, they could still find the place where family jewelry or gold had been buried.

In preparing for the deportation journey, Armenians faced anguishing decisions about what to take with them, as is illustrated by one survivor's comments:

> When they came to tell us to leave, they took us by surprise. Just three days before, we had gone to see the grapes to see if they were ripe enough to be blessed [this was a ritual performed by the Apostolic priests]. Everything was so peaceful then. Only three days later, the town crier called out that we had to leave the town and that on August sixth, they were going to bring us wagons to help transport us. They said they would bring a wagon or cart in front of each house. In those three days, we had to get ready and sell whatever we could. Oh, all those beautiful things, antiques, rugs; we could not carry them with us. We had one cart, but my parents had six children, and with them we were eight people.

Other decisions were even more painful. For example, one young woman had to choose whether to stay with her parents or be deported with her fiancé:

> My future sister-in-law came and talked to my parents. My father would not think of it [i.e., allowing her to go with her fiancé]. But as my parents reasoned between them, they realized that they already had four girls, and that it would not be too easy to protect each, and possibly my fiancé could better watch over me and protect me than they could. We cried and cried. My grandmother gave me rings and gave me her wedding earrings. She gave them to me because they could not do a wedding for me.

Parents were sometimes faced with the terrible dilemma of whether to leave a child behind, especially if there was a Turkish family willing to keep him or her. For example, Nartouhie, a survivor from Palu, recalled that she had gone with her mother to a church for protection when one of the Turkish officials, the *kaimakan* of their village, entered the church:

> His daughter was my age and was learning Armenian, too. In fact, after school, when our servant used to pick me up from school, he used to stop and pick up his girl, too, and we would come home together. Many times she would spend the night at our house. The kaimakan used to like me a lot. He would often make me sit on his lap! [So] when he saw me [in the church with my mother], he said, "Nartou, are you here, too? Come and sit on my knees." When I did, he asked me what I was doing there. I told him that some Turks brought us here, telling us that they were going to save us. He asked me where my mother was. And then he said to me that he was going to take me so that I could play with Saide [his daughter]. Meanwhile, my mother kept signaling

to me to go with him. "No, No," I said. I told him that if he took my mother as well, then I would go with him. So he left, and I stayed behind.

In another instance, Khoren, a survivor from Jibin, recounted that his father resisted letting him remain with a Turkish neighbor who wanted to keep him. He said that the deportation caravan had barely started moving when someone called out his father's name:

> It was Yashar, a partner to my father in the fields. He told my father that since we were all marching to our death, his dad asked if Khoren would stay with us and help us with the fields. I remember my father's answer very well: "If we all die and Khoren is alive, what is the good of that for the family or the nation? He will become a Turk like you. I won't give him," he said. But the gendarme hit my dad with the butt of his rifle; they snatched me and placed me on Yashar's horse, who then took me to his house.

It is unclear from this account whether Khoren's rescuer was motivated by altruism or by the desire to add another servant to the work force.

Some Armenians faced another moral dilemma: they were given the option of converting to Islam and remaining in their homes while their neighbors were deported. Our interviews indicate that very few Armenians elected this option—in fact, only one survivor's family did so out of our sample of one hundred interviews. More characteristic was the following statement made by a survivor from Eskishehir: "Turkish officials came [to my father] and said that he need not be deported, but he must become a Turk [by converting to Islam]. But he refused and said that since they had already drafted his sons and brought them to that condition, he would not give up his Armenian identity. He also said that he would not give his daughters to Turks. On this, they made us leave."

The individual who survived because his mother converted to Islam began to weep during the interview as he told how his neighbors left their town. Very few Armenians from his city survived the deportations, although his entire family lived.

Occasionally, Armenians avoided deportation for reasons other than conversion to Islam. For example, a survivor from Konia said that her eldest sister was allowed to remain because her husband was a tailor who sewed clothes for one of the pashas. Another woman told a similar story—her family remained because her mother was an expert seamstress who was needed to sew uniforms in the local factory for Turkish soldiers. Yet another survivor's uncle was a specialist in making paint and, therefore, was not deported. Also, on occasion, a father might be excused from deportation if his son was serving in the Turkish army, although apparently this was not the regular practice.

REGIONAL RESISTANCE

In the course of our interviews, we often wondered why there was so little resistance to the deportations. This is a complex question, and we have already touched on some of the answers. First, the Armenian leadership had been imprisoned or killed; second, weapons had been confiscated; and, third, the young men most capable of defending their communities had been drafted into the Turkish army. But there are other factors to consider as well.

Because of our own advanced state of technology, we often forget that early in the century, and especially in remote parts of the Ottoman Empire, communication was slow. Consequently, Armenians could not immediately perceive the master plan of extermination that was unfolding, even when caravans marched through their towns from other areas; the full picture emerged only after the worst atrocities had been committed. As one survivor from Kharpert reported: "About this time, deportees also came from Erzerum and Erzinjan to Kharpert. They told us to die in front of our doors and not to leave. I remember that. But the poor women used to think that if they were deported they would be saved."

Finally, the Armenians had evolved a political self-identity over hundreds of years that they were "the loyal *millet*." Thus, when informed that they were to be deported, they obeyed—just as their leaders had reported to Turkish government offices when instructed. However much the Armenians had modernized, they were still obedient citizens of the Ottoman Empire.

Nevertheless, resistance to the deportations did occur in a few places. Among our sample of respondents, we have testimony of defense activities in two areas, Van and Urfa.[14]

VAN

The most notable case of resistance by Armenians was in Van from mid-April to mid-May, 1915. During a five-week period, the poorly armed Armenians of Van fought for their lives in an unequal battle against the Turkish army.[15] Ashkhen offered this account of her experience in Van:

> Gradually we got news that Turks wanted to finish off all the Armenians by massacring them. . . . Every night, taking turns in homes, we had secret meetings to figure out when this was going to happen and how we could prepare

to resist and defend ourselves. They [groups of Armenians preparing to resist] came to our house many times. They would do drills to get used to the rifles. Suddenly word came to us that the Turks were going to attack in three days. Everyone got ready; the men, who were the only fighters, positioned themselves in the basements and were ready with their rifles by small windows. . . . The Protestant churches opened up their meetinghouses for the people to take cover, and waited for the outcome.

Shavarsh, also from Van, recalled the actual fighting in detail:

The whole population was involved, because even we children used to go from house to house to gather the brass candle bars to make shells for the bullets. They even learned to make the powder. Everyone was involved. Sometimes the fighting was at a very close range, from one house to the other. The Turks had all the ammunition and ours was very limited, so we had to be very, very careful not to waste any. Some of the Armenians had the ingenuity that, when a Turk was killed, they pulled him in with a long pole to get the ammunition he was carrying.

Shavarsh recalled that the Armenian resisters were encouraged by the playing of a band that had been organized by a music teacher. He said, "The more he played the more the Armenian fighters were enthused." He also commented that this tactic forced the Turks to keep using their ammunition. In addition, he remembered his own close brush with death during this fighting. He was sweeping the church with a large broom when, suddenly, a cannonball fired by the Turks dropped through the dome onto the floor in the exact spot where he had been standing. While telling this story, he recalled further that when cannonballs fell, the youths would run to them and immediately douse them with water in order to extract the powder before the ball exploded.

On May 14, the Turks started to retreat from Van as Armenian volunteers and Russian soldiers approached the city, and for a brief period the Armenians buried their dead (especially in the surrounding villages) and waited to see what would happen. But when the Turks returned with reinforcements about six weeks later, it became clear that the Armenians had no alternative but to flee. Ashkhen, quoted earlier, recalled how for several days they frantically packed, renting a cart to carry their household goods. They also took their cattle with them and fled toward the Russian border, where they believed they would be safe from further attack. Upon reaching the border, they headed for Yerevan and were among the refugees who, with the Armenians indigenous to Russia, became part of the Republic of Armenia in 1918.

URFA

In our sample of survivors, the only other pocket of Armenian resistance was Urfa. Megerdich explained why the Armenians there decided to fight:

> I remember very well. Several caravans began appearing in the village. They were coming from Dikranagerd, Kharpert, and Severeg. It was a very pathetic sight. . . . We started hearing, as people came to tell us, about massacres: that men were being killed and that they were making everyone leave their houses, women and men, sending them to the deserts. Later, some young boys were brought to our towns. They filled Urfa and the villages. Many Armenians took them into their homes. They brought a small boy to us, too—a little younger than me. He had lost his mother and father and was bewildered, always crying for his mother. He wanted his mother.

At the same time that caravans began passing through Urfa, some government officials demanded that Megerdich's brother give them a dozen donkeys that he owned. His father, against the brother's advice, accompanied these donkeys to the village of Severeg, where the Turks wanted them delivered. The father was presumably killed, for he never returned from that journey.

Megerdich said that his brothers then joined a small cadre of young Armenian men who had escaped from the Turkish army and returned to Urfa. They decided to defend their city from attack and went to train on nearby Mount Saint Hovhannes. Megerdich's task was to take food to his brothers. But resistance was not tolerated:

> One day a large troop came—with thousands—and with bombs. They arrived at our village at about four-thirty or five in the afternoon and headed straight for the mountain. They surrounded it and began firing. We could hear the bombing and rifles. This battle started and we were petrified that they would now come and massacre all of us. Until midnight, the firing poured out. Our men, too, were firing back, but you couldn't tell where it was coming from, but it was pouring.

Late that evening, one of his brothers appeared at their door, having escaped down the back of the mountain. The next morning, however, the resistance was finished:

> The head of the army ordered all males, from youth up, to gather in the local stone church. All the men, like sheep, obeyed and did so. They [the Turks] brought the few that they had captured. My brother went, too. "Why do you go, brother?" [Megerdich asked] but he went. They made the captured ones go by every male and identify who else was at the top of the mountain. From among them, they [the Turks] separated out thirty-five young men from our village, tied them with rope in twos, and took them to Urfa.

These young men were consigned to work on a road crew with a number of other Armenian men. Most of them were killed, however:

> One morning in a place south of Urfa, about one to two hours away, these men worked building a road from Urfa to Rakka. In the morning, thousands of these young men reported to work. They were asked to strip to their shirts and underwear, line up, and be tied. Overlooking them was an Armenian official with a sword. When he realized what was happening, and understanding that they were all going to be killed, he drew his sword and yelled out loudly for all of them to run away. So they all ran, and the Turks opened fire on them.

Megerdich also heard of a similar incident from another Armenian who ended up on a pile of dead bodies that had been stabbed and then pushed over a cliff. This fellow had survived and managed to make his way back to Urfa, covered with blood.

According to Megerdich, however, the general population of Armenians in Urfa was attacked after several Turkish gendarmes were shot in the process of searching for Armenian young men. Violent fighting broke out, and Armenian men and women joined together to defend themselves against the attacking Turkish soldiers. Those who were less able-bodied cooked food for those who were fighting, and the elderly women gathered to pray "Lord have mercy," over and over again. The poorly armed Armenians were no match for the Turks, however. Cannons were aimed at the Armenian quarter, and finally Megerdich's mother, along with other Armenians, decided to surrender. So they dressed Megerdich like a young girl and gave themselves up.

They were put into a *khan* (inn) with a number of other Armenians. Everyone was extremely thirsty, and Megerdich recalled women clamoring for water from a bucket that was brought to them. After living there for a few days, his mother bribed one of the Turks with four gold pieces, and they were transferred to another *khan*. This *khan* was not much better, however. Armenians were dying from typhus daily, and Megerdich recalled how they threw the dead bodies off the roof onto the street below. He summarized their emotions, saying: "We had lost our feelings; our feelings had become numb."

THE PROVOCATION THESIS

Resistance to deportation occurred in a few other areas, such as Musa Dagh. This incident became the basis for Franz Werfel's famous novel, a fictionalized account of how a group of Armenians resisted the Turks in hand-to-hand combat and then escaped down the back of a mountain, to be rescued by French ships.[16] Given the broad scale of the deportations, there was, however, relatively little resistance. Nevertheless, one of the defenses offered by those who seek to deny the Armenian Genocide is that if the Turks did commit any abuses, they were prompted by Armenian threats of sedition.[17]

Talaat Pasha, a central figure in planning the deportations, first propounded that view. However, an alternative interpretation was offered by Henry Morgenthau, the American ambassador to Turkey who had numerous conversations with Talaat.[18] In concluding this chapter, it is appropriate to compare their differing interpretations of events.

In his memoirs, Morgenthau responds directly to the official justification from Talaat that the Armenians were a rebellious people, as demonstrated by their battle with the Turks at Van. In contrast, Morgenthau interprets this legitimation of deportation as part of a centralized plan to settle the Armenian question, once and for all. Morgenthau bases his information regarding the events at Van, in part, on the eyewitness testimony of the American missionaries Dr. Clarence D. Ussher, his wife, and Grace H. Knapp.[19]

Early in the spring of 1915, the Turks and Russians had been locked in battle when the Russians temporarily retreated. Rather than pursuing their enemy, Morgenthau states:

> The Turk's army turned aside and invaded their own territory of Van. Instead of fighting the trained Russian army of men, they turned their rifles, machine guns, and other weapons upon the Armenian women, children, and old men in the villages of Van. Following their usual custom, they distributed the most beautiful Armenian women among the Moslems, sacked and burned the Armenian villages, and massacred uninterruptedly for days. On April 15th, about 500 young Armenian men of Akantz were mustered to hear an order of the Sultan; at sunset they were marched outside the town and every man shot in cold blood. This procedure was repeated in about eighty Armenian villages in the district north of Lake Van, and in three days 24,000 Armenians were murdered in this atrocious fashion.[20]

These events were the prologue to the Van "rebellion." The actual armed conflict began when Djevdet Bey, the brother-in-law of Enver and governor of Van, demanded that the Armenians supply him with four thousand soldiers. Given what had just transpired in the outlying villages, the Armenians interpreted this request as a stratagem to deprive them of the means to resist massacre, and they refused. Morgenthau continues:

On April 20th, a band of Turkish soldiers seized several Armenian women who were entering the city; a couple of Armenians ran to their assistance and were shot dead. The Turks now opened fire on the Armenian quarters with rifles and artillery; soon a large part of the town was in flames and a regular siege had started. The whole Armenian fighting force consisted of only 1,500 men; they had only 300 rifles and a most inadequate supply of ammunition, while Djevdet had an army of 5,000 men, completely equipped and supplied.[21]

Together, men, women, and children fought for a month until the Russian army returned to engage the Turks, at which point the Turks fled and massacred still more Armenians in the surrounding villages. Morgenthau cites Dr. Ussher as stating that some fifty-five thousand bodies of Armenians killed by the Turks were collected by Russian soldiers and cremated.

Morgenthau concludes his summary of the events at Van with these words:

I have told this story of the "Revolution" at Van not only because it marked the first stage in this organized attempt to wipe out a whole nation, but because these events are always brought forward by the Turks as a justification of their subsequent crimes. . . . The famous "Revolution," as this recital shows, was merely the determination of the Armenians to save their women's honour and their own lives, after the Turks, by massacring thousands of their neighbors, had shown them the fate that awaited them.[22]

CHAPTER 4

The Deportation Marches

Beginning in the spring of 1915, Armenians were killed in a number of different ways. As described in the last chapter, many Armenian leaders were imprisoned and tortured to death, while Armenian soldiers were either massacred after being disarmed or worked to the point of exhaustion and death. The predominant method of extermination, however, was somewhat more subtle. Armenians were deported from their homes and forced to march hundreds of miles to the deserts of Syria and Mesopotamia. Along the way some were killed outright, and tens of thousands more died of dehydration, hunger, exhaustion, exposure, and disease. Although deportation might not have been as technologically sophisticated as gas chambers and ovens, it was equally effective at destroying human life.

The pattern that emerges from survivors' descriptions of the deportation marches is complex, however. In some areas, the intent appears to have been the brutal extermination of everyone in the caravan. But in other areas, for some portion of the journey, at least, relatively little violence was directed against the deportees. The experience of caravan members seems to have depended greatly on the attitude of gendarmes who were escorting them. Because the same set of gendarmes seldom accompanied a group throughout its journey, it is possible that some differences in treatment can be attributed to the idiosyncrasies of the individuals who supervised the deportation. Survivors offered instances in which individual gendarmes seemed genuinely protective, but in many cases the gendarmes appeared to collaborate with the Special Organization and local Kurds and Turks who attacked the caravans.

In spite of these variations, the overall effect of the deportations on Armenians was not only dislocation from their historic towns and villages, but also the death of a large percentage of them. Deportation proved to be merely a euphemism for extermination. Scarcely an Armenian family was left untouched by the events of 1915, and many survivors we interviewed reported that they lost half or more of their family members.[1]

TRANSPORTATION

Most Armenians were given a period of a week or two to prepare for their deportation journey, although in some instances they had only a few days. Believing it to be an actual deportation (as opposed to extermination), those with financial means hired carts, donkeys, or mules to carry their possessions. The wealthier a family was, the more carts or animals it could afford. In fact, some families actually contracted with Turks to provide their transportation. Poor families, however, took only what they could carry, which was very little, since many of them had infants and children who needed to be cared for. In a few areas, such as Konia, deportees were transported by train in extremely crowded, wagonlike cars.

A survivor from Chanakkale, in the Constantinople area, described their family's situation: "We had one donkey, where my little brother would sit on one side with a water pot, and I on the other side to balance; otherwise, mother and father would take turns carrying us on their backs."

A survivor from Zeitun recalled a somewhat similar arrangement: "They had made us two boxes, one for my brother, age four, and one for me, age seven. They put these boxes on the mules and did the same for my brother's children. My mother had sewn us bags, and in them placed things like raisins and walnuts, sandwiches. We were to take them with us in the boxes." A wealthier family's arrangements were rather more elaborate, as described by a survivor from Darman: "We had horses and mules carrying the household goods—anything that we could take and anything that was valuable. We had about three carts, two mules, and two horses. This was for both parents, six children, my two uncles with their wives and children."

Realizing that security might be a problem, deportees often attempted to conceal money by sewing it into their clothes or hiding it among their possessions. One survivor said that her family had rented five donkeys to carry their possessions, but her father hid their money in his clothing and shoes and wore ragged clothing to conceal their wealth.

Although most of the interviewees said that they had to supply their own transportation, survivors from both Dort Yol and Kessab said that the government gave them carts and animals. One survivor from Hadjin said that because his brother was a soldier, his family was given a mule cart. Whatever the means of transportation, however, most caravan members were soon reduced to common circumstances.

The deportations might have begun as fairly orderly processions—or at least as orderly as hundreds of families with small children, as well as elderly people, could be. The situation quickly deteriorated, however. Survivors repeatedly told us that a day or two into their journey, those from whom they had hired carts and animals refused to go farther. Deportees were left to continue with whatever they could carry. Moreover, once they had left the borders of their town, the gendarmes often appeared to be in complete complicity with local Kurds and Turks who attacked the caravans, carrying away valuables as well as abducting children and sexually assaulting the women.

SLAUGHTER OF THE MEN

In many, but not all, of the deportation caravans, the men were separated from the women and children during the first few days of the journey and were killed.[2] And because Armenian leaders had already been imprisoned and massacred, and numerous young men were in the Ottoman army, many of the caravans consisted mostly of women and children. A typical account of the deaths of the men was offered by a Konia survivor:

> They asked all the men and boys to separate from the women. There were some teen boys who were dressed like girls and disguised. They remained behind. But my father had to go. He was a grown man with a mustache. As soon as they separated the men, a group of armed men came from the other side of a hill and killed all the men right in front of our eyes. They killed them with bayonets at the end of their rifles, sticking them in their stomachs. Many of the women could not take it, and they threw themselves in the River Euphrates, and they, too, died. They did this killing right in front of us. I saw my father being killed.

Later in the interview, this survivor described a second incident in which many of the boys who had escaped death, as well as the few men who had survived, were massacred. Their caravan had made its way near Der-Zor when an announcement was made that food would be passed out to the men. She described the events that followed:

> When the people heard this, all the disguised boys and men came out and became men again. We gave our donkey to the boy next to us who was from Konia. He used to sing in the church. He was to bring their food and ours. His mother put on his *shalvar* [loose, baggy pants] so that he could stuff it with food. Just as they had killed my father and the other men, so they killed all of these boys and men who came out for the food.

In this case, she said, it was Arabs who lived near Der-Zor who massacred them.

Many of the survivor accounts are similar, differing primarily in the age of the boys who were taken. Sometimes they were fifteen, other times as young as nine or ten. Often, the men and boys were taken away from the main caravan so there would be no direct eyewitnesses to the massacres. For example, a survivor from Sivas stated: "Early in the morning, they took boys over ten years of age and elderly men, and in caravans they took them to the field outside the city. Shortly afterward we heard gunshots and found out they were all killed." Similarly, a survivor from Kharpert said: "They took all the men over fifteen years of age. Once they were taken, they never returned. We heard afterward that they were all killed."

A survivor from Mezre remembered how her father tried to give the family money before he was separated from them. But he was rushed away. The next day they heard gunshots for a long time and knew that the men were being killed. Men were not always slaughtered by shooting, however. In an apparent effort to preserve ammunition, they were often axed, bayoneted, or slain with farm implements.

THE DEPORTATION JOURNEY

The deportees were in despair as they left the villages and cities where their families had lived for generations. A survivor described their departure, saying:

> We got farther away from the houses and reached an open field. We noticed that all the animals were gathered there—our sheep, cows, horses, and so on. I remember my aunt jumping over the fence and going to our cows and hugging them. It was a very sad scene for me, a child. Thus, we left everything behind. There were crowds from every street, all going to the same place. We walked and walked until dark, and I noticed how all the people coming from

different directions would end up on the same road. There were gendarmes on both sides of the road to make sure that no one swerved from his line or fell behind.

In a more abstract manner, this survivor went on to describe the journey: "Anyone who would fall behind would be shot on the spot. They took us through desolate places, through the deserts and mountain paths, so we would not be near any of the cities where we could get water or food. We got wet at night by the dew and were scorched by the sun during the day. I remember going and going."

We frequently heard the statement that Armenians were marched away from populated regions. A survivor from Keghi made the point very clearly: "They didn't take us via regular roads, but instead we would go from village to village and stay outside of them. They would take us through the mountains so that their people would not see us; otherwise, the people would wonder what was going on."

It is difficult to capture in words the human anguish that accompanied the deportations. But imagine, for example, such simple problems as trying to protect one's children's feet: "These were all desolate and wild places, thorns and mountains, uncultivated. I remember well that my mother had made for me something like shoes with cloth; we had no shoes. But in one day that ripped and was the end." Another survivor, from Hadjin, described how her mother cut out little booties each night from a blanket she was carrying until there was nothing left, and the children were forced to walk barefoot.

The recurring image in our interviews is that of caravans walking all day, camping at night—often in fear of being attacked—and then walking again, day after day. A survivor from Chanakkale concisely summarized the deportations by saying, "Walk, walk, walk; the world didn't seem to end." A survivor from Belikesir elaborated on this image:

> Once we left, we started walking and walking for months. We had no donkeys or carts. My legs became all swollen because I was so tired. Sometimes my mother would carry me; otherwise, my older sister did. We had no shoes. We would walk seven or eight hours during the day. After that, you sit and eat bread or whatever is available. We'd cling to each other. Often the young girls would sit below, hiding, and the older girls sat over us.

At night, deportees had little or no protection, because usually tents or other forms of shelter had already been stolen. Typical of their plight was an evening that a survivor from Hadjin singled out for description: "At night we had one blanket which we placed on top of all six of us, but it never quit raining all night. We were soaked from underneath and on top. We were simply shaking—from fear, hunger, and cold."

Questioning a survivor from Sivas, we asked if they had tents, and she replied: "No, no. [We slept] on the ground. Without shoes. And even if you had anything, they used to come and steal it from us." Another survivor described the situation in this way: "At night we slept out in the open with rocks as pillows for our heads."

Deportees were reduced to almost subhuman conditions. Many had been stripped of their clothes, and their hair and bodies were infested with lice. Their skin was not only filthy but often burned from exposure as well. Typical of the self-descriptions we heard was that of a male survivor who said, "I had a child on my back, had on women's clothes, my face was covered with mucus, and I was limping." Describing the attempt to cope with lice, a survivor from Kaiseri said, "[They] would not leave us alone. They would get in our eyes, nose, mouth." She also told of her physical condition: "I had gotten so weak that I couldn't stand up. I was reduced to bones by this time, half dead."

By the end of the deportation journey, according to several survivors, deportees had lost everything, even their clothing. A survivor from Aintab said that his father had wrapped a piece of cloth in front of him, and his mother was clothed in only a shirt. Two different survivors from Hadjin said that caravan members were totally naked by the end of the deportation march and that many of them had turned nearly black from sunburn. Another survivor said that many of the dead bodies along the deportation routes were unclothed. In her words, these bodies were "all blown up, turned black, naked, covered with worms, [both] women and girls."

Indeed, the sight of deportees who had preceded them on the road was a grim foretaste of their own fate. A survivor from Hadjin recalled one of the first groups to have been deported: "Before us the people of Zeitun were taken to Katma and had already started dying of starvation, so that when we got there we saw so many of them dead, in a sitting position. We saw bones everywhere and saw many others who were dying, or on the verge of death, simply sitting and waiting for their turn."

And another survivor from Hadjin gave further details about the earlier deportees from Zeitun: "When we came to Kotma, we noticed that the people from Zeitun had dug up the sand and sat in it and covered themselves up to their chests with it. 'A little water,' they used to want. You couldn't even understand what they were saying. They had buried themselves like that, with the whole family." There were so many dead bodies strewn along the deportation route, said another survivor from Hadjin, that "we used to try to avoid stepping on them."

It was not just the Zeituntzi who littered the road, however. A survivor from Marash recalled the scene he had witnessed as they neared Der-Zor:

> At the first station, we saw a lot of Armenians who had gotten there much earlier than us, and they had turned into skeletons. We were surrounded with skeletons so much that it felt like we were in hell. They were all hungry and thirsty, and they would look for familiar faces to help them. We became terribly discouraged, so hopeless that it is hard to explain exactly how we felt. From grief my father became ill.

It is important to note the frequent reports of starving and dehydrated Armenians, for they suggest that lack of food and water might have claimed as many lives as outright massacres did. A survivor described what she had seen near Bab and Meskene: "There were so many people left on the roads, starving and begging for a bite of bread. Children everywhere, crying, begging. What did we have to give them? Oh, it was pathetic. They were mostly children and old people. Many, many of them, on the sand, wasting away. The old ones could not continue to walk, and the children could not be carried by their parents any more."

The number of dead created a health problem, and the Turks faced the dilemma of disposing of the thousands of corpses that littered the roadways. A survivor who had witnessed the remains of caravans from Moush, Erzerum, and Bitlis commented on this problem:

> When we were going to the village, the road on both sides was filled with dead bodies. I have seen with my own eyes thousands of dead bodies. I did not see how they got killed, but I saw the dead bodies. Women who had long braided hair—their hair comes off the head and their bodies were all swollen. It was summer, you know, so the fat from the body would be melted around the body. And the hair would be like that, intact. It was so bad that it began to stink everywhere, so that they [the Turks] gathered up all the corpses and burned them by pouring kerosene on them.

In other instances, Armenians were burned alive. In our interviews there are examples of deportees being burned in *khans* and caves. For example, a survivor from Aintab described how her cousin was killed: "They took part of our group at one point to a cave and killed them. My cousin was in that group. The way they killed them was to put them in the cave, place wood in front of it, and burn them. They burned them alive, and there was no way to escape from it." We also have accounts of children being burned in a large hole near Der-Zor, and near Misis a group of Armenians who were in hiding was burned, as well as several hundred or more Armenians who had gathered in a *khan* near Kaiseri.

However sadistic it may be to burn people alive, other brutal means of annihilating Armenians were also cited by survivors: for example, cutting off women's breasts and nipples, opening the stomachs of pregnant women, and decapitating people with pruning instruments. Many survivors, however, experienced more prolonged forms of suffering.

HUNGER AND THIRST

Repeatedly, survivors said that the gendarmes prohibited the caravans from drinking, even when they were near water sources. We can only speculate that there must have been an official policy of killing Armenians through dehydration; it is difficult otherwise to imagine denying a child a cup of water. A typical incident was described by a survivor from Sivas: "We finally came to a place, after walking hours without water, where there was a large tree. Under the tree there were dirty puddles of water accumulated from rain and where animals had urinated. The people threw themselves on the water, but the gendarmes began shooting and wouldn't allow anyone to drink. Just think, they would not even let them drink the dirty water."

A survivor from Arabkir offered a similar account: "At one point we got to a place where there was a spring of water. Thousands of people ran to it to drink water, and others drank from any puddle they could find. My mother had me on her back and she too bent down to drink some of the dirty water which was mixed with animal urine. The gendarme nearby came and hit her in the breast. She fell back and I fell off of her. They would not let us drink even from the dirty water."

A survivor from Kharpert described how an Armenian boy was killed in his attempt to get water from a well: "We continued on, but on the way they would not let us drink water, even though we would be walking right by the river. Then we came to a place where there was a well. [A boy] was trying to tie many belts together so that we could get some water. The gendarmes noticed him. Even though he was dressed like a girl, they could tell from his walking that he was a boy. 'Gâvur,' they yelled out to him, and threw him in [the well] and killed him."

Even when deportees were allowed to drink, it was immensely difficult for them to get water from wells without implements. One survivor said that they would tie together articles of clothing and put a tin can on the end. However, people were so thirsty that they would frequently "yank and pull at it to get a drink so that nothing would remain in it."

The ingenuity of a mother who was still trying to provide for her children is revealed in this statement: "We reached a place where water had accumulated where the camels stand. It had frozen, so it was shining. My mother took her head piece and spread it on this icy water and told us to suck water from it. Oh, how we drank. We all drank." This same survivor described how difficult it was for her younger sister to have patience when she was thirsty. She recalled her sister crying out, "Mama, please, some water." And her mother would tell her to be patient. At one point they walked eight days without a fresh supply of water. Another survivor, from Hadjin, told a similar story regarding one of her siblings:

> Now this sister was so thirsty, so thirsty. "Mairig, I am dying, a drop of water. Mairig, I am dying." My mother took her on her back—she was nine years old—and I held her leg so that it wouldn't be too heavy for my mother [the girl had fainted]. [Then] we saw that there was a caravan going ahead of us. We asked them to give us a cup of water for ten cents. They said "no" to the money and gave us a cup of water, and we gave it to this girl. That little bit of water revived my poor sister.

Some of the accounts involving water depicted exceptional altruism. For example, one survivor recalled that her mother kept a little bottle of water with her to wet her daughter's lips but refused to drink any of it herself. She added that whenever she now sees a similar bottle, she relives this memory of the deportations. Another survivor, who was ten at the time, described how his mother had fainted from dehydration. He left his mother and went on ahead where some members of the caravan had discovered water. He drank his fill and then noticed that people were taking water back to those who had fainted. He recalled his mother and went back and found her.

Starvation—as well as dehydration—was a common cause of death. Local Turks were apparently prohibited from giving food to passing caravans of Armenians, and after the Armenians had been plundered, they lost not only the supplies they were carrying but also the means of purchasing more. As a result, they were forced to eat the grass that grew alongside the road. One survivor said that they lived like grazing sheep. Sometimes the grass was boiled and mixed with cracked wheat (bulgur), but often it was simply eaten raw. One survivor remarked that when you are hungry, grass is better than honey or steak. Indeed, a survivor whose father was able to secure some flour described the process of preparation: "We would knead that flour and wash and boil the grass, chop it, add salt and pepper to the flour, and we would eat it."

But survivors also ate anything else they could find, including dead birds, fish, donkeys, and other animals that had fallen along the deportation route. Several survivors said that they picked the grains out of animal dung and ate them: "We used to go and gather up the grains from the animal waste, wash them, and then in tin cans fry them to eat. We used to say, 'Oh, Mommy, if we to to Marash again, just give us fried wheat and it will be enough.' "

One enterprising survivor, who was a teenager at the time, said that she and her sister were sitting hungry, without food, while they watched others eat. So she decided to take matters into her own hands and went in search of food along with several friends. Eventually, she found a year-old calf:

> Slowly, I led it to a small valley, and there I butchered it. I said a prayer to God that what I was doing was sinful and that if we had not been brought to this condition, I would never do this. I begged God to forgive me for this wrong. So with these words and crossing myself in the name of God the Father, the Son, and Holy Spirit, I killed the calf. There were three of us, so I divided it into three sections. The head and the legs I buried there. We took the sheets that we had with us, placed the meat in it on top of sticks and grass so that the blood wouldn't come through, and walked with it. It was quite an uphill that we had to climb. We took it back to the camp and fed it to the sick there. When people asked me where I got it, I said that it was dying, so I killed it.

Early in the deportation process, Armenians who had not yet been deported gave food and clothing to passing caravans. For example, one survivor told how they took extra coats and shoes to Armenians from Zeitun. Also, after the caravans reached the deserts of Syria, the local people sometimes took pity on individual survivors who begged at their doors.

THE ROLE OF THE GENDARMES

The role of the gendarmes was, ostensibly, to escort caravans of Armenians from their local villages to the deserts of Syria. At one level, one can appreciate the vast scale of the task of moving more than a million people hundreds of miles on foot. Even if there had been a humane motive for the deportations, the logistical problems of feeding and transporting so many people—including pregnant women, young children, and the elderly—would have been immense.

Several themes emerged during our interviews on the role of gendarmes in the deportations. Retrospectively, many survivors wondered aloud how it could have been possible for a handful of gendarmes to escort hundreds and thousands of Armenians to their deaths without rebellion. A survivor from Marash told us that there were only two gendarmes escorting their caravan. As she told her story, she pondered, "Was there not a single young person among us who could have killed those gendarmes? We were going to die anyway. What does it mean for so many people to follow two gendarmes so sheepishly?" A survivor from Belikesir expressed the same sentiment: "Just think, there were only two gendarmes walking with us, one in front and one in back on horses. In between, thousands of people were walking. What kind of people were we that we could not kill these guys and be free?"

Other survivors offered answers, however tentative, to these questions. For example, one of our respondents asked reflectively: "Where would we go? Are we going to remain hungry in these mountains? So we kept walking." Once they had left their homes, often in good faith, thinking that they were going to be relocated, how were they to return? Furthermore, some survivors continued to believe that the deportations were temporary. For example, a survivor from Erzinjan said, "We used to actually believe that we were going to another town to resettle. Perhaps the older folks knew better, that we were marching to be killed, but they did not tell that to us." Yet another reason deportees did not revolt is that they had reason to fear the gendarmes. A survivor from Keghi commented, "It used to be said that if we harmed the gendarmes, then others would come and harm our women."

Whether the gendarmes were responding directly to government orders to annihilate the Armenians or were committing atrocities of their own accord, our interviews provide substantial documentation of actions that resulted in the deaths of thousands of deportees. The lowest level of involvement was complicity between gendarmes and local Kurds, Turks and soldiers. For example, a survivor from Konia stated:

> The soldiers would come and give us a bad time. Others from the hills and mountains would come and snatch girls and baggage, or whatever they could. You scream, "Gendarme, gendarme," but there was no help, because they [the soldiers and abductors] were all together in this. I saw all of this myself. I saw them snatch girls and goods right from the horses or wagons, dragging them by force. I can still picture the whole thing right now. They would kidnap more of the older girls. They had brought some deportees on the cliff. They would tie them, shoot them and throw them in the river. There were gendarmes among them, civilians and soldiers. Sometimes it would be

the turn of a pregnant woman. They would look at each other and say, "boy or girl," and pierce her belly with the sword.

Violence was also perpetrated in the very act of herding the caravans. Several survivors indicated that anyone who lagged behind the caravan was shot. For example, a survivor from Mezre recalled how the donkey on which her mother was riding kept dropping behind the rest of the caravan. This little girl repeatedly urged her mother to leave the donkey behind, but she refused because all their money was sewn into the bedding that was loaded on the donkey. The girl left her mother to catch up with her brother and the rest of the caravan. A short time later she heard a shot and then saw her mother's donkey, without its rider, being led behind the horse of a gendarme.

Another survivor told us how the gendarmes used to beat them as an inducement to continue walking: "My mother could not carry my baby brother anymore, so she tied him to my back to carry. While we were walking, the gendarmes were going along, too. They would rush us, and when they'd tell us we could rest a bit, they would quickly then hit us with clubs to get up and continue walking."

A survivor from Aintab recalled his father's being struck by gendarmes after he had grown very weak: "The next morning, very early, the gendarmes got up the deportees to continue, but my father wouldn't get up. They came and said, 'Get up,' and he wouldn't. So they beat him up so very badly. They beat him with their whips until his body was bleeding, and he fell down as though he were dead. Thinking that he was dead, the gendarmes left. I saw this with my own eyes."

Two different survivors from Marash told us about an incident they had witnessed in which a mother was hit by gendarmes because she was slow in packing her tent. After this incident, her daughter, then eight years old, said she used to fervently pray, "Lord, just give us four walls around us."

There is also indication that gendarmes engaged in extortion from members of the caravans they were deporting. For example, a survivor from Gurin recalled this scene: "On the way, the gendarmes—a few of them were taking us—wanted money. They spread a sheet on the ground, and the women, one by one, threw down what they had. They filled a whole bag." From the testimony that we heard, it appears that such greed was often mixed inseparably with violence.

In summarizing the actions of gendarmes, however, we do not want to leave the impression that all were evil. Scattered throughout our interviews are references to gendarmes who carried water on their horses for children to drink, gendarmes who allowed deportees to purchase food, and so on. Just as there were "good Turks" who sheltered Armenian children or families from deportation, there were also humane gendarmes who understood their role to be that of escorting the caravans, rather than annihilating them.

CONFLICTING VIEWS OF TALAAT AND MORGENTHAU

In seeking to understand the motives that inspired the deportations, we can start by examining the statements of Talaat Pasha, one of the chief architects of the plan. After fleeing from Constantinople to Berlin following World War I, he penned a manuscript containing many of his personal reflections on Turkey's entry into the war, its relationship to Germany, and other issues, including his justifications for the deportations of the Armenians. After Talaat was assassinated by Soghomon Tehlirian in revenge for his treatment of the Armenians,[3] the manuscript passed into the possession of his wife, who allowed parts of it to be published in a liberal Turkish newspaper in Constantinople. Even though one would not expect Talaat to assume responsibility for the genocide of the Armenians, the manuscript nevertheless contains some interesting admissions.

For example, Talaat does not challenge the fact that deportations occurred. However, he blames the victims for their own deaths, a theme that recurs in most justifications by perpetrators of genocide. He states that the Armenians collaborated with the Russians on the Caucasian front. In response, the government took the following actions:

> The Porte, acting under the same obligation, and wishing to secure the safety of its army and its citizens, took energetic measures to check these uprisings. The deportation of the Armenians was one of these preventive measures.
>
> I admit also that the deportation was not carried out lawfully everywhere. In some places unlawful acts were committed. The already existing hatred among the Armenians and Mohammedans, intensified by the barbarous activities of the former, had created many tragic consequences. Some of the officials abused their authority, and in many places people took preventive measures into their own hands and innocent people were molested. I confess it. I confess, also, that the duty of the Government was to prevent these abuses and atrocities, or at least to hunt down and punish their perpetrators severely. In many places, where the property and goods of the deported people were looted, and the Armenians molested, we did arrest those who were responsible and punished them according to the law. I confess, however, that we ought to have acted more sternly, opened up a general inves-

tigation for the purpose of finding out all the promoters and looters and punished them severely.[4]

Talaat divided the "looters" into two categories: those who pillaged out of personal hatred and for individual profit, and those who sincerely believed that they were serving the common good by punishing the Armenians for their allegedly traitorous acts. Regarding this latter group, Talaat states: "The Turkish elements here referred to were shortsighted, fanatical, and yet sincere in their belief. The public encouraged them, and they had the general approval behind them. They were numerous and strong."[5]

Talaat offers the following justification for his government's unwillingness to punish these individuals: "Their open and immediate punishment would have aroused great discontent among the people, who favored their acts. An endeavor to arrest and to punish all these promoters would have created anarchy in Anatolia at a time when we greatly needed unity. It would have been dangerous to divide the nation into two camps, when we needed strength to fight outside enemies."[6]

What is noteworthy in Talaat's reflections is that he does not deny the deportations, nor does he deny that crimes were committed against the Armenians. But he distances himself from the abuses by blaming the Armenians for the necessity of deporting them, implying that any atrocities that occurred in the process of deportation were carried out by fanatical local Turks who were pursuing a personal vendetta, and he excuses himself from punishing these Turks because it would have been politically divisive.

Yet Talaat's remarks do not answer several significant questions: (1) why it was necessary to deport Armenians who were far from the Russian front; (2) why women and children had to be deported; (3) why the government armed the Special Organization and encouraged them to attack Armenian caravans; and (4) why events were orchestrated to make Armenian resistance practically impossible. (As discussed previously, some of the preliminary actions included disarming Armenians serving in the Turkish army, arresting Armenian political and religious leaders, seizing all weapons at a local level, creating hysteria among the local Turkish population toward the "traitorous" Armenians, and removing *valis* [regional officials] who refused to carry out abuses against the Armenians.) In Talaat's version of the events, the government did what was required, but the local Turkish population got out of hand.

The memoirs of Henry Morgenthau, the American ambassador to Turkey, offer a contrasting interpretation of the role of the Young Turk government in annihilating the Armenians. Because the United States was neutral in the war at the time he was ambassador, Morgenthau had open access to government officials, as well as free communication outside of Turkey. He spoke on a regular basis with Talaat and less frequently with Enver, as well as with the German ambassador, Baron von Wagenheim. Morgenthau's memoirs, published in 1918, recount many conversations with fellow ambassadors and Young Turk leaders and provide a detailed overview of the genocide of the Armenians. This four-hundred-page book is based on his personal daily journal and on the considerable volume of reports that he received from American consuls in other parts of Turkey, some of which were cited in chapter 1.

Morgenthau relates many of the conversations he had with Talaat on behalf of the Armenians, drawing directly from his diary for the details. Reflecting on his visits with Talaat, Morgenthau states:

> "He gave me the impression," such is the entry which I find in my diary on August 3d, "that Talaat is the one who desires to crush the poor Armenians." He told me that the Union and Progress Committee had carefully considered the matter in all its details and that the policy which was being pursued was that which they had officially adopted. He said that I should not get the idea that the deportations had been decided upon hastily; in reality, they were the result of prolonged and careful deliberation.[7]

In a subsequent conversation, Talaat elaborated on the basis for the policy against the Armenians. Morgenthau quotes Talaat as having said:

> "I have asked you to come to-day," began Talaat, "so that I can explain our position on the whole Armenian subject. We base our objections to the Armenians on three distinct grounds. In the first place, they have enriched themselves at the expense of the Turks. In the second place, they are determined to domineer over us and to establish a separate state. In the third place, they have openly encouraged our enemies."[8]

Morgenthau summarizes the rebuttal that he made to Talaat on each of these points. To the first objection, he argued that massacre is certainly a novel way of destroying business competition, but hardly a fair way of treating people who are industrious. To the charge that the Armenians sought political independence, Morgenthau responded that the Armenians would not contemplate secession if there were an orderly system of government that treated all of its citizens equally. To the charge that the Armenians were sympathetic to Turkey's enemies (such as France, Great Britain, and Russia), Morgenthau asserted that, given the history of massacre and outrage against the Armenians, it was hardly blameworthy that they might appeal to powers that had the potential of protecting them against such assaults.[9]

Among the conversations with Talaat that Morgenthau recorded, one that struck him as particularly outrageous was a request for a list of all Armenians who had life insurance policies with American companies. Talaat intended the Turkish government to collect the insurance payments on the Armenians they had massacred. Morgenthau reports that he nearly lost his temper with this request.

Morgenthau, writing in 1918, estimated that between six hundred thousand and one million Armenians perished.[10] In his view, the events of 1915 were not only a disaster for the Armenians, but they also spelled the "economic death warrant" of the Turks.[11] As a result of the deportation of the Armenians, fields laid uncultivated, skilled labor was at a premium, and those capable of giving financial leadership were dead. The short-term gain of seizing the property and valuables of the "infidels" was past. But gone, also, was one of the most economically productive segments of the population. While Talaat's boast to a friend might have been correct—namely, that "I have accomplished more toward solving the Armenian problem in three months than Hamid accomplished in thirty years"—his policies had also created an economic catastrophe for the Turks.[12]

CHAPTER 5

The Experience of Women and Children

It is perhaps inappropriate to argue that women suffered *more* than men during the deportations, but, in general, they had a significantly *different* experience from the male population. Many of the men were killed relatively early in the deportation process, often experiencing brutal and violent deaths. In contrast, women were left alone with their children to suffer for months on the deportation routes. They were raped, their children were abducted, and they were forced to make excruciating decisions. For example, Was their own life to be valued over that of their children? Would their children have a greater chance of survival if given (or even sold) to passing Turks or Kurds? Should they sacrifice the life of a weaker child in order to preserve the life of a stronger son or daughter?

The story of Aghavni, one of the oldest survivors we interviewed, can help to give insight into the experience of Armenian women during the genocide. In this chapter—as well as the next two—survivors' accounts will be organized to illustrate specific themes. In each case, we will attempt to provide enough context to link the survivors' particular experience of the genocide with the complex historical background.

THE STORY OF AGHAVNI

Aghavni was an infant during the massacres of 1895. Although she remembers nothing of the following incident, her mother and several other women from Sivas told her repeatedly as a child that she was instrumental in saving their lives.

Sivas was attacked in October 1895, and Aghavni's mother and several other Armenian women were running down the street, fleeing Turkish soldiers. A Turkish neighbor was about to take them into her house when she saw three soldiers approaching, and, instinctively, she closed the door. These women, one with Aghavni in her arms, were left standing alone in the street. The soldiers approached the terrified huddle of Armenian women, and to their surprise, one of them spied Aghavni and kissed her on the cheek, saying to the women, "We give your lives to this baby girl."

Aghavni's father was not so fortunate, however; he was killed in 1895. The death of her father reverberated deep in Aghavni's consciousness as she told us about the events of the genocide. Like most of the survivors we interviewed, it was impossible for her to separate the experience of the genocide from the larger context of family history.

In 1915, about a month before Sivas was deported, Aghavni recalled, many of the local Armenian political leaders were imprisoned. Sixty Armenian men were hanged one day, followed by thirty the next, and twenty-five more the following day. Aghavni also reported that at night many of the men who had been imprisoned were chained together, taken outside the city, and killed. Her husband, Bedros, who was in the army, was also killed.

An eyewitness to his death reported that a group of Armenian soldiers was collectively shot. The witness himself was among those shot, but he pretended to be dead and crawled out from under a pile of bodies hours later. He remembered seeing Bedros in the same group of Armenians who were hit and presumed that he did not survive.

Sivas was deported with very little warning. Aghavni said that they had a two-days' supply of bread in the house, which they took with them as they started the deportation journey. At the time, she was twenty years old and had two children: a nine-month-old boy and a three-and-a-half-year-old girl. Together with her uncle's wife, Aghavni rented a donkey, and they put their children and a few provisions on its back. They had gone only three days, however, when the donkey tired and refused to move. So Aghavni and her mother-in-law took the children down and began carrying them.

Aghavni's mother was leading another donkey with some of their possessions. However, she lagged behind the rest of the caravan, and from some distance, Aghavni observed a gendarme shoot her. Immediately, Aghavni rushed to her mother, but when she approached the body a gendarme threatened to kill her also, so she was forced to return to her children and mother-in-law. Together, the mother-in-law and Aghavni alternated carrying her three-year-old on their backs, while the baby was carried in one of their arms.[1]

For seven months they walked. Her grandmother was drowned by gendarmes in the River Euphrates. Along the route, two of her aunts were also killed. Her uncle and a neighbor had their throats slit by Turks. Her brother fled from the caravan and was presumably killed; she never saw him again. Food and water were extremely scarce. In fact, Aghavni remembered wetting a little gown her infant son was wearing and wringing water into his mouth. When telling us this story, she asked rhetorically, "Can you forget that? Every day that I drink water that [image] comes before my eyes." At night they slept in the open, without any protective covering. She remembered women in the caravan being raped by gendarmes at night. But her mother-in-law kept comforting her by saying, "My son was good, and no one will enter his bed."

While being deported, Aghavni observed hundreds of young women commit suicide by drowning themselves in the Euphrates. She said the rivers were awash with bodies of people who had been killed by the Turks, as well as those who had drowned themselves. At one point, in despair, she left her children on the riverbank and threw herself in the river, but a relative saw her and solicited the assistance of a kind gendarme who pulled her out of the water. As she had lapsed into unconsciousness, the next thing she remembered was the gendarme slapping her on the back trying to revive her, and her young daughter crying in a thin voice, "Gendarme, don't hit Aghavni. Don't hit Aghavni." This gendarme was an older man with a real conscience, she said. In fact, he gave Aghavni three gold pieces and instructed her, "Take it and don't throw yourself in again."

Her good fortune was short-lived, however. They had traveled for barely three hours the next day when the caravan was attacked by Kurds. The three gold pieces were stolen, as well as a shawl that she had folded inside of her son's diaper; it had been a prized wedding present. Stripped of everything but their lives, Aghavni and her mother-in-law continued to carry her children as they were herded toward Der-Zor: "We went by way of the mountains; we did not go on the correct routes from town to town. We went up and down mountains. Up and down. I had an apron and I used to wrap my baby in it and hold the other end with my teeth, and climb the mountains that way." Both of her children died on this journey, and perhaps because it was too painful, she did not give the details of their deaths. Her mother-in-law also died, but not until the two of them had almost reached Der-Zor.

All alone on the outskirts of Der-Zor, her resources—physical, mental, and spiritual—were spent. Exhausted, she lay down naked on the bank of the Euphrates River, ready to die. But as she lay there, two elderly Turks came upon her: "[One of the Turks] took his stick and poked me with it. You know, even when you're dead, you still don't want to die. So I turned when he poked me. When I moved, he said 'Tabour, take this girl home. She is a sweet one. Bring her up, and when your son returns from the army, give her to him.' . . . I was lying down, dead. I got up, but I could not walk. . . . Also, I was all naked. And I was embarrassed."

One of the men took Aghavni home. While his wife bathed her, he went out and bought her clothes. She lay in bed for three weeks, and after that, she was sent to live with a servant and his wife who continued to nurse her back to health. When she remarried several years later, she named her firstborn son Bedros in memory of her deceased husband, and her second son after her brother who had escaped the caravan and was presumed dead.

Aghavni's story exemplifies many themes that characterize the experience of women during the deportations. By the end of the deportation journey, all her support structures had completely disappeared. Her husband had been killed, her mother was shot, and her mother-in-law was dead from exhaustion. By the time she reached Der-Zor, she was completely alone. She had struggled against insuperable odds to care for her children, and after their deaths she lost all sense of meaning in her life. She survived, however, because someone cared for her. These themes reverberate throughout our interviews, with substantial variations.

CARING FOR CHILDREN

Children posed a substantial dilemma during the deportations. Whose life should be given priority: an infant who was being carried and nursed or a child who was older and strong enough to walk? Given the circumstances of the deportations, mothers continually faced the terrible question of whether to give their children to passing Turks or Kurds in the hope of enhancing their chance for survival or to struggle ahead together as a family unit, despite the probable outcome that both mother and children would die. Such are the tragic moral choices that genocide so often requires, although it is perhaps an overstatement to call them "choices." In these circumstances, people respond rather instinctively to what seems best given the requirements of the moment.

For example, a survivor from Aintab recalled that both of his parents were accompanying him on the deportation when it started to hail. For a while they continued to plod forward in spite of hail the size of walnuts. Hagop, however, said that he began to freeze and simply couldn't walk any farther:

> I said to my mother, "Please leave me here and go on." She said, "How can I do that?" "I can't [go farther]," I said. "My legs don't move anymore." So with tears, crying, they left. I cried and they cried. It was dark.
>
> In the morning I woke up, and in the midst of all the water, the sun came up—a sweet sun came out and I stood up and now I am crying, saying, "Mommy, Mommy," and eating whatever grass I can. All alone, with no one around in the desert, I am walking, calling for mother. Crying and eating grass.

At one point in his wandering, he heard his name being called. Years later, he learned that his mother had walked a little farther after their separation but then, unable to tolerate the thought of abandoning her son, had said, "If my son is going to die, let us stay here. We'll die, too." According to Hagop: "They slept a little bit away from me and in the morning, they too got up and started my direction, while I went theirs. They called 'Hagop,' and I called 'Mother,' but we missed each other and lost each other." Twelve years later, Hagop was reunited with his mother as a result of a newspaper advertisement that she read listing the names and birthplaces of hundreds of orphans.

Survivors told us numerous stories about babies they had seen abandoned along the deportation routes. Sometimes they were put under the shade of a tree, and other times they were simply left along the roadside to die. On occasion, they were also left on rocks in streams, from which they would tumble into the water and drown—a merciful death, perhaps. One survivor justified these actions by saying that mothers simply could not carry their infants any longer. Furthermore, she explained, "They themselves had nothing to eat, so that they didn't have milk for their infants [whom they were breast-feeding]. The child screams, so what is the mother to do? . . . They would simply set them down and go on." Occasionally, mothers apparently acted collectively in deciding to part from their infants. Two survivors told us independently that in front of a *khan* (inn) in Urfa, perhaps dozens of mothers placed their infants under a tree and walked on.

The moral anguish experienced by women in circumstances that forced them to break the primal bond between mother and child is almost unimaginable. But in story after story we heard accounts of such extreme conditions. For example, a survivor from Belikesir offered this account of discovering an abandoned infant while they were camping one night during the deportation:

> We were in the tent at night when we heard a baby crying and crying without stopping. My uncle said to my mother, "Mariam, let me go and see this baby." He returned to tell us that he saw a little baby boy alone, who apparently had been left behind. We tried to feed him and tried to care for him a bit. My uncle had him in his lap and was walking with him. Then there was another woman on the way who kept crying and crying. We asked her why she was crying. And she said to us that she had an only child, a baby boy, and that she had left him behind. So my uncle's wife asked her if she would recognize the baby if she saw him. [Upon seeing the infant] she answered that it was her child. So my uncle took the baby to her, and she fainted instantly. She finally revived and said that it was her baby. So she took him and began walking. . . . My uncle had several babies, but they all died. He loved children. Many, many babies were left behind like that.

This survivor reported seeing many infants on the deportation routes that had dried up and turned to skeletons. She commented that these sights made her feel that she was going crazy, especially when she saw abandoned children who were still alive. She remembered these children crying as they passed them, "Mommy, a cup of water. Mommy, a piece of bread."

A survivor from Chanakkale told us how they had left her eight-year-old brother behind on the deportation. The donkey on which she and her brother had been riding died along the way, and so she and the brother were walking when he finally declared:

> "Leave me here. I can't go on." He said that his legs were bleeding from rubbing against each other. But how can a mother leave the child? My father said, "Leave him. We will be left behind, too. We will all be left. Armenian woman, leave him."
>
> Now my parents were arguing. My mother can't part from him. Finally, they left him, sat him down, and left some food with him. But no water. We walked on, but my mother kept looking back to the child and kept crying. But my father kept saying, "Walk, woman. We will each stay behind too, one by one. We must. This is our fate."

This survivor said that she remembers this event as clearly as if "it's across from me now." Her mother's eyes, she said, continued to be "behind her," looking back at her abandoned child.

It is clear that these images haunted survivors well into their adult lives. For example, one of the two survivors who told us about the babies left behind in Urfa pondered reflectively in our interview: "Did they kill them, or did they die of hunger?" She finally said, "This scene is always in front of my eyes, you know." She remembered, in particular, an abandoned infant whom she described as a "cute, chubby baby." "What was his fate?" she wondered.

Because most of our respondents were young at the time of the genocide, we can document how these scenes of abandonment affected surviving children, but we have little firsthand evidence of the emotions of mothers who left their children. However, we do have one striking account of a mother's tortured reflections after the deportation:

> Our neighbor used to come over sometimes and say to my mother to come and listen to this poor Miriam Hanem. I, too, used to go to look. She would be sitting on the floor, crying and crying, pulling her hair. She would tell her story, over and over: "I killed two of them. I killed two of them," she would repeat. Apparently, she was walking, holding one child's hand and holding the other in her arms. On the way, they would eat grass or nothing at all. From all of this, they had diarrhea and, meanwhile, they could not stop because the gendarme would beat them and make them walk. So she let go of one of the kids because he kept dragging her behind. She couldn't walk on with him pulling her back. So he was left behind. Meanwhile, she walked on and on until the child in her lap died. She buried this one, but then would cry to us, "What happened to the one who was alive? The wolves ate him; the wolves ate him. One died, I know. The other one the wolves ate."

For the mothers who abandoned children and survived themselves, we can only assume that, as with Miriam, tremendous guilt must have overshadowed their conscious and subterranean emotions, even though from a utilitarian standpoint, abandoning an infant might have been the only reasonable thing to do.

We heard several accounts of children being sold for a loaf or two of bread. Although the motives for these transactions are complex and not entirely clear, it is doubtful that parents sold children simply to assist their own survival. Indeed, the sister of one survivor protested when her father sold two orphan neighbor children who were accompanying them, because she, also, wanted to go (thinking that a surrogate family might at least have food to eat). Another survivor argued that his parents gave up his twelve-year-old sister and nine-year-old brother on the calculation that they would be better off than staying with them. However, his seventeen-year-old sister begged to be drowned rather than given away because she feared being sexually abused. She protested, "Brother, throw me in the river, but don't give me away." This survivor asked us rhetorically, "What could we do? If we resisted, they would shoot us on the spot."

Other children were forcibly abducted. Local Turks and Kurds went among the deportees taking whomever they wanted. Sometimes girls were abducted at night; other times children and women were treated as if they were animals for auction, we were told repeatedly in our interviews. A survivor from Jibin said that there were about 150 people left in their caravan when they entered a Turkish city and were commanded to sit down under some trees: "While we sat to eat, the gendarmes came to take money from us. Also, the villagers began appearing and taking away young children. They would grab them, and holding them by the hand, lead them away. Someone came and took my hand, too. But my grandmother grabbed me and would not let me go." A gendarme who was guarding the caravan saw this and hit this survivor's grandmother with the butt of his rifle. She fell to the ground, and the boy was taken away, along with a number of other children.

On occasion, however, resistance was successful. For example, a survivor from Keghi described how her mother had taken her to the river to wash. Up to this point, her face had always been covered. However, a gendarme saw how pretty she was and grabbed her. Although her mother fainted in the scuffle, somehow the girl managed to break free and mingle with the rest of the people in the caravan.

The emotional, physical, and spiritual stamina required to attend to children day after day was extraordinary. A survivor from Hadjin stated that every morning on the deportation journey, her mother would start the day with prayer and read a passage of scripture from the Bible. Her Christian faith played an important role in giving her strength and confidence. And at night, she remembered her mother sitting between her and a younger sister, covering the three of them with a comforter or blanket. She wondered when her mother slept, commenting: "When I used to open my eyes, I saw that my mother was awake and not sleeping. She used to be afraid, because they used to kidnap girls—many." Describing her mother's strategy for preserving her daughters, she said: "My mother used to keep us dirty intentionally—in the face especially—and would wrap rags on our heads. She did such things. She used to put dirty clothes on us, two or three sets of clothing at once."

Women also had to cope with childbirth on the deportations. A survivor who had been raped by a gendarme said that months later, after the child was born, she still had to find food while living as a vagrant refugee. Revealing her conflicting emotions toward this child, she recalled that she would lay the baby on a rock, unattended, and go off to gather grass to eat. When she came back hours later, the baby would be there crying. The child lived only about a week, and when he died, there was no burial—they simply put the child aside and went on. The survival rate of newborns appears very low, based on references made to childbirth in our interviews. Typical of the comments we heard, a survivor from Aintab stated rather matter-of-factly: "My mother was pregnant on the way. So a little sister, Mary, was born. But since there was no food to eat, the baby died."

One of the most difficult tasks for parents must have been coping with the deaths of their offspring, and more specifically, what were they to do with children who died? Were they simply to cast them aside? If not, how were they to bury them? We were told a poignant story of a father who held his dead daughter throughout the day, wrapped in a blanket on a horse that she had been riding, refusing until they stopped for the night to tell his wife that their daughter had died. When they reached their destination at the end of the day, he took the child down from the horse and laid her on the ground: "My mother threw herself on her body. After all, it was her daughter. We had to leave the next day. We only had a knife and nothing else to dig with to bury her. So we wrapped her in cloth and left her that way. The rest of the way, my mother used to weep and weep. My dad used to try to comfort her and used to say that we were all going to die."

All of the structures that normally give support in times of birth and death had been stripped away from these deportees. Yet something deep in the human spirit continued to crave for rituals of closure and transition, such as burial. A survivor who was a young boy during the deportations told us how he and several friends had buried eight small infants who had washed up on the shore of the Euphrates. They dug shallow graves with whatever implements they could find, faced east and crossed themselves, and then drew a cross in the sand next to each grave. Another survivor told us that, lacking any implements for digging, they placed a cloth over the face of a child who had died, as an act of burial.

RAPE

References to sexual abuse abound in our interviews,[2] but one of the most graphic accounts was of a young girl who was raped by one of the Turkish leaders of a town through which their caravan passed. Gendarmes went through the caravan and found an especially pretty twelve-year-old girl. They dragged her away from her mother, telling the weeping woman that they would return her. And, in fact, the child was returned, but she had been terribly abused and died. The witness to this event said that the women gathered around the mother, attempting to comfort her. Several of them dug a hole near the wall of the city of Dikranagerd. They put the girl's body in this shallow grave and on the wall of the city wrote, "Shushawn buried here." This event made an indelible impression on the survivor who offered this account not only because of the violence of the rape but also because of the attempt of the women to comfort one of their own.[3]

Another survivor told us that he and his Turkish *agha* happened on a soldier who was raping a young Armenian girl along the roadside. He said that "she was bleeding, beaten up, [and was] in bad shape." However, what is distinctive in this account is the fact that the survivor's adoptive Turkish father, who was a leader in the community, challenged the soldier, saying that such acts were against the Koran, and threatened to take him to court. Meanwhile, the girl kept crying through this exchange, saying that the soldier had thrown her mother in a well, and she begged the *agha* to dispose of her, likewise.

One woman told us that she had been forcibly taken as a wife by a Turk and against her will had borne a child. However, when the orphanages opened after the war, she ran away from her "husband"—which also meant abandoning her child. Such decisions obviously involve profoundly conflicting feelings: on the one hand, the child was "tainted" by the rape; yet on the other hand, it was her child, born of her womb. Although this survivor decided to abandon her child and flee to the orphanage, we will never know the number of Armenian women who had been forced into marriages yet *did not* leave their Turkish husbands.

SUICIDE

Echoing through our interviews are recurring references—sometimes only a sentence or two—to young Armenian women committing suicide.[4] Although we obviously could not interview those who had died, we speculate that many of these young women killed themselves out of fear of being abducted as wives and/or raped. The method of suicide in most instances was drowning in the Euphrates River. In fact, this practice was common enough that several survivors told us the words of a song which was sung in the orphanages that included the phrase "Virgin girls holding each others' hands, threw themselves into the River Euphrates."

Hundreds of girls often drowned themselves in a single day, according to survivors' accounts. It appears that a form of group hysteria developed in which groups of young women elected to die together. As best as we can reconstruct, these girls would link arms or hold each others' hands and leap from a bridge or cliff into the turbulent waters of the Euphrates or other rivers. Their motives must surely have included some of the following factors: the girls were physically and emotionally exhausted; they had witnessed tremendous violence during the deportations, including rapes and abductions; many had lost family members; their support structures were minimal; and, perhaps, most important, they had abandoned hope of survival.

In carefully reviewing our interview transcripts, we also identified three other types of suicide: *altruistic suicide, despair-motivated suicide,* and *defiant suicide.* Although these types of suicide were mentioned less frequently in our interviews than young women's suicides, it is appropriate nevertheless to offer brief examples of each in order to illustrate some of the tragic moral choices made by deportees.

Altruistic suicide was motivated by a deeply felt commitment to a person or an ethical ideal. Typical examples of this type of self-sacrifice were mothers who gave their portion of food or water to their children, ignoring their own need for sustenance. In other instances, mothers (or relatives) elected to die with their children rather than to abandon them on the deportation route. For example, a survivor from Amasia told us about a grandmother who elected to stay behind with a child whom the family had decided to abandon. It was clear that the child would die soon, but the grandmother insisted that she would rather die with her than leave her to die alone.

Despair-motivated suicide took place when deportees gave up the struggle of their journey and drowned themselves or simply sat down on the road to die, even though they might have been physically able to continue. A survivor from Gurin told how his mother went twice to the Euphrates to attempt suicide. The first time she returned, obviously not having the heart to abandon her children. But the next time, this survivor told us that he found a little bundle with his name on it next to the river where his mother had left it before taking her life. When we asked him how he responded to her death, he replied quietly, "I cried a lot. Wasn't she my mother?"

Defiant suicide occurred when deportees took their own life in anticipation of being killed, as if to cheat an aggressor of the sadistic pleasure of murder. For example, a survivor told us how his mother died:

they were being deported over a mountain pass, and at a point high above the Euphrates, the gendarmes were stripping the deportees of their clothes and shoving them to their deaths in the river below. When it was his mother's turn, he observed her taking some gold from a bundle that she was carrying, hurling it into the river, and then grabbing her four-year-old son and jumping to her death with the child in her arms.[5]

In reflecting on suicides that occurred during the deportations, we see them all as involving tragic moral choices, paralleling those faced by parents in deciding whether to abandon their children. In both cases, the tragic acts of suicide or abandonment would never have occurred except under the conditions created by the deportation marches. Suicide is always morally ambiguous, but the extenuating circumstances, and the deportees' complex motives, preclude indiscriminate condemnation of the choices that they made.

THE EXPERIENCE OF CHILDREN

Just as we opened our discussion of the experience of women by offering a portrait of one of the oldest survivors we interviewed, we can begin to assess the experience of children by examining the story of one of the youngest survivors.

Anaguel was born in Mezre and was six or seven at the time of the genocide. Before her family was deported, her uncle had been badly beaten and tortured, and her aunt had also been tortured in an effort to elicit secret papers related to her husband's activities as a member of the Dashnak political party. Early in the deportation from Mezre, Anaguel's father was separated from the caravan, along with the rest of the men, and shot. Her mother was also killed when she lagged behind the caravan. From this point forward, Anaguel survived on her own, attaching herself to whoever would offer her shelter and food.

When the caravan arrived in Urfa, Anaguel was graciously taken in by the family of an Armenian baker. While staying with them, she recalled women gathering in a room and singing over and over again, "God have mercy, Christ have mercy." She also recounted a scene from Urfa that had made a strong impression on her: as they were being deported out of the city limits, she saw a group of young Armenian men who were tied together and being stoned by Turks, whose wives were standing nearby and chanting as if it were a wedding or celebration. The next thing Anaguel remembered was finding herself in a large barn that

was filled with sick people as well as corpses of Armenians who had recently died.

Those who were still ambulatory were allowed to leave the barn,
and as Anaguel was exiting from the place, a Turkish man approached
and asked if she would like to go home with him. Weak from dysentery
and lack of food, she readily agreed to his offer. However, when Anaguel
arrived at his house, the wife rejected her, realizing that she was sick.
One of the sons then took this young child to a desolate place, removed
her jacket, and left her there. Anaguel was completely alone, not just orphaned but also separated from the caravan of deported Armenians.
What was she to do?

She started walking, and after a while encountered some extremely
poor Turkish women who were living in caves. She approached one,
kissed her on the hand, and was eventually taken in by a woman who
was childless. Anaguel recovered her health while living among these
women and was instructed to go beg for her portion of food. This was
so contrary to Armenian custom that she found it extremely difficult at
first, but hunger overcame her reluctance.[6] Later, the only problem was
that she often consumed the food she obtained from begging before returning home.

The women with whom Anaguel was living were barely able to eke
out an existence, and after a while her adoptive mother died. Once
again, Anaguel was on her own. She continued to beg for food as well
as to cope with a recurrent eye problem that had troubled her even
before the deportation. As she struggled for survival, she told us how
she used to fantasize that her mother was rocking her in a cradle and
comforting her, especially from the pain in her eye. But Anaguel could
not dwell on these thoughts for long—she had to concentrate on feeding herself.

One day she went to a large *khan* where food was being distributed,
and a woman singled her out and gave her a whole loaf of bread, saying
to her, "You are a *gâvur*." She denied the statement and insisted that
she was a Turk. But this Turkish woman continued to give her a generous portion of food whenever she came and also offered her a quilt on
which to sleep. But this woman was not the only one to single her out
for special treatment.

Another time, as Anaguel was sitting on a rock trying to warm her
feet, a well-dressed Turkish woman saw her, realized that she was an
Armenian orphan, and offered to take her home. Food was plentiful in
the woman's home, but it was also so rich that at first she couldn't digest

it. The woman treated her extremely well and gave Anaguel to her daughter, who had recently married. She lived with the daughter until an older Armenian orphan in the household persuaded her to run away to an orphanage that had been established.

Our interviews are filled with stories like Anaguel's. The feelings of utter aloneness and abandonment that survivors had experienced during childhood marked them for life. As an adult, Anaguel was distinguished by two characteristics, both rooted in her childhood experience. She was a very fearful woman, always worried about being attacked. But another characteristic was at least as prominent: she was constantly feeding people or taking them food. She undoubtedly had little control over her fears, given the insecurity of her childhood; but her generosity in feeding others was volitional, and a wonderful symbol of her attempt to overcome her own childhood deprivations.

A CHILD'S VIEW OF ABANDONMENT

A number of the survivor-children we interviewed spent months and sometimes years nearly completely alone, without parents or other significant adults to nurture them. The feelings of loneliness and loss that survivors reported are very poignant; some of the most emotional moments in our interviews occurred when survivors described the death of, or separation from, their parents. For example, a survivor told us that a Turkish man was volunteering to take Armenian boys, and his mother decided that this was best for him:

> That night, I and two other boys slept at this Turkish *agha's* house. In the morning my mother brought a bundle of clothes for me and left it with a Turkish woman whose husband had worked in my father's bakery and who had lived with this *agha* for years. I was there when she came to the house to leave my clothes. I was sitting there and I saw her, but it was as though I was in a trance. We never talked, and she never kissed me. I don't know if it was because she could not bear it from sadness. I never saw again any of those clothes or anything that my mother might have left in them for me. The deportation caravan now went on without me; they still had two hours to make it to the River Euphrates. When they got there, [we heard] they were all killed.

Such moments are never forgotten, and survivors frequently wept when they told us about their final memories of a father or mother.

Before telling us how her own mother had given her up, a survivor offered an account of an infant who had been abandoned by its mother.

Their caravan had stopped to rest, and an aunt had taken her by the
hand to investigate the remains of belongings left behind by previous
caravans. They noticed a little tent, and inside of it was a hammock
holding a crying infant, who had obviously been abandoned. Nearby,
they also saw a bundle in a blanket; it was the tightly wrapped body of
an old woman. After recounting these desolate images, the child-
survivor told us of her own separation from her mother:

> About this time, Turkish or Kurdish women would come and take children
> away. They approached my mother, too. Realizing that there was nothing but
> death facing us at that point, she gave me to them. . . . She said to me that
> we will come later and join you. So these two women held my hand and took
> me away. . . . I kept looking back and wondering how I could let go of their
> hands and run back. So I kept walking—with my eyes and heart behind me.

This survivor remembered being taken to a room where there were children speaking Turkish, which she didn't understand. She sat and
watched the children play, feeling utterly alone. At the end of the day, the
children left and she was truly alone, with no one coming to take her
home—so she simply fell asleep on the floor. Experiences such as this are
burned into the conscious and unconscious life of the child-survivors we
interviewed.

Sadly, similar stories of separation are repeated again and again, although each has its uniqueness and poignancy. For example, a young
Armenian girl was being watched over by her grandmother when a
Turkish man told the grandmother that he wanted her. She remembered
the man telling her grandmother that all of these children were going to
die and that at least she would have a chance to survive if she went with
him. So the next morning the man returned: "When he came, I remember my grandmother sitting like a dead person, crying and crying. The
man took me and another Armenian girl away. He gave me to another
person, a young woman who did not have a child."

She remembered sobbing and sobbing, and she could not be comforted. Her adoptive mother told the girl that she would take her to her
grandmother the next day, but the woman was merely deceiving her to
quiet her, because "day after day no one took me to her." She stayed
with this family for about three years, during which time she forgot the
Armenian language, and in her words, "I became a Turk."

Not all of these partings were resisted by children, however. A survivor from Marash recalled that they were very hungry when they observed some Turks nearby selling *madzoon* (yogurt). She described the
trade that was made: "So they said that if my mother would give us girls

to them, they would give them *madzoon*. So my aunt does, in the absence of my mother and grandmother who were away grinding wheat. It was my older sister and myself. My aunt said to us that we would be fed well and that they would bring us with them once a week and give them more *madzoon*. We were hungry, so it sounded good to us."

Shortly after they arrived at the home of the new family, she began to cry, "I won't stay here." Meanwhile, her mother had returned and was furious when she discovered that the aunt had sold the children for a serving of *madzoon*. Fortunately, the children's discontent with their new Turkish household provoked the wife to tell her husband to return them. As they arrived back with the other deportees, they found their mother praying for their return. Describing their reunion, this survivor began to weep.

Children who were abducted, abandoned, or sold to Turks or Kurds had many conflicting feelings. For example, a survivor told us of his disappointment that, when a group of Kurds took children away, he was overlooked: "I remember standing by the wall and crying that I did not get to go with them." On the other hand, another survivor said that he asked himself what was wrong with him that his mother had kept his brother but had abandoned him. But even as he uttered these words, as if he had spoken heresy, he immediately countered his question with the comment, "But what could we do? Everyone had to fend for himself." And another survivor described her emotions after she was nearly abducted but struggled free, only to see another girl taken in her place. She said that she felt very bad and, upon revealing her feelings to her father, was told "to be quiet and to look after my own self, because they may still come after us."

FEELINGS OF LOSS AND LONELINESS

Albert was born in the village of Ailanji, near the city of Yozgat. He remembered it as being filled with orchards and trees, and this area was known especially for the wheat grown there. His house was on a hill, with a river flowing in front of it. His father was a farmer, but a progressive man, and in 1912 had gone to the United States with the intention of bringing his family as soon as he was established in business. The deportations, however, interrupted these plans.

Albert's earliest foreboding of the impending disaster came when a number of Armenian soldiers were murdered in a valley near their village. His mother went to investigate but was told to return or she, also, would be killed: Shortly after this incident, the Turks started looting their village at night. Although only nine or ten at the time, Albert remembered joining others to defend Ailanji: "Like David and Goliath, we, too, would take small stones and our slings and at nights protect ourselves against these people. There was no one around to guard us." But their situation was hopeless, so they fled with other families to another village about an hour away: "So by night, having informed everyone by bells, we all got up to go to Koungouy. In one night we all moved to this village. We walked through desolate fields, all quiet except for the cry of infants. We got there at night and slept. In the morning, when we woke up, my sister asked my mom if we were ever going to return home. She answered that we were not. My sister began to cry."

In a nearby village, the Armenians were also attacked. They tried to defend themselves, but the Turks retaliated by burning the village. Having few options, Albert and those from Ailanji decided to return home: "We traveled quietly all night through the fields until we reached the edge of our village. They [the Turks who had taken over their village] opened fire on us. It was pitch-black and we couldn't see one another. They took us and put us in a torn-down house. There we were in our own village, yet captive. All the women were crying and grieving." At this point in the interview, Albert began to weep quietly as he recalled his house and his chickens that he loved.

Albert and his mother and sister were then deported along with other Armenians from their village. After many days of walking, he remembered, they were all gathered in a large field and a *mounedig* (town crier) was announcing: "Whoever wants a woman or child, come and get them." Albert said that people came and took whomever they wanted, comparing the scene to sheep being sold at an auction. Remembering his own situation, he stated: "A man came and grabbed me. My mother began to cry and cry and would not let go of me. He slapped her and yanked me away." Weeping softly, Albert told how he and his mother ended up, quite fortunately, living in the same village. His mother was taken as the wife of a Turk, and Albert was taken to a separate home where his job was to graze sheep. Albert's sister was able to stay with his mother, earning her keep by taking care of the turkeys in the household. On occasion, Albert would go to visit his mother, and he recalled her saying: "I stay alive for your and your sister's sake."

For three years Albert lived with this Turkish family, and although his adoptive father was good to him, the man's wife used to beat him. Sometime in 1918, Albert's mother came to visit him. She told him that a new orphanage had opened in Yozgat and that she and his sister were going there:

> We went to a barn to talk. That barn became a palace for me. There my mother talked a long time to me, giving me advice. She kept assuring me not to worry, and that she would have me brought to the orphanage, also.
>
> Early in the morning my mother had to leave. She was going to walk. My mother kissed me and gave me advice. We walked together to the edge of the road, both of us crying. When we came to a hill, we separated. My head and eyes were continually looking back to my mom.

When Albert returned to his Turkish home, he said that everything looked so different. The very fact that he had been able to visit his mother occasionally had given him comfort. Now he felt totally alone.

So Albert decided to run away from his home to try to find his mother and sister in Yozgat. A few days later, quite fortuitously, he found his sister sitting on a rock, all alone, not far from where he used to graze sheep. She explained that on the way to Yozgat, she and their mother had wandered too close to a herd of sheep and were attacked by several of the guard dogs. His sister said that their mother had wrapped her body around her so she would not be bitten and, in the process, was terribly mutilated herself. As their mother lay dying, she told the girl to go back and find her brother. After the mother died, Albert's sister placed an apron over her mother's face as a burial cloth and went in search of Albert, with no idea where to find him.

Albert recalled that after his sister finished her account, together "[we] cried and cried, grieved and grieved." With pain in his voice, Albert summarized their feelings by asking, "Who cared for us? Who was concerned for us? We were all alone." Albert said that his life had lost all meaning—the only thing he could think about was finding his mother's body.

So he sent his sister with a passing caravan that promised to take her to the orphanage in Yozgat. He then stole a horse and went searching for his mother's remains, but to no avail. By this time, Albert might have been eleven or twelve and, having failed to find his mother, he began looking for the orphanage where he believed his sister was living.

Arriving in Yozgat, he encountered another orphan boy like himself. This fellow had been surviving by stealing bread from a bakery, and so together they decided to find an orphanage that might take them in. After trying an orphanage that had been closed because of a louse infestation, Albert found his sister in yet another orphanage. Although they had not been separated for long, he described how they hugged and hugged, both feeling very alone in the world. The orphanage she was living in had no beds but only simple wood planks on which the children slept. Albert declared: "The only thing to say for the place was that it was safe, that no one would come and snatch us away."

There is much more to Albert's story, but these few glimpses into the relationship between a mother and son, as well as a brother and sister who struggled to find their way in a world that had lost meaning and predictability, are paradigmatic of the experience of many orphaned children. Emotions of loneliness, loss, and grief are common to many of the survivor-children, but there is nevertheless a unique poignancy in each articulation of these feelings.

For example, a boy of eleven or twelve who was living alone with several of his sisters described a typical evening: they had found an abandoned store in which to sleep, and after moving the stones aside on the floor to make a place to lie down, he said that he put his face on the dirt and slept. Or consider the case of an orphan boy who, at about seven years of age, decided to return all by himself to his hometown of Aintab. Making his way to a crowded train station, he described how he boarded the train after waiting some time for his turn: "finally, they threw me on top of the heads of the people. I fell through and found a place on the floor [of the train], after being shoved around." Eventually, he teamed up with another orphan who was a few years older, and after arriving in Aintab, they went together in search of relatives who might have survived.

Somewhat surprising to us was the frequency with which orphan children living in Muslim homes would strike out on their own at the first opportunity, rather than clinging to the security offered by the adoptive family. For example, a girl who had been taken in by an Arab family stated: "They treated me like a daughter. It was a nice house they lived in. I stayed with them for about one year. Then I ran away. I reasoned that no matter what, I was Armenian and they were Arabs. If I remained there, I, too, would become an Arab and lose my Armenian identity. I thought that if I ran away, some Armenians, someplace, would take care of me."

Some time passed before this survivor was reunited with her people. She first encountered a group of Kurds, and although they were friendly to her, she believed that it was because she was a likely bride. So she stole some bread and continued her flight until she finally found an Armenian who arranged for her to serve as a maid to a German family.

Another survivor remarked, "Anytime someone came to take me to another place, I went willingly, looking for a better place." She described a series of homes she lived in after being orphaned:

> Initially I was with a Turkish family where the man had two wives. One of them had children and the other did not. The wife without children used to take care of me, but the other one was envious, saying that she was taking care of a *gâvur*, taking the food away from her own children. The man being the cause of the strife between them [the two women] took me to another house. Here the woman was paralyzed and very thin. She had a child and couldn't take care of her. So I was to do all the chores around her. I was so young myself and didn't understand her language [Turkish].

One day she was sitting on a wall holding the paralyzed woman's baby on her lap. This wall adjoined a large house owned by a Turk who had taken an Armenian as his wife. By this time, the survivor-child had forgotten Armenian and could speak only Turkish. The Armenian woman told her that she knew a family who had a little girl she could play with, and asked if she would like to live with that family. They arranged a meeting time, and she left the baby she was tending to go to this woman's house.

> When I got there, two effendis were talking. The woman made coffee, put it on a tray, and had me carry the coffee to the men. I remember walking so slowly and carefully with the coffee in the tray. The woman must have washed me and put clothes on me, because I don't remember if I was still wearing the rags from the desert. But I must have looked presentable. The effendi took me with him to another town, and I didn't return to the family with the baby. I lived with this family. They had a garden and two older daughters.

In offering this account, she reiterated her previous statement about continually hoping for a better situation and being willing to leave one family in order to join another in pursuit of a better life.

SURVIVAL SKILLS OF CHILDREN

Armenians use the word *jarbig* to describe someone who is clever and able to manipulate circumstances to his or her benefit. In listening to the stories of interviewees, we frequently heard the expression *jarbig* in reference to children who survived. A child who was passive, allowing circumstances to dictate fate, did not live long. Children who survived were not only aggressive, but they often had to be clever, as well. This meant taking risks that could easily have led to death and making choices that gave them control over circumstances. Children who survived learned how to charm the Turks they encountered and to exploit opportunities for their own advantage.

One very *jarbig* survivor offered several examples of how he fed himself. It was summer, and he noticed a Turkish man and his wife asleep in the courtyard of their house. They had left the door ajar, and the boy sneaked in, grabbed the blanket off of them, and ran. The man pursued him, but he evaded him and took the blanket to the marketplace where he exchanged it for some bread. This survivor said that he became a "first-class" thief in order to stay alive, and he offered several other examples of his craftsmanship. One afternoon he was working with a Turk who had six pieces of bread, and being extremely hungry, he secretly took several pieces of bread from the man's lunch. He ate one of the pieces, and then another half. The other half he shredded into little pieces next to the man's lunch to make it appear that a mouse had eaten the rest. In another instance, he had a job cleaning stables. For this work, he was given a small piece of bread each day. Unable to survive on this limited amount of food, he took some of the tools for grooming the horses and traded them for bread. He concluded these accounts by saying that "wherever there was the possibility of getting bread to eat, I would go to serve."

Other interviewees also offered a variety of accounts of survival that included stealing, although they were sometimes hesitant to tell these stories. One elderly survivor recalled, after some urging, how he had stolen a woman's purse in the market as she was buying halvah. He also remembered pushing a container of *bekmez* (a thick syrup) from the hand of a woman on the street. It spilled, and after hiding, he went back to lick the syrup from the pavement. And he recalled stealing grapes off of a donkey. The owner caught him and started beating him, but he continued to eat the bunch of grapes as he was being hit.

Another survivor lived as a servant with a wealthy Turk. She was well provided for, but she would steal money from her employer and give it to two poor Armenian women she knew. Yet another survivor who was a servant arranged for her brother to come beg at the Turkish home where she worked. Whenever he came, she would fill his hands with cracked wheat, oil, and other things, and he, in turn, took them to their mother. Some months later, she decided to run away. Before leaving, she removed the nice clothes the family had given to her, folded them neatly, and put on the rags she had worn when she entered the home. In her mind, it was right to steal food for her brother and mother, but it was wrong to take the clothes that her employers had given to her.

Rather than elaborating on these individual incidents, we will conclude this chapter with the story of Megerdich, who, at the time of the deportations, was an eight-year-old child living in Garmouch, a village outside of Urfa. It is an excellent account not only of a child's survival skills, but also of his overriding desire to reunite his family after the deportations.

THE STORY OF MEGERDICH

Megerdich remembered very distinctly caravans from Dikranagerd, Kharpert, and Severeg passing through his village before he was deported. In fact, his family had taken in a small orphan boy from one of these caravans. Megerdich recalled, "He had lost his mother and father and was bewildered, always crying for his mother." Megerdich's father had been killed prior to the family's deportation, and when they set off on the march from Urfa, Megerdich's mother dressed him as a girl.

The caravan's first destination was Rakka. They expected to be resettled there, but upon arrival, they were marched through town to the shores of the Euphrates. They spent fifteen days there in horrible conditions, said Megerdich, and hundreds more deportees arrived daily as they waited. They were then informed that they would be sent to Der-Zor and that whoever had money could hire a boat for transportation. So with his uncle's family, they rented a boat and went all the way to Der-Zor. The boat must have been a luxury that most deportees could not afford—or else they were not given that option—since we heard numerous accounts of Armenians arriving in Der-Zor on foot, naked and exhausted, having lost many members of their caravan on the way.

After they arrived, this eight-year-old assumed the role of father and husband. He bought a horse as well as a donkey, and placing his sisters on the animals, he and his mother walked beside them, along with another brother and some other relatives. For days they walked, often along the Euphrates River. He stated that they saw many bodies floating in the river, and when they washed up on shore, "The soldiers used to ask us boys to go and throw the bodies back in the river."

They were then ordered to go toward Mosul, which required crossing the desert, away from any water sources. He recalled that one cup of water sold for a red gold coin. For days they walked without food, and, indeed, a vivid image stood out in his mind from this portion of their journey. A man had fallen down on his back during a rainstorm, and he was so tired that he could not get back up. He kept saying, "Please, come and help me up. I have valuables to give you. Please come and help me." But Megerdich asked, "Who would listen? Everyone is concerned about *his* life."

At this point in the journey, his brother could no longer walk, "so we left him behind by the side of the road. He yelled and screamed after us." A few days later their grandfather died. He had been carrying a grandson, and Megerdich was left with this small boy. However, they couldn't care for him, and a Turkish woman offered to take him, "so we gave this little grandson to her, hoping that God would look after him. We wanted to give our little sister, too. But she would not part from us."

Finally, they reached Mosul. They paid a man to let them hide in his barn and were thereby spared further deportation. Still, life did not improve substantially. Megerdich said that there was a terrible famine, and it was difficult to get flour for bread, so they survived by eating grass mixed with flour. Under these conditions, his mother died suddenly: "We used to gather up grass together, and she always wanted me to live and used to give me her portion. It got to a point that her body could not take it, so one morning we got up and found her like an angel, with her spirit gone. We took her and buried her. I know the grave to this day. It was behind a church." Megerdich was now alone with his sister-in-law and two younger sisters.

Still on the move, they went to Tell-Afar, and there someone told him that his two older brothers were alive in Aleppo. He said that his "heart jumped" when he heard that he might see them. But he pondered, "How was I going to go there?" After some consideration, he decided to walk. His sisters and sister-in-law, however, decided to stay in Tell-Afar.

What followed was a remarkable account of an eight-year-old taking on the world in an attempt to reunite what was left of his family. Mingling with a caravan of Arabs, he walked for six or seven days to Nisibin, where he found some relatives who were working for the Germans. They cleaned him up, gave him clothes, and helped to rid him of the lice that were crawling all over him. He then went to the train station, studied how the system worked, and decided that this was the best way to get to his brothers:

> When I saw that all the cars were lined up in a long line and the whistle blew, I went and grabbed the outside of one of the cars. They were open animal cars. I grabbed on hard until it reached the next station, where it blew the

whistle long and then stopped. I jumped off and walked around as though I were a porter. I was dressed like a porter, and my head garb was like what the Kurds wore. It was nighttime, and I waited for the train to move again. I did this until it went quite a few stations.

As he traveled on this train, Megerdich soon learned that freeloading was not appreciated:

One time when the train started moving again, and I had grabbed on, all of a sudden a man came to me. He was a train official and asked for my vesica [ticket]. "What is a vesica?" I asked. He asked me how I could be on the train without a vesica. I told him that I was a porter and that my brothers were also in another station. He said that would not do. So he asked me for money. I had none, but I told him that if he took me to the station where my brothers were, I would go and get money from them and pay him. "All right," he agreed. But I had no idea where my brothers were! He must have been a good man. He told me to follow him so that he would take me to a safer place.

The train official, in fact, notified him when it was time to get off, and Megerdich continued to search for his brothers: "It was dark. All I knew was that my brothers worked in a garden near the border. So I walked on and on, looking for a garden. In the distance, I saw some greenery and yelled out. Someone came out and asked who I was. I said it was me and asked who they were. He said that he was Hovhannes. It was my oldest brother! Benjamin was there, too. We hugged and I told them all about what had happened to us."

Megerdich remained with his brothers for about two weeks, and then began to worry about his sisters: "After I had rested a little, I sat in the garden and I wept, thinking about my sisters. My heart could not take it. My oldest brother came and asked me why I was crying. I told him that I was afraid they would die. So he said that one of us should go and bring them. As I thought about it, I knew that they couldn't find the way [even though they were considerably older], and that it had to be me." So, together, Megerdich and his brothers decided that he should be the one to return to the sisters.

The brothers negotiated with the same train official whom Megerdich had previously encountered. They settled on a price for him to go, as well as to return, so for fifteen hours he rode the train back toward his sisters. And through numerous negotiations he returned to his sisters in Tell-Afar. He convinced them that their brothers had food and were living relatively comfortable lives, and despite many difficulties, he and the sisters retraced the journey to be reunited with their brothers.

CHAPTER 6

Orphanage Life and Family Reunions

In 1895, Hayastan's grandfather was killed with a hatchet. Her mother said that for three days he struggled to breathe, with air escaping from a wound in his lungs. However, during the tragic events of 1915, her immediate family was spared deportation. Her sister's husband was the personal bodyguard to American consul Leslie Davis, who lived in Mezre,[1] and when the deportation was announced, Consul Davis took pity on Hayastan, three of her sisters, and her parents, all of whom were allowed to move into the consulate building. Her older sisters and their families, however, were deported, and of that group, the only person she heard from again was her maternal aunt.

Hayastan's vantage point in the consulate gave her a unique opportunity to observe events as they occurred. After the deportations began, Mezre was filled with orphans from caravans that passed near the city. Hayastan's mother was extremely compassionate toward these children, imagining the fate of her own grandchildren who had been deported:

> We used to gather these kids up without the consul knowing it and place them in the large stable, which was for the horses and the cows. We would let them sleep there, and in the morning my mother would give them a piece of bread and send them out from the back door so that neither the consul nor anyone else would see them. They would go out and beg and wander around during the day, but at night they would return.

The children were infested with lice, and as they slept in the barn, the animals all became infested, too. Hayastan's older sister would cut the orphans' hair to rid them of their lice, bathed them, and gave them clean clothes. They carried on this work of charity until 1918, when Near East Relief opened a number of orphanages, including one supervised by Mr. Henry Riggs, that cared for many of the orphans they had nurtured.

The plight of these orphans was extremely pathetic. Hayastan recalled that during the cold winter months, they huddled outside the doors of Turkish homes, seeking what little heat might escape under the threshold. She remembered orphans frozen stiff by morning. And even in the consul's barn, the children often did not fare much better, although the heat of the animals' bodies helped keep them warm. She specifically remembered Antranig, a thirteen-year-old boy who died of pneumonia. Many such children died in the stable, she said.

But she could not forget the face of Avedis, a good-looking young man who had come to them with an injured ankle. He couldn't walk and, in addition, had dysentery:

> One day we were doing the wash and they told me to take Avedis some milk that my mother had boiled, along with some cheese, which they thought would help his intestinal problem. . . . I went there and what I saw was not Avedis at all. His eyes were wide open, his mouth open. He was dying, and I did not know it. I went back to my mother and said that Avedis did not talk to me, and he was making a funny sound. My mother ran to him, and he had died.

Hayastan said that for a long time, and especially at night, Avedis's face appeared before her, and she would cling to her mother for comfort.

On September 7, 1922, Hayastan's family left Kharpert, along with 250 orphans. Mr. Riggs and orphanage personnel all over Turkey were evacuating Armenian orphans from their native land. Hayastan's father helped supervise the caravan of children, first taking them to Aleppo and then on to Beirut. Two weeks later, Hayastan's uncle followed with another group of 300 orphans who were transported by wagon. In addition to Beirut, orphans also went on to Greece and elsewhere.

Hayastan's mother did not make the trip, however, She died at sixty-three—of a broken heart, according to Hayastan, who believed that her mother simply could not cope with the deaths of her older daughters and their families, who had been deported.

MISSIONARIES AND RELIEF EFFORTS

The first Protestant missionaries went to Turkey in the early 1830s, sent by the American Board of Commissioners for Foreign Missions (ABCFM). By the turn of the century, the ABCFM had 12 stations and

270 outstations in Asiatic Turkey, with 145 missionaries. In addition, 114 Protestant churches, 132 high-grade schools, and 1,100 lower-grade schools, as well as 6 colleges had been established by the missionaries.[2] Many missionaries refused to leave when Turkey entered the war, and consequently, they witnessed atrocities connected with the genocide. Even more important, however, they were able to provide the infrastructure for the relief efforts that began as soon as news regarding the plight of the Armenians spread to the United States and a number of European nations.[3]

Near East Relief was born of an appeal for $100,000 by James L. Barton, foreign secretary of the ABCFM, and Cleveland H. Dodge, vice president of the Phelps Dodge Corporation and a close friend of Woodrow Wilson. The money was raised in a month, with the aid of a $60,000 donation by Dodge, and transferred to Henry Morgenthau, the American ambassador in Constantinople.[4] Morgenthau stated that this was a "good beginning," but drawing on information from the United States Consul in Aleppo, he said that $150,000 a month would be required for that one region alone. Subsequently, Barton, Dodge, Charles Crane (eldest son of the founder of the plumbing equipment company), and other influential people formed the American Committee for Armenian and Syrian Relief (ACASR)—later called Near East Relief—and by the summer of 1916 there were ACASR committees in thirty-eight U.S. cities.[5] The central organizing committee, headed by James Barton, mobilized public opinion effectively by sending news releases to major newspapers based on information they received from missionaries and relief workers stationed in Turkey and Syria. In response, philanthropic organizations such as the Rockefeller Foundation gave more than $300,000 between 1915 and 1916, and the cause attracted the public spirit of compassion to such a degree that even the proceeds of the Harvard-Yale football game of 1916 went toward Armenian relief.

Between April 1917 and October 1918, donations to Near East Relief averaged $500,000 a month. By October of 1918, the group had raised $11 million, and by the end of 1919, nearly $20 million had been given for the rescue of the Armenians.[6] Churches were targeted for fundraising, and Near East Relief supplied ministers with resource materials for their congregations, including the following lyrics, sung to the tune of "America the Beautiful":

> Oh! Beautiful for martyr feet—
> Whose weary, bleeding stress
> A line of life in death hath beat
> Across the wilderness!

> Armenia! Armenia!
> To God thy dead arise
> And low at evensongs of heaven
> Acclaim thy sacrifice.[7]

Through well-organized appeals, Near East Relief had raised over $40 million by the end of 1920.

The United States government also made grain available and provided transportation to help save the starving remnant of Armenians. Thus, in February 1919, one of three U.S. Navy ships, the *Mercurius,* unloaded 2,000 tons of flour, 2,500 cases of canned foods, 500 cases of condensed milk, 18 trucks, 20 ambulances, 500 sewing machines, 200 oil stoves, 1,750,000 yards of cloth, 50,000 blankets, 800 hospital cots, 26 tents, 78 X-ray machines, and 200 tons of coal.[8] Some of these ships also carried relief workers, such as the *Leviathan,* which left New York on February 16, 1919, with 240 mission and relief personnel, including 30 physicians and 60 nurses.[9] Between 1916 and 1929, nearly a thousand Americans served overseas in relief efforts; many, but not all, of them assisted the Armenians in Turkey. Twenty of these volunteers and five missionaires died from typhus, pneumonia, and other diseases.[10]

Referring to the efforts of Near East Relief, President Calvin Coolidge stated:

> Not only has life been saved, but economic, social, intellectual and moral forces have been released. New methods in child welfare, in public health and practical education have been introduced. A new sense of the value of the child, a new conception of religion in action and a new hope for a better social order have been aroused. All this has brought enduring results, a promise of a brighter future to replace the despair of years of fear and hopelessness. The work of the Committee has demonstrated practical Christianity without sectarianism and without ecclesiastical form, recognizing the rights of each and all of their ancestral faith, while expressing religion in terms of sacrifice and service that others might live and be benefitted. Its creed was the Golden Rule and its ritual the devotion of life and treasure to the healing of wounds caused by war.[11]

The United States was by no means the only nation to come to the aid of Armenians. Several European nations, particularly through their missionary movements, built orphanages and offered medical assistance and food. Names such as Papa Kuenzler, who along with his Swiss wife gave their lives to helping the orphans, will long be remembered by the Armenians.

The two hundred orphanages staffed and operated by Americans played an important role in rebuilding the lives of the children who survived.[12] Although the administrators of these orphanages could have been cultural imperialists, they in fact recognized the importance of teaching the orphans about their own history, as well as helping them relearn their native language, which many children had forgotten while living in Muslim homes. The orphanages were also vital in offering children educational opportunities; indeed, the few survivors we interviewed who were illiterate were those who had lost their parents in the genocide but did not grow up in orphanages.

Because American and European orphanage personnel encouraged girls, as well as boys, to achieve educational goals, the girls benefited from opportunities that might not have been available to them otherwise. Many of the girls left the orphanages to pursue nursing or teaching careers, and some of the survivors we interviewed indicated that they had somewhat resented getting married and adopting more conventional Armenian gender roles.

Hence, it is difficult to overestimate the importance of these institutions in healing the wounds of the children they nurtured. The orphanages functioned as "families" for the survivors who had lost parents as well as siblings. Here, orphans bonded to each other, seeking to recreate the closeness they would otherwise have enjoyed with their own family.[13]

GATHERING THE ORPHANS

By the time relief efforts began, Armenian children were scattered at many points along the deportation routes, with many of them living in Turkish or Kurdish homes as a result of abduction or abandonment. The younger ones had forgotten their native tongue, and many were confused about their national identity, particularly if they had been adopted into relatively nurturing homes. The older children, on the other hand, often maintained their sense of nationalism and better understood the dynamics of the genocide they had experienced.

After the war, concerted efforts were made to locate these children and move them to orphanages. In many instances, children were living on the street and naturally gravitated to the orphanages for food and shelter. And in other cases, children ran away from the family with whom they were living upon hearing that an orphanage had opened in their city. But it is also true that some children were removed forcibly from the homes in which they were living.

Hagop, one of the older survivors, assisted in the process of collecting orphans from Turkish homes: "When the English came, they started to gather up all the Armenians, so I and another woman, who spoke Turkish really well, went to the surrounding villages to gather up the Armenians. We would go where we knew there was an Armenian and say, 'This girl here, you give her back or you go to jail.' That way we gathered about two hundred or so people and brought them all back to [the town of] Homs."

When gathering these orphans, they also encountered Armenian women who were living in Turkish homes:

> We found a woman who was gathering grass from a field to cook and eat. I noticed that she was looking at us strangely while we were speaking Armenian. So I told the woman with me that I thought that this woman, too, must be Armenian. But she had gotten married and was pregnant. When we asked her if she was Armenian, she said, "Yes, yes, shush, be quiet. They'll hear you from there." We asked her what she was doing there. She said that she was left starving and thirsty, so she got married. When we asked her if she wanted to go back to the Armenians, she said, "Sure!" She said she must have brothers somewhere and would like to go and find them. We planned to meet her the next evening secretly and, sure enough, after we waited about fifteen minutes, she came and we took off and were safely away.

After they returned to the city, an English army captain saw that the woman was pregnant, and he found a bed for her, as well as a woman to care for her, paying the expenses from his own pocket.

Not every separation was so simple, however. Some Armenian women had been married to Turks for several years and had borne them children. A survivor told us, "I had girlfriends who had married Turks. They used to say 'I want my effendi.' They wanted their husbands. They had a comfortable life." Indeed, this survivor remembered several Armenian women who escaped from the orphanage and returned to their Turkish husbands. But she also recalled that some of these same women later returned to the orphanage and were accepted back gracefully.

Some children also resented being taken from their Turkish homes, both because they had formed attachments to their surrogate parents and because conditions in the orphanages were difficult, with food often being scarce, especially when the orphanages first opened. A survivor recalled that once, when all the children were hungry, some of the older girls began to shout, "Why did you bring us here? Let us go back to the Turks." Another survivor said that her uncle's wife found her playing on the street, and recognizing her, said: "You are the sole survivor [of your family]." The aunt took her to an orphanage, but three days later she ran back to her Turkish mother, who hid her. Eventually, however, she was taken back to the orphanage and not allowed to run away.

A survivor from Kharpert recalled how she was taken to Papa Kuenzler's orphanage:

> One day while I was sweeping the floors with water, two soldiers walked in.
> Apparently orders had come that Armenian children had to be gathered from
> the Turks. These soldiers told me that I was Armenian and that I had to go
> with them. I was all wet and shivering. Then I said from fear that I was not
> Armenian, but Turk. Apparently on a hill above the city they had rented a
> large building and were gathering up all the Armenian orphans from the city.
> Some of the older ones, ones who understood, had actually run away from
> their adoptive homes to go there. Little ones like us, of course, did not know,
> so they gathered us up themselves.

Recalling her first evening in the orphanage, this survivor said:
"Some were crying, others confused. At night they took us to that building that was like a *khan*. There was no food. No beds. They just laid us
on blankets in groups of four or five children. This did not last long,
though."

Orphanage personnel struggled with overwhelming circumstances,
both in terms of the number of children they were serving and the resources they had to offer. One woman described her early experiences at
an orphanage:

> I was not accepted for two days, but the third day an orphanage took me in.
> They took me upstairs, but I didn't know anyone. There they were all lying
> down in dirty beds. Some had a blanket, others had only half a blanket. I
> remember that they cut all my hair with a little machine. Up until then, my
> hair had not been cut at all. There was not much food or much clothing. So
> we were hungry and cold. They only gave us food in the morning and night.

For some children the move to an orphanage represented, at a purely
physical level, a decline in their circumstances. Minas, for example, described his home life with a young Turkish couple who took good care
of him:

> I was very happy there. It was after this that the English came and gathered
> us up. The French announced that they would pay money to any family who
> gave news of any live Armenians. They came and found me too and wanted
> to take me away. You should have seen how this poor lady [his adoptive
> mother] cried and did not want to part from me. So I told her not to worry,
> that I would run away and return. She really could not stop crying.

His new orphanage home was not particularly inviting, however. There
was very little food to eat, and the orphanage was infested with lice from
the children.

On the other hand, some children ran away from Turkish or Kurdish homes to join an orphanage. In particular, older children—who had not lost their sense of Armenian identity—seemed more inclined to exercise initiative in leaving comfortable circumstances in order to rejoin their fellow Armenians. For example, a survivor from Darman remembered having been picked out of a pile of dead bodies by a Turk. This man took him home, and he became his servant, grazing the man's herds. He lived with him for five years, but when he was perhaps seventeen or eighteen, the idea of running away to an orphanage occurred to him:

> This man had to go to Kharpert, so I went with him and saw in the business district that there were people who were speaking Armenian. I asked someone if there were some Armenians there, and they told me that there were a lot of Armenians, as well as an orphanage run by Near East Relief. I kept that in mind and when I came back, I decided one day that it was time for me to leave these Turks and go to Kharpert. So I left and traveled about fifteen days, all by myself, walking. There was nothing to eat. I ate any grass that looked good. I finally reached Kharpert and went directly to the Near East missionaries and told them who I was. It just happened to be that the head of the orphanage, Mr. Riggs, said to me that he had been to my home so many times. He had known my mother and father.

Because this survivor was older than the rest of the orphans, Riggs placed him in charge of food distribution within the orphanage.

ORPHANAGE LIFE

Despite some children's ambivalence about going to the orphanages, they served an extremely important function in gathering the survivors and thereby became the basis for establishing a new generation of post-genocide Armenians. For the orphaned children, these institutions were a bridge from disorder, trauma, and chaos to relative order, stability, and structure.[14]

The orphanages nurtured a semblance of family life. Children were divided by sex into different groups, and *mairigs* (surrogate mothers) were assigned to each group. These *mairigs*—often widows or older orphan girls—were usually in charge of about a dozen children. Survivors who described their orphanage experiences to us in some detail included this young girl from Sivas:

> I was very happy in the orphanage. We all had the same story in that we all were Armenians who had gone through the deportation and had lost family. It was very clean, and they took special care to keep us very clean. I had hair that was past my waist, never cut from the time I was separated from my

mother. They cut all of that. The food was good and regular. Every morning
we had a brief prayer meeting, and then we went to classes. In the morning
we had breakfast, at noon only bread, and at night we had bread and cheese.
But it was such good bread. We were all healthy. We had medical help as
well, and in the summers they took us on retreat to another village.

Of her first few days in the orphanage, she remembered being ushered
into the "living room" of the orphanage where one of the older *mairigs*
was in charge. The girl had completely forgotten her mother tongue,
and the *mairig* taught all of the newcomers a hymn in Armenian. The
song was number 14, "What a Friend We Have in Jesus." The survivor remembered singing the hymn without understanding any of the
words. Also in that first week, everyone was given a physical and assigned a number.

When they entered an orphanage, some of the younger children knew
very little about their background. For example, one man told us that he
didn't know his name, so he made up a name and told them it was
"Tashjian." Later, when his uncles were looking for him, they wondered
where he had gotten that name.

In spite of troubled beginnings, the survivor children we interviewed
generally had very positive recollections of their orphanage experience.
Many remembered getting a good education in their orphanage. The
teachers—who themselves were survivors—were often very nationalistic, and they put their heart and soul into redeeming this orphan remnant. Resources were scarce; one survivor recalled that there was only
one book for every four or five students. But apparently the curriculum
was rigorous: "Within a short time, they gave us a crash course in language, and those who were in music, they taught music, and brought us
up to better than our age average. I even learned algebra. They were fan-
tastic. They couldn't do enough for the orphans."

Discipline was seemingly strict, both formally and informally. For example, several survivors said that they were punished if they spoke Turkish, while another respondent said that the older boys used to beat the
younger children if they caught them speaking Turkish. Yet the moti-
vation for discipline emerged from a deep concern for the children's welfare. A survivor recalled one of his teachers in the orphanage:

We really had some very good teachers. They used to look after us like their
own children. We had a teacher from Van whose name was Gostan Bandi-
gian, and we never saw him sleeping at night. He used to go through the halls
at night, covering the children who needed it. He also used to try hard to stop
our fighting among ourselves. When we would not listen to him, he used to

throw his jacket aside and say that he was going to throw himself in the sea. Then we would all stop fighting, surround him, and apologize.

We heard contradictory testimony regarding how orphanage personnel dealt with the children's psychological trauma from the genocide. Several female survivors told us that they were forbidden to talk about their deportation experiences, while others said that they were encouraged to relieve themselves of the burden of these memories. In fact, in some orphanages, the children even wrote songs commemorating their experiences. Likewise, they sang nationalistic songs that provided a sense of collective strength in this time of rebuilding and despair. In some orphanages, Armenian nationalists came to give speeches to the children.

In the midst of the positive experiences, there were also painful moments, as children attempted to cope with the reality of being alone in the world. What their mothers would have done unthinkingly, these children had to manage for themselves. For example, a survivor said somewhat plaintively: "We used to try to comb each others' hair. We were young; we couldn't manage too well." She also said that her eyes sometimes hurt so badly that she couldn't open them, and she lamented that she did not have a mother to comfort her.

Sometimes orphans were invited to their relatives' homes on Sundays or holidays, which was a great boon to their spirits. But many other orphans had no relatives. When we asked Rebecca what the most difficult moment of her life was, she replied: "It was a Sunday. A lot of relatives of orphans came to the gate to see them. One by one, they called out the names of orphans if there were relatives waiting for them. I sat there, too. No one called my name. That day I can never forget. How much I cried. 'Why am I left alone? Why me? Why is there no one asking for me?' That day kept me very sad." Another survivor voiced the same poignant reflection: "Many of the other students had relatives who used to come and visit them. We would all stare at the reunions, thinking how lucky that they had an aunt or uncle."

Physical nurture was easier to provide than psychological mediation to help reconcile the orphans to their experiences. Feelings of loss were common to all the orphans, but many of the children also had to struggle with an abrupt change in their social status. The following statement expresses both feelings:

I was the son of a very wealthy man. Why should I now be in an orphanage and fight over a piece of bread, or not even have one? Why should I not be with my brothers and family, living as we used to? Why not have a mother? Whenever someone would say "mother," my heart used to break into pieces. I couldn't take it. Sometimes some mothers [obviously widowed] used to come to the orphanage to bring things to their sons. I used to watch, lower my head, and wonder and ask why was I not to have a mother. Why should I not have a mother?

Balanced against such moments of anguish were the good times that helped rebuild the children's spirits. In the words of one survivor: "There was a nice community in the orphanage. We used to dance and sing. We would sing a lot of sad songs and cry together. We used to teach each other the dances we knew according to the places we came from. We were sad, but happy with each other."

FOOD IN THE ORPHANAGES

One way of glimpsing into the daily routine of the orphanages is to look at their food and meals. Because orphanages were operated by different funding sources, supplies and services were not uniform; furthermore, conditions in the orphanages were more stringent in the initial months of operation than after they had become better established. Survivors we interviewed offered varying images of orphanage life. For example: "They used to wake us up early in the morning and take us to church. After church, we ate breakfast: tea and a piece of bread. For lunch, we had soup and bread. At night, we had pilaf and beans. They cooked in huge pots. There were a lot of orphans."

Other descriptions indicated a more spartan diet. For example, a survivor stated that "they would divide up one bread in four ways, giving us only a quarter piece. At night we had only three walnuts to eat and a few raisins." Another respondent said that they used to get cookies in tin cans from the United States, but more typical fare was bread and sometimes an onion. According to another survivor: "They gave us raisins and bread in place of a meal, or sometimes nuts and bread. On occasion, we even had some meat in our food, with string beans."

The source of meat, however, was often questionable: "One day there was a dead donkey in front of our orphanage. They brought it in, cooked it well, and served us soup. We were very hungry." Another survivor related a similar story, saying that orphanage personnel killed a mule they found and made soup from it—but some of the girls were apparently afraid to eat the soup, thinking that since mules are sterile, it would affect their own childbearing capacity.

Fruit was rarely included in the orphans' diets, and a number of survivors mentioned their various attempts to obtain oranges or apples. The most common method was to use their bread, especially if they had extra, to barter for fruit: "I used to get one and a half bread, while my sister got only one. It was more than we needed, so we used to exchange some of it for fruit and vegetables that other Armenians grew." Similarly, another survivor said: "They never gave us fruit, so we used to gather all our bread, sell it, and with the money buy enough fruit to fill a skirt. We'd bring it back and eat them."

This survivor also recalled an anecdote reflecting the compassion of Mr. Riggs, the missionary who oversaw several of the orphanages in their town. "One day, apparently when he was going by, one of the orphans asked him for an apple. He went to the orphanage and asked why they were not given fruit. So that noon, when we went in for our bread, we all found apples waiting for us. He was a very kind and gentle person. He loved the orphans, and the orphans in turn felt very comfortable talking with him."

Not all orphanages had the resources to respond to the children's cravings, however. For example, a survivor told us that they were frequently hungry and that orphanage personnel dealt with the problem in the following manner: "Since we were young, they used to put us to bed so that we would not feel our hunger. Sometimes we'd get bread, and other times they's make soup with cracked wheat and water."

SPONSORS AND MISSIONARIES

Much of the money raised to support the orphanages came from individual donations. One striking example of the connection between orphans and sponsors was offered by a survivor who was able to attend school because a Sunday school class in the United States sent a monthly donation for her education. At one point, Khatoun was informed that she could no longer attend school, and when she asked why, she was told that the class which had been supporting her had stopped sending its donation.

Another survivor described the interaction between sponsor and child: "Most of the orphans had a sponsor. They used to have us write letters so that they could translate them and send them to the sponsors. We would write simple, childlike letters. They also used to take our photos and send them as well." The orphans also did needlework for their sponsors in the United States: "We used to study and go to school until noon. In the afternoon, we had to do needlework. They used to tell us that the work we did they sent to the United States, so the Americans would send money with which we could be fed." Although the interaction between children and their sponsors was sometimes very direct, it is equally true that thousands of people gave donations simply in response to images of "starving Armenians."

While some people gave money to support the orphans, others gave their time and even their lives. For example, a survivor recalled a Miss McPherson, an Englishwoman who came to Turkey at the age of eighteen: "She worked voluntarily and was not paid, and she stayed and died there, too. She apparently was a wealthy person. But she was a deep Christian. She made us pray a couple of times a day, and if we did not, she would tell us not to rebel, but to thank God, even just for sunshine."

Another woman who gave her life for the Armenians was a Miss Jacobson. According to a survivor: "She became a great Armenian mother. She used to counsel the orphans as they would leave, giving them advice on how to get along on their own and in their new places. She, herself, could speak Armenian, so she brought the orphans up with a spiritual and Armenian spirit. After her death, on her grave, they called her Miss Hagopian, which is Armenian for Jacobson."

The non-Armenian mentioned most frequently in our interviews was Papa Kuenzler, a Swiss missionary.[15] Survivors told us of his love and concern for them, as well as of an incident that resulted in the amputation of his arm:

> We had a girl who had TB. Papa Kuenzler used to like her a lot and felt sorry for her. He visited her often in the hospital. One day she died. We were asked to pray for her. Papa Kuenzler dug the grave and buried her himself. While doing this, he got a thorn in his finger, and traveling up, it infected his arm. He did not pay attention to it until it was too late. He had to go to Beirut for surgery. We used to cry and pray for him, and we were told that important doctors were brought in to work on his arm. They amputated his arm, and after a while in the hospital, he returned to the orphanage.

When Papa Kuenzler died some years later, a survivor offered this account of his burial: "They [Armenian orphans] carried his coffin on their shoulders all the way from Ghazir to Beirut. This was in the winter, in the rain, but they did it out of respect for him."

THE ORPHANS LEAVE TURKEY

Papa Kuenzler played an active role in helping escort the orphans out of Turkey when it became apparent that they would continue to face persecution if they remained there as adults. This exodus required moving thousands of orphans, in caravans of several hundred at a time. One survivor's extended account of their journey reveals a great deal about both the process of the evacuation and the role of orphanage personnel:

The Americans got our papers secured to have us leave the country. They hired wagons to carry our bedding and belongings, and by school grade level we started off. Some on foot, others in the wagons. They placed our clothes on our backs, along with names and numbers. On the way, they took pictures. It was April first the day we left for the journey. It might have been 1922 or so. Papa Kuenzler was with us, too. We walked and walked. Every few hours they made us lie down and rest, with the packs on our backs. They also would give us a bit to eat. Then up, and we'd be running again. After all, we were kids.

We then reached a place where Papa took the boys somewhere to relieve themselves and left us girls behind. We joked about that, because we were not sure what we were supposed to do. We reached a place in Urfa that was called Maghara, which was known to be a bad place filled with *chétés* [the Special Organization]. We had to sleep there in the open. At about midnight, it began to pour! We had no place for shelter, so we got soaked as did our clothing and bedding. We had walked long and were tired and sore. The rain would not quit. We took our bedding back into the wagons and people scattered everywhere. No one knew where they were going. I could not walk any longer. Finally, I got in the wagon. Things fell apart there. Kids going in different directions. The next day, the whole day, it rained and poured. Until about dark again, the rain did not stop. We finally reached a place called Souruj.

Many people had lost their belongings, including their bedding. Some kids themselves were lost. That night the Armenians in Souruj came to take us into their homes. I did not go with anyone, so I remained there and, trying to sleep in my bed, wherever I placed my feet, it was wet. Finally, morning came, and all the orphans once again gathered together. God sent us sun, and we hung all our belongings and stayed there one week, until everything dried. We cleaned all the mud, too. Papa Kuenzler, whom we used to call Yacoub, divided us up into twos and sent one couple to one side and the other to the other side. I ended up on the side that had to continue on the journey. We were eight girls and four boys in our wagon. All our belongings were first placed in the wagon, and we were to sit on top of them.

After a cup of tea and bulgar pilaf, we started off. It was mud everywhere. At one point, on one side of the mountain, our wagon wheels got stuck in the mud. We looked up and saw a *chété* with his rifle on top of the mountain. The other group was walking on the other side of the mountain. The boys in our group left and walked on. In a minute, the one *chété* had turned into what seemed like thousands. We forgot our belongings, the wagon, and ran. We ran not knowing where we were going. We were sure that those people were going to kill us all. Seeing us run away, they apparently went to the other side of the mountain, to the other caravan. But when they got near, the gendarmes stopped them, saying that the orphans belonged to the Americans, not to dare come close or they would shoot. They were saved, too.

Meanwhile, we continued to run and run until we saw some train tracks. Then we heard Papa's voice shouting, "Children, stop!" There he fed us. Our wagons caught up with us. We boarded them again, crossed over the tracks and felt that we were on safer ground. We went all the way to Djerablous. That night the Armenians there cooked pilaf for us and brought us *madzoon*. We rested well that night. The next day we crossed the River Euphrates, since the bridge was broken. There we boarded the train and went to Aleppo, where we waited fifteen days for the other caravan. We were located in a *khan*. We washed our clothes and did whatever we could.

With the evacuation of the orphans from Turkey, a chapter in Armenian history was closed. Not only had the orphans left their homeland, but they had also begun a process of psychologically distancing themselves from a trauma that they associated with Turkey. A survivor recalled her relief once their caravan had arrived safely in Lebanon: "When we got there, we all said, 'Oh boy, away from the Turks, finally. We're saved from the Turks.' I had sworn that when I left the land of the Turks that I would fast one day. And I did." Although the act of physically crossing the border could not eliminate the scars of the deportations, it symbolized the crossing of a new threshold in Armenian history.

LEAVING THE ORPHANAGES

Orphanage personnel recognized that the children they were nuturing would one day leave the sheltered environment of the institution. To that end, they taught the older orphans trades that would enable them to be self-sufficient. The girls often learned needlepoint or rug weaving, or else they were trained to be nurses or teachers. The young men typically were apprenticed to become tailors, cobblers, or sometimes carpenters. As the orphans reached their late teens, they were encouraged to move into private housing. And the young women were often visited in the orphanages by potential suitors, some of whom came specifically because they wanted to marry an orphan girl.

Orphanage personnel also made a concerted effort to find relatives of their children. If the children had become separated from their parents during the deportation, there was still some possibility that a survivor's mother, father, or other relatives might be alive. To locate them, the orphanages published advertisements in various newspapers with as much information as possible about each of the children, including name, parents' names, city of birth, siblings' names, and so on. In one typical case, a child had a mother living in Baghdad, unknown to him: "One day a boy named Hovsep got hold of an Armenian newspaper and read the information about me to my mother. All the information matched my history, so my mother knew right away that was me. So when I was in Juni, I received a letter from my mother. [Thus] I knew that she was alive. It had been nearly twelve years."

Our interviews include poignant images of children embracing siblings and parents at these moments of discovery, and such reunions were frequently referred to as "the happiest day of my life."

SIBLINGS REUNITED

In earlier chapters, we presented several accounts of how family members had become separated from each other; occasionally, survivors of family units also rediscovered each other. The story told to us by Perus combines both of these elements, illustrating the joy of reunions as well as the haphazard manner in which they often occurred.

Perus and her family were deported from Chanakkale. On the road to Der-Zor, her eight-year-old brother, Hovsep, said that he could not walk any farther, and the parents reluctantly left him behind. In Der-Zor, her mother died. Her father continued to take care of Perus and two brothers, Boghos and Harutiun. In fact, she remembered her father making soup for them in a small can and heating it with whatever trash he could find to burn. They finally reached the city of Sinjar and found an empty room to occupy. Then, without warning, all of the men were gathered. Her father was killed, and she became separated from her brothers, one of whom ran away to a Kurdish village. Perus was left alone on the street where she had been playing. Unaware of what had happened, this five-year-old child kept returning to their room, looking for her family. After she did this about a dozen times, it began to get dark. Not knowing what to do, she began to cry. Finally, some women heard her and offered to let her sleep with them.

Much later she discovered that her brother Boghos had been adopted by a Kurdish family that took excellent care of him:

> Now my brother's feet are all swollen and cracked from the cold and sand, so much so that he can't walk. They take him, bathe him really well in cold water. Apparently, they were very wealthy, but the wife was blind. They put my brother down on a very comfortable and soft mattress to sleep. There he gets well completely and grows to be a very nice young boy, their only son.

They take such good care of him, giving him the best of everything. He be-
comes the light of their eyes. . . . Finally, they ask him to participate in their
religious rites of washing and praying three times a day. He agrees. He says
that he will do whatever they want him to. So now he is a Muslim.

Unknown to her, Perus's other brother, Harutiun, was tending sheep
in a nearby village. She, however, was still all alone, except for the
old women who allowed her to sleep with them at night. In her words,
"Every night we would gather on a narrow street by a broken wall
and sleep next to each other, sitting up." She was infested with lice
and was filthy, but the women did what they could for her: "I was the
youngest in the bunch, so the women used to say, 'Oh child, don't cry.
Come to us.' They would put me on their laps. I spent the days on
my own and joined them at night on the narrow street. I used to get
happy seeing them."

One day the women gave her some soap, and she went down to the
river to wash her face and hair. An older boy approached and asked her
if she was an Armenian. She replied to him in Turkish. He asked her the
names of her family members. She told him, and he then asked her if she
wanted to see her brother, Harutiun: "He took me to a village. I was
running to get to him [her brother]. Then I saw him. He had become a
shepherd. He had gotten several sheep, some goats and donkeys. I saw
him from far off. I could see him crying. We hugged and hugged. He
asked me where the rest were. I told him what I had heard, that they
took all of them away [and killed them]."

The Turkish family for whom her brother was working refused to
take in Perus, but the siblings would nevertheless meet secretly at night
on the roof of the house where he slept. Describing their meetings, she
said: "He would get up on the roof and reach down his arms, and I'd
put mine up and he'd pull me up. He used to comfort me and instructed
me not to cry."

Some time later, the English liberated the town where they were living. Harutiun told his Turkish boss in these words that he was going
to leave them: "I did not come out of a wall. I have a family. I am going to go and find them." So, together, Harutiun, Perus, and the friend
who had reunited them set off to find Boghos, who they speculated
might be living in Tell-Afar. The brother and his friend helped carry
Perus, and they walked for a number of days. Upon reaching Tell-Afar,
they asked every Armenian they saw if they knew someone by the name
of Boghos from Chanakkale, their hometown. Finally, someone said
he knew him, but thought he was dead. So after a few days, they left

and started walking toward Mosul. Having no money, they begged for food along the way.

They felt relatively safe on their journey because of the presence of English soldiers. And once in Mosul, they discovered that the English were placing refugees in homes: "They would give one room to every four families. In each family, either a brother is left, or a mother, or a child; but all are missing members. We gathered our few belongings of a blanket and a few rags. We stayed there for a while."

The English further assisted the refugees by giving them soap, disinfectant for their lice, and medication for their sores and wounds, as well as clothing, pots, utensils, and rations of oil, rice, sugar, and tea. Perus's brother got a job doing cement work, and they discovered an aunt in Mosul who took care of Perus.

It was also in Mosul that they finally found their brother Boghos. When he heard that Armenians were gathering in Mosul, Boghos decided to leave the Kurdish family that had adopted him. For three days his adoptive mother cried for him not to leave, but the family finally sent him on his way with a large sack of food. Once in Mosul, he went among the Armenians asking if anyone knew of Harutiun or Perus Hagopian, from Chanakkale. Perus described her initial reaction to Boghos:

> When my brother came to me, I didn't recognize him. . . . He looked very handsome, and he had a sack on his back. He said, "I'm your brother." But I ran away from him—he looked like an Arab to me. He kept saying he was Boghos: "Don't you recognize me?" Then he named all my brothers and my parents. I said, "I know them, but I won't come to you." Finally, it clicked, and we hugged and kissed, and he showed me all the food he had brought—for me, he said.

Perus ended her description of the reunion with the simple but eloquent words, "Here we reconciled to life."

While children in the orphanages had some structure for making their way into adulthood, the narrative Perus told about her next few years is typical of refugees who struggled without institutional mediation. From Mosul, the three siblings decided to go to Baghdad. There, Boghos got a job washing dishes for an Indian cook, and Harutiun again found a job doing concrete work. Perus described her typical day: "While my brothers were gone during the day, I used to play with children, used to gather up rags and make dolls." The English, she said, continued to give them some food, especially bread. She recalled heating tea in tin cans over the ovens where the bread was baked.

As the years passed, the Armenian refugees moved from tents into *khans*, which the English rented for them. Perus described the process of economic advancement: "Both men and women continued to work, anything they could do—drive cars, or be servants. And thus with the help of the English, the Armenians began to move ahead and find themselves. After enough Armenians earned money and became self-sufficient, they rented small places for themselves and lived in separate quarters."

Meanwhile, Perus recalled her brothers taking care of her, including the small tasks such as bathing her. She said that they would do the "top" part, and she would do the "bottom." She never lived in an orphanage, but she wished that she had. In Baghdad, Perus went to school briefly, but her principal memory was that "one day the teacher asked me why my dress was torn, and if I could not sew it. And he hit me; slapped me really hard. I got scared, and, of course, I did not have any encouragement at home. There was no mother, no father. No one encouraged me." Perus said that she might possibly have continued to go to school, but one of her brothers got married, and she became a helper to his wife. They all lived together, in one room, until Perus was seventeen, at which time she married another refugee living in Baghdad.

CHAPTER 7

Emigration and Resettlement

After the war ended, some deported Armenians—especially from the Cilicia region—attempted to return to their native villages or towns. Penniless, they hoped to recover the homes, fields, and possessions they had left behind. But survivors were often disappointed: their homes had been ransacked and destroyed or were being occupied by Turks or Kurds; their fields were untended; and many of their churches and schools were burned. Thus, in spite of strong desires to begin life anew, there was little on which they could build.

The testimony of our survivors reflects the dismal condition of the homes they had left. For example, a survivor who returned to Misis said that "our house was still there, although no two stones remained on top of another in that town." Another survivor went back to her town of Kessab and found: "There was no house. It was burned and destroyed. The Turks had destroyed the churches, too." And a survivor who had grown up in a large house in Bor said their home was in ruins, so they lived in the streets. In describing their homes, survivors also commented on the culture that they had left behind. It, too, had been gutted. There were no schools and no businesses; the infrastructure of the community had been destroyed.

Yet some survivors attempted to reestablish their homes, and we will begin this chapter by focusing on three short case studies of survivors from Marash, Smyrna, and Zeitun. We will follow with some representative accounts of Armenian immigrants in America.

RETURNING HOME

MARASH

Substantial numbers of Armenians returned to their homes only to be massacred. Ghevont's story is typical. In 1920, his family went back to Marash, thinking that they would be safe.[1] They had great hopes for starting life over again. When they arrived at their home, a Turkish family was living there, but to their surprise, the occupant actually paid them a few gold pieces for the several years his family had lived there. Indeed, said Ghevont, it appeared that the Turks living in the Armenian quarter of Marash actually felt somewhat intimidated by the number of Armenians returning to claim their homes; moreover, there were Armenian volunteers as well as occupying French soldiers, whose task it was to protect the deportees who had returned to their native soil.

However, shortly after Ghevont's family returned to Marash, fighting broke out between the French and the Turks. The Armenians, fearing for their lives, gathered in churches for protection. Ghevont said that he and many others had been in a Catholic church for about three weeks when something quite unexpected happened. Under the cover of darkness on February 10, 1920, the French began to flee the city, leaving the Armenians defenseless against the Turks. Ghevont saw the French soldiers wrapping rags around their boots so that they could slip away noiselessly during the night. Observing this, he decided that he would try to escape, also.

> That night it had snowed a lot and there was a full moon. This made escaping dangerous. My father was very much against it, but I did not listen. I am glad that I did not listen. So ten or fifteen of us started walking without knowing our way. We passed one hill and then another and another. Then we lost our way. We weren't sure which was south, north, east, or west. I just knew that south was toward the fields. We walked through rice fields which grow in water, knee high. It was so cold that if we raised our feet out of the water, they would freeze. We walked and walked and then spotted the campfires of the French, so that by morning we joined them.

When daylight broke, Ghevont saw four or five thousand other Armenians had likewise escaped with the French army. From a distance, they could see that Marash was in flames.

Stanley Kerr, an American official of Near East Relief, witnessed these events, and in the concluding paragraphs of his autobiography, comments on the fate of Armenians in Marash:

When I left Marash on 29 July 1922 with the remaining members of the NER [Near East Relief] staff and one young lady whom I was abducting from the mission to be my bride, we were told that not more than ten Armenian families remained in the city. Of the eighty-six thousand Armenians living in the district of Marash in 1914, only twelve thousand were known to have survived. The fate of the few hundred Zeitunlis deported to the north in 1920 was never learned. Undoubtedly some of the sixty-two thousand who disappeared during the 1915 through 1918 period of exile may have survived and remained in villages of Syria and Palestine, but certainly most of them died. Of those who fled with the French army, twenty-four hundred reached Islohia in February 1920. During the two years that followed the 1920 insurrection the ninety-seven hundred survivors in the city of Marash abandoned their homes, fearing to remain after being deserted by France. Of these the last three thousand willing to live under Turkish rule had finally been forced to yield to Turkish threats of immediate harm and migrated to Lebanon, dispossessed in spite of assurances given in the Accord of Ankara.[2]

The final sentence of Kerr's autobiography states, "The ancient city of Marash, with a history extending far into the dim past beyond the Hittite period and once largely populated by the Armenians, had finally become purely Turkish."[3]

SMYRNA

Because the Armenian population of Smyrna (Izmir) had not been deported in 1915, Armenians went there in considerable numbers after the war had ended. It had been occupied by Greeks and was viewed as a relatively safe haven for Armenians. However, in September 1922 the Turks reoccupied the city and burned the Christian district in order to drive out the Greeks and Armenians. Annalin, one of the survivors we interviewed, offered this account of what she witnessed in 1922.

When the Turks began to enter Smyrna, Annalin said that many Armenians fled the city. But her uncle had started a restaurant that was beginning to prosper, and he kept asking, "Where am I going to go? I have no relatives anywhere." Annalin described the events that followed:

As it got worse, all of us, and all the people, began gathering in our school. The word came around that the Turks were going on the streets and killing all the Armenians and leaving them on the streets. I, myself, was in school already, so I simply stayed there. Then orders came from the school that we, too, should run away. But where? All the buildings were on fire! The Turks were burning everything. There was a whole group of us running away from the school.

Attempting to escape the raging fire, the Armenians headed toward the port on the Mediterranean, in total chaos:

> There were Armenians all over, coming in cars and jumping out of them and yelling and screaming. Meanwhile, the Turks were seeking out the Armenians to kill them. There was the stench of dead bodies coming out of the houses and buildings. Some people threw themselves in the water and began swimming toward ships a distance away, but apparently people from the English ships dumped boiling water on them. We heard some men who swam back saying how they had poured hot water on them as they sought help.

Another survivor provided additional details of the panic that ensued as the city went up in flames. Khatoun told us that she saw some newly married couples tying themselves together and drowning themselves in the Mediterranean Sea, saying that it was better to die together than at the hands of Turks. She also corroborated Annalin's account of Armenians trying to swim out to the ships in the harbor. Khatoun said that the ships turned their searchlights on the swimmers, which made them easier targets for Turks who were shooting at them from shore. She also said that many Armenian girls were kidnapped in the chaos.[4]

ZEITUN

Araxie was a survivor who returned to Zeitun, one of the first areas to be deported in 1915. She was only seven or eight at the time of the genocide and ended up in Aleppo, where several of her surviving brothers had started a butcher business that sold meat to the orphanages and soldiers, first German and then French. Life was finally going well for Araxie and her brothers when they heard at the end of 1918 that Armenians were returning to Zeitun. But they had left behind a new and spacious house in Zeitun and decided to attempt to reclaim it. Although a number of houses had been burned, their home was still standing. For a year they lived in Zeitun, during which time Araxie contracted malaria. However, when the French began leaving Turkey, the Armenians—as described earlier in this chapter—were again under attack. Zeitun was viewed as something of a haven for Armenians, and Araxie remembered the population increasing dramatically. She said all the Armenians took refugees into their homes, and they made huge pots of soup for the impoverished survivors who came to Zeitun. During this time, one of her brothers was killed by Turks when he ventured out of Zeitun, attempting to get supplies of salt, sugar, and other things they had to import.

At this time, the political situation deteriorated badly and a decision was made to evacuate the elderly, as well as the sick, lame, children, and infants, from Zeitun. The Turks discovered this caravan about a half-hour from Zeitun and deported it to Marash. Araxie and her family were in this group, although several of her brothers remained in Zeitun to defend it. Along the way, her father was hit in the head by a gendarme for walking too slowly, and he became permanently deaf in one ear. When the deportees arrived in Marash, the Armenians living there were told that their houses would be burned down if they harbored anyone from Zeitun. The one act of kindness Araxie remembered was that of a Turkish pharmacist who gave several of the women medication for their eyes.

Araxie became separated from her family in Marash. She lived with a widowed aunt whose husband had been burned to death during the 1909 Adana massacres. This was a very lonely time for Araxie, and she said that her face was constantly swollen from crying. Her parents had been deported to Kharpert, and two of her brothers had been killed in Zeitun, attempting to resist another Turkish invasion. The man who later became her husband was almost killed in Zeitun—the Turks had set fire to the area where he was hiding, but he survived miraculously, even though everything around him was burned. After this incident, he escaped from Zeitun and went by foot all the way to Adana. By the time he reached Adana, he was nearly naked and had been without food for three days.

By the end of 1922, only a small number of Armenians remained in Turkey. Those who had returned to Zeitun, Marash, and other areas either had been deported once again or else forced to leave because of the hostility they encountered. As previously mentioned, even the orphans were removed from Turkey in 1922. Surviving Armenians faced the problem of finding a safe place to settle. It is to the story of their emigration that we now turn.

HOVAGIM—AN EMIGRANT FROM
THE 1909 MASSACRE

Armenians came to the United States in several different waves.[5] Although a few Armenians were brought to America in the seventeenth century—chiefly to help grow silkworms—the first noticeable trickle of Armenians to America started after American missionaries went to

Turkey in the early part of the nineteenth century. Some of these Armenians came to the United States for theological education, but by the 1870s and 1880s, Armenians were also developing an Oriental rug industry in America. Approximately 1,400 Armenians emigrated to the United States from 1869 to 1890, with another 5,500 emigrating in the following five years.[6]

The first substantial wave of emigration came after the 1894–96 massacres. In both 1896 and 1897, approximately 2,500 Armenians came to the United States.[7] This rate of emigration continued into the twentieth century, and immediately after the 1909 massacres in Cilicia, the number jumped to a record 5,500.[8] As the stream of immigrants increased, the boat fare from Constantinople to New York decreased, from approximately $34 in 1900 to $24 by 1913. The earliest immigrant among the survivors we interviewed was Hovagim, who left Adana a year after the 1909 massacres.

Hovagim, born in 1893, was sixteen at the time of the massacres in his town of Adana. He vividly recalled fleeing to a church where his family and other Armenians stayed for several weeks. When they returned to their home, everything had been stolen from it. Subsequently, he took a job sweeping the floors of a factory for a few cents a day. But his brother-in-law ridiculed him for working at such a low wage and told him to try selling *tán,* a yogurt drink, on the streets. He tried that and increased his earnings. He next started picking cotton, and while doing this work, he got the inspiration to go to the United States: "One night it rained terribly. We all went under the tent—both men and women. Everyone was telling a story. So I said, 'Tomorrow I am going to go to America.' They said, 'The hungry child sees a dream in his dream. How are you going to go to America?'"

In the morning, he asked his mother for clean underwear and a clean shirt and started for Adana, where his father was. He informed him that he was going to America, and then found his little sister and told her the same news. The only impediment was that he had no money for his fare. So he asked his sister if he could have one of the gold chains around her neck. She said no, but gave him five gold coins, which was the equivalent worth. His other sister gave him two gold pieces, and his father, realizing his seriousness, gave him eight. Putting this together with a little money he had saved, he had eighteen gold coins.

With this money he set off for Greece, and there he boarded a ship for New York. After paying his fare, he had exactly five and one-half gold coins left—which he understood to be the minimum for entering the United States as an immigrant. When he arrived in New York, he cashed his Turkish gold for dollars and entered the United States with exactly $20.56.

He made his way from New York to Boston and found an Armenian restaurant where a stranger helped him buy a suitcase, a hat, and a ticket to Middleboro, Massachusetts, where his grandmother was living.

> He put me on the train; it was a freight train. On the train, I kept saying to the conductor, "S'il vous plaît, montrez moi Middleboro." The man replied, "Sit down." Whenever the train stopped I would say, "S'il vous plaît, montrez moi Middleboro." And each time, he would say, "Sit down." Finally the man said, "Middleboro." I got out to see that my grandmother and her husband had come to the depot. She started to yell to me in Turkish: "I didn't want any of you to come to America."

For three months Hovagim lived with an uncle in Middleboro, but because he didn't know English, it was difficult to find employment. Finally, he was placed in the home of an American doctor. The doctor's wife took him on as a project:

> She used to explain to me, "Dinner plate, cups and saucers, napkin . . . ," whatever was on the table. Then she would take me to the kitchen, cook two eggs, coffee, and oatmeal. She would eat it, and give me two eggs and oatmeal, too. There I stayed for three months. In those months I had a dictionary with me. From that dictionary I would learn about forty words a day. I would write them down. I would write down the Armenian, like *havgit*, then next to it "egg." Gradually I started to learn English. I began to speak English with the lady. After three months I said to the doctor to get me a job, because I could speak English.

The doctor was unsuccessful at finding him a job, so he stayed for another three months with the family, who started paying him one dollar a week.

A number of images stand out in Hovagim's memory from his first year in the United States. On one occasion, his adoptive "grandmother" took him to a friend's house, and he offered the blessing for the food in French. This impressed his host and affirmed Hovagim's belief that he was worthy of some respect, in spite of his difficulties with the English language. But he also recalled being ridiculed by a small boy who stared at the way he ate bread with his hands. Finally, the doctor found him a job on the farm of an Armenian, where he was to earn fifteen dollars a month. But at the end of the first thirty days, the farmer refused to pay him, saying that he had broken some tools and that Hovagim actually owed *him* money.

He decided to leave that job and go to Boston, where he heard that an Armenian who did not speak English had opened a hotel. He worked two weeks for this man as a translator, as well as making beds and helping with the cooking. But once again, when it was time to be paid, his boss refused to give him the eight dollars that were promised, saying: "You eat and drink and sleep. What more do you want?" However, Hovagim got some Armenians to pressure the hotel owner; eventually, he was paid and in time was able to save a total of ten dollars. When he had accumulated this money, he sent the entire ten dollars to his mother in Turkey, leaving nothing for himself.

He continued to work at the hotel until he had saved thirty dollars. With this money, he went into partnership with another Armenian who wanted to open a restaurant. Gradually, he learned how to cook, and after awhile his partner wanted to buy him out for sixty dollars, but Hovagim in turn proposed to pay the partner sixty dollars to own the restaurant himself. He became the cook, the waiter, and the cashier.

Unfortunately, the business declined, but he was able to sell the restaurant for fifty dollars, and return to Boston in search of a job. There, after buying into another restaurant, he decided that it might be better to work for someone else, so he got a job as a cook for nine dollars a week. But Hovagim preferred to be self-employed, and he became a partner in still another restaurant a few years later, which he then sold for seven hundred dollars.

He promptly took six hundred dollars and sent it to Adana to a woman who had been identified as a potential wife. After waiting several years for his bride to arrive, he went to the train station to meet her: "I went and was looking for a big girl. I was looking all around me. Then I saw a small girl come to me and ask me if I was Hovagim. She said that she was Sona. . . . My friend took us to a department store so we could buy clothes for her. . . . We went there and the manager looked at my wife-to-be and said that we should go to the children's department to buy her clothing."

Sona was seventeen when she arrived in Boston, and almost immediately she made it clear to Hovagim that she did not want to marry him. Taken aback, he tried to match her with a friend, but the friend was saving money in order to help his two brothers and was not interested in marriage. However, Sona finally told Hovagim although she didn't love him, she would marry him anyway. He told her that love would come later, and so they made their vows at a friend's home.

In our interview, Hovagim continued to recite how he went from job to job, always searching for a new financial opportunity. By saving a few dollars every month, he finally accumulated five thousand dollars, which he used for down payment on a house.

HENRY—MAKING IT IN AMERICA

Many accounts could be offered of survivors who came to the United States after the 1915 genocide, but the story of Henry, who eventually owned several toy stores in Pasadena, California, demonstrates the initiative exercised by those who succeeded financially. Henry was nine at the time of the deportations. His father, an influential man in the region of Sivas, had died of typhus shortly before the atrocities of 1915 began. After his father's death, the family was cared for by Ali Effendi, a Turkish friend and business partner of his father. Ali Effendi comforted Henry's mother by saying that terrible things were about to happen to the Armenians, and he was not sure he would have been able to spare her husband much suffering.

Ali Effendi was a commissioner in charge of controlling prices of products for the region of Sivas. Henry said, "He was a real human being." In fact, when Henry first referred to Ali Effendi, he stated: "I want to mention his name, because he was directly responsible for my being in this country today. He was a Turk, but a beautiful man, a man with a soul."

As the officials started to imprison and kill the Armenian leaders in Sivas, Ali Effendi brought Henry's mother and all five children to his own home. Henry's family left everything behind, except for a block of sugar that his mother took with her.

> In Ali Effendi's house, we were all grouped together in one room with one mattress and one quilt. We had to be completely quiet so that no one could tell that we were there. He'd lock and go and at night bring us food. We were there like a jail for three months. [Then,] the new orders came that any Turk hiding Armenians would be hung along with them in front of the house. So he was frightened and came to talk to Mother, in the proper way—with a wall separating them. He said that the only way to save ourselves now was to become Muslims.

At this point in the story, Henry broke down and cried as he described his mother's dilemma. At first, she said a definite no to the idea of converting. But Ali Effendi insisted that he knew they would be deported, and he said that they would kill all the children in front of her and force her into a marriage with a Turk. Henry summarized her response as follows: "So after thinking about it, my mother, a devoutly Christian woman, decided to go through with it for our sakes, taking the advice of Effendi that she would do it externally only, her heart and prayers remaining Christian." Henry then recounted the process required of each of the children:

> We went to the city hall and a judge asked each of us questions like this: "Son, your religion is a very bad one. It should be denounced. Do you denounce it?" And we would say, "*Evet, effendi*," which means, "Yes, sir." "Do you accept the real religion, the Muslim religion?" "Yes, sir." Then he would say: "Son, your name will be henceforth Abdul Rahman oghlu Assad, and no more Vartanian." Then they gave a fez and a turban. I was to wear it so everyone would know that I was Muslim. . . . Then all the boys had to be circumcised. So we did that, too. It was done by a religious leader. After all this, we could go out on the street. But even then, they [Turkish boys] would harass us and call us "*dönme*," meaning "turncoat."

After this ceremony of conversion, Henry's family was not allowed to return to their home, which had been turned into a hospital for soldiers. Instead, Ali Effendi rented them a one-room house, with a dirt floor and dirt ceiling—quite a contrast to their own home, which had running water, a swimming pool, and large bedrooms, and was situated in a garden surrounded by trees.

Although living in extremely humble circumstances, Henry's family was spared from the ordeal of deportation. He went to a Turkish school and completely forgot how to speak Armenian. He also remembered being extremely ill with a high fever and because all the Armenian doctors had been deported or killed, he had no medical help. During the last dream before his fever broke, Henry recalled hearing trumpets and devils that were chased away by a group of angels.

After the war ended, Henry's family received a letter from his mother's sister, who had emigrated to the United States after the 1895 massacres. She said to send Henry and another son to Istanbul, and she would in turn send money for them to go to the United States.

When he arrived in Istanbul, Henry stayed with another aunt who insisted that he should learn Armenian before going to America. But instead of sending him to the local Armenian school in Istanbul, the aunt placed him in an orphanage. Henry remembered being heartbroken: "Here I have a mother in Sivas, and I'm in an orphanage!" However, in the orphanage he learned Armenian, as well as algebra, music, and other subjects. Henry said that his teachers were very nationalistic, and in his words, "They couldn't do enough for the orphans."

Henry stayed in the orphanage for more than a year until his brother, who had preceded him to America, sent money for his passage. But because Henry was still a minor, he needed someone to sign a release for him to emigrate. His aunt refused, wanting him to learn more Armenian in the orphanage. So finally, after some manipulation, Henry persuaded a well-known doctor to certify that he was nineteen, instead of fifteen.

In July 1921, Henry dressed in his best clothes—his Boy Scout uniform—and set sail for America. He went third class, and while many of his fellow Armenians were seasick, Henry joined with those who were singing and dancing. Thirty days later, on August 4, 1921, he landed at Ellis Island. Henry made August 4 his birthday, declaring that on this day he was born again—born into freedom. He took the train to Chicago, and then a cab to the house of the cousins who had sent the money for both his and his brother's passage to the United States. He stayed with them two weeks, receiving gracious hospitality.

He then located his brother, who had become a barber in a Jewish neighborhood. When his brother asked whether he wanted to work or go to school, Henry unhesitatingly said that he wanted to continue his education. But this proved to be an awkward experience:

> So my brother put me in a public school. This was very distressing, because I was with little kids. Here I am fifteen and a pretty big kid. I said, "No, this won't do." I could understand English a little, I had learned some in the orphanage, and I had a dictionary in my pocket. In the class, when we'd stand up, I would be towering over [the children]. I was so ashamed. I said, "What am I doing here?" So I decided to get work and learn the practical language, and then go to night school.

Shortly after he dropped out of school, his brother found him a job at Rosen's Bakery, across the street from the barbershop. His job—hauling out coal cinders and dumping them in the basement—proved too taxing for his strength. Hoping to be an electrical engineer someday, Henry began working as an apprentice to an electrician who had a contract to convert old gaslights to electric lights. His boss paid him ten dollars a week, but after two or three months the electrician's contract expired, and Henry was in quest of a new job. Through an Armenian doctor he got a reference to work as a busboy in a cafeteria. This job paid him nine dollars a week, and also gave him breakfast and lunch. In the six months he worked there, he managed to save a hundred dollars. From their paychecks, both Henry and his brother faithfully sent ten dollars a month home to their mother. During this time, he lived with his brother in a room behind the barbershop.

Finally, Henry got a job that offered some room for advancement. He started working in a chain restaurant as a busboy, and after three months, he asked the manager for a new position. He was given a raise to sixteen dollars a week and was put in charge of the steam table and making coffee. A few months later, he went to the manager once again and told him that he wanted to be an assistant manager. His boss smiled at him and said that the position required a college degree, but asked if he would like to be a short-order cook. This was a demanding job, and Henry remembered getting up at two in the morning to prepare for the day cook.

Always looking for a path to economic advancement, Henry next worked for an Oriental carpet dealer, but grew restless and decided to try driving a taxicab: "I used to love to drive. As soon as I could, I said I was going to get a car. So the only way to drive now was to drive a Yellow Cab. I passed all the tests, passed the chauffeur's test, and got my license. Some Armenians who would see me [driving the cab] told me that wasn't a very nice job. But I was doing it so I could earn enough money to bring my family over." Then a cousin suggested that they buy a car together and drive for the Checker Cab Company. So they bought a Buick, and in order to keep the car busy both day and night, they alternated shifts.

By this time Henry had learned English fairly well. He was pursuing his dream of becoming an electrical engineer and was attending night school. But his cab-driving days ended when an Armenian from his hometown of Sivas suggested that his parents would not be happy if they knew what kind of work he was doing. After selling his share of the car to his cousin, he started working once again in an Oriental carpet store, for twenty-four dollars a week. Although Henry was only an employee, he thought the store would be more successful in a different location, so he suggested to the owner that they move to a more prominent street. By 1929, he had become an American citizen and was making seventy-five dollars a week.

In spite of his financial success—he had even bought a Dodge car with wire wheels for thirteen hundred dollars—Henry continued to think about the family he had left behind. He was able to bring two of his sisters to be theology students at Union Seminary. But his mother posed more of a problem because of immigration rules, so he suggested that she attempt to come to America via Cuba, a route that many Armenians were taking to the United States at that time.

Meanwhile, he heard of a cousin who had been found among some Bedouins. His aunt told him that the only way she could come to the United States was as the wife of an American citizen. So Henry took a three-month leave from the carpet business and went to Paris:

Shnorig looked like an Arab. There were tattoos all over her face and lips. How could we make the consul believe [that she should be allowed to immigrate]? So I had my aunt make a beautiful dress for her and took her to a doctor who was married to another one of my cousins to remove the tattoos. He removed some, but not all—not on the lips. We got married in the city hall [in Paris] and then had to wait thirty days. When time came to present her to the American consul, I had my aunt make her up really well, so that she looked presentable. We got the visa right away. But she was very naive and uneducated and didn't know how to eat. [On the boat] I told her to watch me as to when and how to use a fork, spoon, knife, and so on.

Waiting six months, Henry then did the paperwork to get a proper divorce, having discharged his duty of getting her to America.

Henry continued to struggle to get his mother into the United States. In 1930 he went to see her in Havana. He spent considerable money in Cuba trying to get her a visa, but at that time, only one hundred people a year were allowed to immigrate to the United States. After several more years, he finally grew impatient with the immigration laws and wrote a letter to President Hoover. Henry summarized his letter stating, "I sent him [the president] copies of my income tax returns and all the money that we had and were sending to my mother, and asked why should we be living apart and sending American dollars to be spent in Cuba when we needed them here." He received a reply shortly, and a few months later, his mother was in Chicago.

In 1932, Henry married an Armenian girl he had met in Wisconsin. This was in the midst of the Great Depression, and his pay had declined from $75 to $30 and then to $15 a week. But he borrowed $100 from an insurance policy to take his new bride on a honeymoon. Times were very rough. For a while he went into partnership with his brother in a barbershop. When that didn't work out, he opened a restaurant called "BBQ A LA KING" with a cousin. Although it was successful, it required such long hours that he sold it and borrowed $400 to open a rug business. He sold Oriental carpets in the front of the store and cleaned rugs in the back, where he lived. There was no place for his wife, however, so he sent her back to live with her parents. After about a year, he managed to buy the entire building—on very good terms, he said—and brought his wife back to live with him in an upstairs apartment. Henry sold the business and moved to California in 1946 and eventually established three toy stores in Pasadena.

Henry's rags-to-riches life as an immigrant is similar to some other accounts we heard, but we also interviewed a number of survivors who were living in extremely humble circumstances when we visited them. They had never really recovered financially from the genocide. Despite the noble intentions of the orphanages' educational programs, many survivors had nevertheless suffered a substantial break in their education. Furthermore, survivors lacked the financial support that many young people receive from family assistance.

ARAXIE—BALANCING WORK AND MOTHERHOOD

The attempt by Araxie (described earlier in this chapter) to balance the demands of work, motherhood, and emigration illustrates a less fortunate outcome of losing one's homeland. After being deported from Zeitun for a second time, Araxie went to Marash and then to Aleppo. In Aleppo she began to earn her own way as a maid in the home of a doctor. By this time she was fourteen, and despite another bout with malaria, she began to gain weight and developed into an attractive young woman. Several suitors approached her brother about marrying her, but he declared that he would give her only to someone from Zeitun. Soon, Toros—who had been one of the defenders of Zeitun—asked to marry Araxie. Although her sister-in-law complained that he was too poor to be a suitable husband, Araxie's brother approved of the match, and she got married before she was fifteen.

At first, the couple did fairly well, but as children were born, their financial needs increased and other stresses developed:

When we first went to Aleppo, we were in such poverty. My mother . . . died. . . . Seventeen days later my daughter was born. Then I became very ill. Not just illness. I became very nervous and anxious. My husband was not successful as a butcher there. He could not pay the cost of the meat. . . . He used to give things away; he felt sorry for the poor. So he became the loser. We couldn't get ahead. I don't know what happened. I took my ring, and whatever jewelry I had, [and] I gave [them] to my husband to sell to make his business go. So we lost those, too. But we still could not succeed. . . . We used to have fifty to sixty sheep and cows. My husband either sold them or lost them. "We sat on water," as the Turks used to say. We had nothing.

After the birth of their first child, Araxie's malaria recurred: "My mouth used to be dry all the time, and my husband would put water in my mouth, and I could not get enough. We were in the village, and they were simply waiting for me to die." Finally, she received some medication that helped her through the malaria. Their poverty was unremitting, however—and still more children entered their household: "In Aleppo, two more girls were born. When I was pregnant with my fourth daughter, I used to work at the convent. My legs were swollen. I was tired. I started labor there and the baby was born there. I suffered with that girl a lot, but it was that daughter who [eventually] brought all of us to the United States. She turned the trouble into happiness." Later in the interview, Araxie said she had seriously hoped for a miscarriage but was reprimanded by a woman who told her that this might be the child who would take care of her in her old age.

After their sixth child was born, they moved to Beirut where they lived for twenty years. Her fourth daughter, the one born in the convent, married and moved to the United States; in 1970, she brought Araxie and, in time, the rest of the family to the United States.

Near the end of our interview, we asked Araxie about the effect of the genocide on her life. At first she discussed its impact on her own education: she had completed only the equivalent of kindergarten. Later she learned to read in order to read the Bible, but she never learned to write or spell. She then talked about the genocide's effect on the next generation. Because of their poverty, only two of her children completed high school; the others terminated their education at the level of fourth or fifth grade. One of her sons, who has a successful plumbing business, once told her that if they had grown up in the United States, he would have been a professor or a lawyer. Araxie said, "He is bright, but what could we do? We could not send him to school, so he followed a trade."

For an Armenian orphan, dolls help express hope for a future with home
and family. Photograph taken at the Near East Relief Center, Beirut, about
1921. Courtesy Project SAVE and the Armenian Library and Museum of
America.

Armenian orphans at the Near East Relief Center, Beirut, about 1921.
Courtesy Project SAVE and the Armenian Library and Museum of America.

Armenian refugees at the Near East Relief Industrial School, Beirut, about
1921. Courtesy Project SAVE and the Armenian Library and Museum of
America.

Armenian deportees returning to their homes in Marash in 1919. Photograph
by E. Stanley Kerr, a medical missionary. Courtesy Project SAVE and the
Rev. Vartan Hartunian.

Armenian survivors from Kharpert on a forced march to Baghdad in 1916,
pictured here on the banks of the Euphrates River at Der-Zor, Syria.
Courtesy Project SAVE and Elizabeth Boyajian Roberts.

Family of Sarkis Agojian of Chemeshgezak, 1911, who was interviewed for this book.

Young Armenian professionals from Sivas, 1910. The man seated on the right is Vahan Vartanian, the uncle of Henry Vartanian, one of the survivors interviewed for this book.

PART III

Analysis

CHAPTER 8

Survivor Responses to the Genocide

Toward the end of each interview, we asked survivors to discuss their personal reflections on the meaning of the genocide. Although the greater part of each interview was devoted to recollections about specific events and experiences, we were also interested in the moral, religious, and philosophical sense survivors made out of the violence and hardship they had witnessed. Survivors had been dealing with these memories for more than fifty years, and we wondered whether the wounds from their childhood experiences were still festering or if there had been some healing. We wanted to know how survivors had coped with the trauma of their childhood, and whether there were identifiable patterns of response.[1]

PREOCCUPATION WITH THE GENOCIDE

A number of survivors said that they had actually become *more*, rather than *less*, preoccupied with the genocide as they became older. They told us that as children and young adults they were so focused on survival that they did not have the time or energy to think about their losses; only in their later adult years did they begin to relive and work through the pain of their childhood. This is not to say that survivors did not feel lonely and isolated as orphans—many did—but it is equally true that many survivors felt their losses more profoundly later, when they had their own children and realized what it meant not to have a father or mother.

Once again, it is valuable to hear the survivors themselves reflect on their experience; for example: "When I was young, I really did not care; it didn't seem to bother me. We were hungry and I used to run around, do any job I could, go from place to place to get something to eat for us. It is now that we understand the value of mother and father [that the sadness and feeling of loss is occurring]."

We heard almost identical statements about delayed emotional response from others, too, as is evident in the words of three different survivors:

> I felt these things as I got older. Even when we were being deported, I did not feel what I do today. After we returned and I saw that others had a mother and I did not, then it hit me harder.

> The older I got, when I started working, and especially when I had my own family, then I really started to think about these things, remembering the past and my hometown.

> When you form your own family, [have] children, you tend to think about that more, because you understand more about the value of the family. Then you feel worse, and you miss your loved ones. Here we are now [in the United States] as total strangers.

We were told frequently that whenever survivors get together, they inevitably discuss the topic of the genocide. In fact, one survivor stated: "Whether you want to or not, you talk about those days. That is where the conversation goes." Another respondent expressed the same sentiment: "When we are gathered, this talk always comes. It just comes." Repeatedly, survivors told us that the events they witnessed are remembered if for no other reason than because the atrocities they saw simply cannot be forgotten: "You know, no matter what we start out talking about around here, we always end up coming to this [the genocide]. This is something that cannot be forgotten. How could I?"

Another survivor was even more pointed in identifying specific memories that she cannot get out of her mind:

> It is impossible to forget. The wound is there and does not go away, no matter what you try to do or even try to ignore it. It is part of your body, and it will not go away. I've tried many times to forget. I've tried many times before going to bed, thinking that I will not dream about [it], but it is impossible. I cannot get it out of my mind. How can you forget? I remember my poor infant, and how he died with no food or clothing.

In addition to its being a common topic of conversation among survivors, the genocide also haunts them in their dreams and personal moments. A woman told us, "Sometimes my husband wakes me up and says, 'What's wrong? What's happening?' I yell in my dreams." And several survivors talked about their past as if it were a movie that replays against their will:

> I think about my past all the time. It comes in front of my eyes like a dream. You don't want to think of those incidents, but they come to your eyes.

> Sometimes, like a movie, I see my past, and sometimes I cannot sleep thinking about my past. I remember the things we saw, my parents, my relatives.

> Sometimes when I am resting on my bed, I recall all that I've gone through, and I can just see all of my past.

Even if survivors try to forget their past, the opinion of many interviewees was that the events were so powerful that they cannot be repressed. "Can one forget such a thing? Look at me. All alone. What business do I have to come to the United States? No father or mother. A family of fifteen to twenty all wiped out. . . . Can you possibly forget that? And why *should* you forget? For the Turks' sake?"

Another survivor vividly stated why forgetting is not an option: "We talk about these things because our hearts have burned." The image of fire was used by another survivor in describing her memories: "Does the fire go out? Does it go out? When ashes come, it looks like it is out. But when you stir it, it burns again."

Whether the appropriate image is one of a smoldering fire or of a festering wound, there is little doubt that the psychological trauma of the genocide profoundly affects all survivors, regardless of their external response to the events of 1915. For example, one man told us how his mother used to scream at night—she had seen a Turk trying to kill her mother by pushing her into an oven: "So poor woman, until she died, she used to scream in her dreams." Survivors also dealt with their pain by crying. We could cite numerous examples, but a distinctive case is that of a mother who was instructed to throttle her tears: "There was a time when I used to cry all the time, all the time for my child. Then a woman told me not to cry, that God might take my other child away. So I used to think of those words often when I felt like crying, and I would try to control myself."

The attempt to moderate emotions was seen even in the orphanages. Although it might not have been a matter of policy, several survivors told us that orphanage personnel refused to let the girls talk about their deportation experiences. And we also have several instances in which relatives or spouses attempted to keep survivors from reliving their experiences. For example, a woman told us that her uncle forbade her sister to talk about the deportations, because she had nightmares everytime she did. Another said that even in married life, she finally decided not to talk anymore about her childhood with her husband, because it always left her disturbed.

TYPES OF RESPONSES

From survivors' comments about the genocide, it is apparent that they responded in very different ways to the trauma of their childhood. Far from evoking mechanical responses, the events of the genocide are always recollected within an individual framework of interpretation that is conditioned by many factors, not the least of which is each survivor's moral and spiritual struggle to comprehend the injustice of the genocide. Hence, analyzing the response of survivors requires entering, at some level, into their experience of "making sense" out of events that defy the ordinary structures of interpretation.

Although each survivor's experience is unique, and every attempt to respond to that experience is highly individualized, we nevertheless were able to identify six definite patterns of response. These are "ideal types" in the sense in which this term is used in the social sciences.[2] Namely, they are abstractions, or artificially drawn categories, that help to illumine social phenomena even though they are not necessarily identical with the experience of any single individual. Indeed, to reduce any one of our survivors to an "ideal type" would be to deny the complexity of the individual's experience. Yet social science is predicated on the assumption that there is value in generalizing beyond the specific case, and so we offer the following sixfold typology as a way to help understand the struggle by survivors to deal with the trauma of the genocide.[3]

1. Avoidance and repression.   The dominant response among some survivors has been to put a lid on their experience, attempting not to think about the genocide and avoiding occasions where genocide is discussed. The wound of their childhood experiences is too deep for them to expose it continually to public attention. In psychological terms, their response might be viewed as one of repression, an attempt to ignore a past that threatens the stability of their emotional well-being.

2. Outrage and anger.   A second response is characterized by outrage and anger. It is the opposite of repression: individuals who respond in this way feel the fire of resentment burning deep within their conscience and consciousness, and they deal with the injustice and pain of the genocide by regularly venting their feelings about those who perpetrated the crime. However, in contrast to the next category, "revenge and restitution," outrage and anger function at a cathartic level and are not manifested in political actions.

3. Revenge and restitution. The third category of response channels outrage and anger into a political and/or retaliatory expression. Hence, some survivors have dedicated themselves to seeking reparation in one form or another; it may involve return of homelands, or it may take the form of revenge against those who are associated with the crime of genocide. Of course, the actual perpetrators of the genocide are no longer living, but because the Turkish government refuses to acknowledge the genocide, its representatives have become objects of retaliatory revenge.

4. Reconciliation and forgiveness. A fourth response by survivors can be characterized as reconciliation. Survivors who appear reconciled do not deny the horrors of the genocide. Nor are they necessarily unsympathetic to the call for reparations and recognition of the genocide by the Turkish government. However, unlike survivors who are still obsessed with the genocide, these individuals seem to have come to terms with the trauma of their childhood. In their view, an injury has occurred, but the wound has healed, despite the visible scars that remain.

5. Resignation and despair. The fifth type of response we have identified is resignation. We encountered survivors who seemed overwhelmed by a sense of despair and projected a genuine melancholy regarding the violence that shattered their lives. They did not deny the trauma of their childhood, nor did they fight against it. Physically, they appeared to embody the pain of their memories, and, psychologically, they seemed to lack the emotional strength to rise above their past— their lives were marked by resignation, despondency, and a certain flatness of emotions, positive or negative, when reflecting on their past.

6. Explanation and rationalization. Finally, we interviewed survivors whose method of coping involved rationalizing the genocide in one way or another. This response took several forms, ranging from stating political reasons for the inevitability of the genocide to offering religious explanations of the genocide as a punishment from God or finding after-the-fact consolation that, because of the genocide and the exodus of Armenians from Turkey, at least they no longer have to suffer at the hands of the Turks. Rationalization was typically a secondary response; that is, faced with the brute fact of the genocide, survivors searched for some positive by-product from these events.

These six responses may apply to a number of different circumstances in which individuals attempt to cope with traumatic events that do not fit routine categories of explanation or understanding. Such events might include natural disasters such as earthquakes and famine, as well as more personal tragedies such as the death of a child or loved one. Stated as a typology, the ways in which individuals may attempt to deal with such events include: (1) ignoring or, in extreme cases, denying that they occurred; (2) expressing outrage at the source or perpetrator of the trauma or tragedy; (3) seeking retribution against or compensation from the person, agency, or group that caused the tragedy; (4) reconciling oneself to the tragedy (e.g., by appealing to a transcendent value or religious experience); (5) resigning to the pain of the event; or (6) rationalizing the event (e.g., as being God's will, serving the common good, or being unavoidable).

FACTORS INFLUENCING SURVIVOR RESPONSE

While we lack the longitudinal data to determine whether survivors progress through different stages with respect to the six categories, we have anecdotal evidence that their responses sometimes evolve. For example, at one stage of life a survivor may be bitter and outraged and then progressively become more reconciled. We are, however, hesitant to suggest that there is an appropriate progression of survivor response which, for example, eventuates in reconciliation. In analyzing survivor response, we should consider several mediating factors.

First, we think it is indisputable that the Turkish government's denial of the genocide has profoundly affected survivor response. In any humanly created tragedy, denial by the perpetrator retards the victims' ability to focus on their own healing. It is difficult to overstate how offensive it is to survivors that the reality of their suffering is denied by the Turkish government. Armenians expend an enormous amount of individual and collective energy in combating this distortion of the truth. Everytime an official denial is made by the Turkish government—or whenever the American government refuses to acknowledge the genocide—the effect on survivors is akin to rubbing salt in an open wound.

At the same time, it is somewhat ironic that the Turkish government's denial may actually promote group cohesiveness among Armenians scattered throughout the diaspora. In the face of the breakdown of Armenian culture in the diaspora (what has been referred to as the "white genocide"), there is at least a common sense of outrage against the Turks for their denial of the genocide. Possessing a common enemy can create considerable social solidarity, but Turkish denial is unfortunate because, to some extent, it has fixated Armenians on a single issue, which has in turn retarded a fuller flowering of postgenocide cultural expression.

Second, the degree of suffering that survivors experienced unquestionably influences their response to the genocide. The child who saw his parents killed, or the mother whose infant or child died in her arms during the deportations, carries a heavier psychological burden than someone who experienced relatively little trauma during his or her childhood. However, suffering is qualitative and not purely quantitative, and so we resist simply counting deceased family members to measure survivor trauma.[4]

We also suspect that children who had at least one parent survive were less wounded than those who were totally abandoned. The images from our interviews that haunt us the most are of children, six or seven years old, who lived totally alone, wandering from place to place in search of a piece of bread or a spot to curl up at night to sleep. Children surely do not emerge unscathed from such experiences. And it is not surprising that some of the survivors we interviewed seemed fearful or otherwise affected by their childhood experience. At the same time, we frequently remarked to each other during the interview stage of this research how "normal" survivors appeared to be, given their history.

As we pondered the apparent emotional health of our survivor sample (particularly in comparison to American children who come from "dysfunctional" family backgrounds), we realized that all the survivor-children we interviewed spent the first five or six years, or more, in what were presumably stable family contexts. Hence, they had already successfully negotiated some of the most important developmental stages before undergoing the dislocation of the deportations.

Another important factor that might have influenced survivors' response is their experience in Turkish homes, as well as in orphanages. For example, some children had witnessed terrible violence and perhaps had lost both of their parents but nevertheless ended up in Turkish homes that were nurturing (it should also be noted that many Armenian children were exploited by their Turkish "families"). Likewise, orphanages differed in the quality of care that they were able to provide children, but, overall, we believe they provided important environments of safety and nurture. Once again, we have no way to quantify the role of these surrogate families, but we believe they must be considered significant mediating institutions.

We believe that three other factors, all related to the adult experience of survivors, should be examined in assessing the impact of the genocide, because each of the three provides a context for interpreting the significance of the genocide. First, we believe that political affiliation in adult life is important. Those survivors who are committed members of the Dashnak Party, for example, often frame their understanding of the genocide within the context of the political platform of the party and its commitment to reparations and return of the homeland. (Obviously, one may ask whether individuals joined the Dashnak Party because of their political inclinations or whether the party provided a template for interpreting their experience; certainly both dynamics may be involved for many survivors.) Second, professional success, as well as the hardship one has endured in making a living as an adult, contribute to the way in which survivors assess the impact of their childhood experience of the genocide. Some of those we interviewed have lived on the financial margin all of their lives, and for them, the genocide looms as the overpowering force that has shaped their destiny. Finally, religion has been a key mediating experience and institution for some of the survivors we interviewed. In their struggle to make sense out of the irrationality of the genocide, they have looked to religious explanations for perspective on their personal experience, as well as on the collective experience of the Armenian people.

In addition to stressing that our proposed typology is a heuristic device for analyzing survivor responses, we must also underscore one final qualification: survivors often have extremely ambivalent and conflicting feelings that preclude classification. For example, we found survivors saying, "As a *Christian* I feel I must forgive the Turks, but as a *human being* I find that I have deep resentments." Alternatively, some people expressed strongly militant views about Turkish reparations and establishment of an Armenian homeland, but when asked if they would return to Turkey, or if they thought Armenians would repeat the pattern of Zionism, the answer was no. Or we might have thought that someone was reconciled, only to discover that his or her first response upon hearing of the assassination of Kemal Arikan, the Turkish Consul General in Los Angeles, was a celebratory "Good!" Also, within a given interview we sometimes found that the context established by our questions—for example, whether we were asking about political issues or religious explanations—dictated the tone and substance of survivors' responses.

In summary, this typology is intended to suggest the *range* of ways in which survivors have coped with the trauma of the genocide, but we have become increasingly hesitant to categorize individuals as responding exclusively in one way or another.

AVOIDANCE AND REPRESSION

In figurative terms, one method of dealing with painful events is to "put a lid" on them and attempt to live in the moment. Repression is an unconscious defense mechanism by which individuals "forget" painful life events. But individuals may, at a conscious level, also engage in avoidance by ignoring situations that provoke painful memories. Neither repression nor avoidance eliminates traumatic events, but both are attempts to keep deeply troubling memories from disturbing everyday consciousness.

We encountered several modes of avoidance among survivors. First, some survivors told us gently that they would prefer not to be interviewed, that such occasions evoke memories that disturb them and make it difficult to sleep. We always honored these requests. Other survivors initially agreed to be interviewed, but later telephoned to cancel their appointment, saying that even anticipating the interview was making them nervous and upset. But perhaps more striking was the fact that some of our interviewees, including those with extremely poignant stories, said that they had *never* told their experience of the genocide to anyone, including their children.

Since our research is based on interviews rather than clinical assessments of survivors, it is more difficult to measure repression, but there were nevertheless references to unconscious forgetting in our interviews. For example, one survivor said that "forgetting" was always mixed with "remembering":

> Sometimes I force my brain to remember, because a lot of things happened to me. But, fortunately, there has been a time when I have blocked those memories and have not remembered everything. It was a life struggle. . . . My existence has caused me more grief . . . every minute those scenes are before my eyes—all bloody. If that American orphanage [hadn't been] there, I would also not exist today. This is the story of the end of my life. The things that

happened while I was very young, those things I will forget, and I have given
them to "forgetting."

For this survivor, repression appears to be a means of coping with events
that are too painful to resolve at a conscious level.

The fact that survivors want to forget—or at least forget specific
events—is not surprising. The survivors we have known most intimately, such as Vahram (described in chapter 1), talked incessantly
about the genocide, but even Vahram carefully guarded certain events,
recounting them only on rare occasions. Yet these were the incidents
that we suspect troubled him the most. There were also times when it
was only after the tape recorder had been turned off that survivors told
us things that deeply disturbed them, which they perhaps had never revealed. For example, on one occasion a survivor hinted that she had
been raped by a Turk and had actually had a child by this man.

"Forgetting," then, is a complex phenomenon. When it occurs un-
consciously in the form of repression, it is a double-edged sword, being
both a defense mechanism and a force that controls moods and actions
at a subterranean level. When it occurs consciously in the form of avoidance, it is a tactic chosen by some survivors in their attempt to preserve
their emotional equilibrium.[5]

OUTRAGE AND ANGER

A feeling shared by many survivors, even those who fit into other categories of this typology, is outrage. Repeatedly, survivors told us that
they were not reconciled to the genocide. They said that whenever they
think about the genocide, their hearts burn with anger. Indeed, the word
"Turk" or the sight of a Turk elicits visceral reactions from some survivors, such as the individual who said: "Sometimes I go to a park near
here. I sometimes hear some Turks speaking. I hate them so much that
I run away from there." Another survivor told us that she gets nervous
whenever she hears the word "Turk." And other survivors were more
blunt in expressing their feelings, such as the survivor who simply said
that he hates the Turks, that the things they have done cannot be forgiven. Indeed, one rather kindly survivor, who didn't know the fate of
some of her relatives after the deportations, told us that she would prefer
them to be dead, rather than living as Turks.

On the other hand, some survivors made a clear distinction between
Turks who were guilty of atrocities and those who were not account-
able. As previously discussed, some survivors owed their lives to the

kindness, and even heroic actions, of Turks and, consequently, often refused to make blanket generalizations about Turkish character. Also, we
encountered survivors who were careful to distinguish between Turks
who carried out the genocide in 1915 and Turks living today who may,
in fact, have little knowledge of what was done to the Armenians. In
the words of one survivor: "They were not the cause of it. They were
not born yet. They did not know what was going on. Why should I
hate them?"

Other survivors, however, extend their rage to all Turks. For example, when we asked a survivor if she would ever want to return to her
homeland, she responded, "I'd love to see Urfa again, but I do not want
to see the Turks. I don't want to see their faces." A similar sentiment was
expressed more strongly by a survivor who said: "I wish we could eliminate the Turks from this earth, but I don't have hope that will occur."

When we probed survivors regarding their feelings of outrage, they
frequently cited specific events that provoked powerful responses. For
example, "They burned infants and children. They gathered them up
saying that they were taking them to an orphanage, but instead they
placed them in a building and burned them. How can a human being
take that?" Another survivor responded to our questions about his anger by saying: "When you think of that poor little boy sitting there all
by himself, crying for his mother and then eventually dropping dead out
of starvation—when you try to picture that, what can you say?" A third
example illustrates survivors' deep feelings on recollecting specific images of horror:

> When we think of what happened, we cannot forget the pain. Your mother
> and father come to mind, your own children. He [referring to a Turk] takes
> the child from its mother's lap and kills it. A wild beast does not do that. Of
> course those feelings remain with us all the time. And by remaining in us, the
> feelings will affect our grandchildren, too. The Armenian's heart is burnt. He
> cannot reconcile with the Turks.

Indeed, as was stated previously, the feelings of anger may actually in-
crease with age. As one survivor said: "You know, as you get older, the
fire burns more fiercely. That's how I feel. Taking my father the way
they did, deporting us, killing my mother on the way."

REVENGE AND RESTITUTION

An alternative to simply feeling outrage is seeking amends for the
wrongs that were committed. In the case of genocide or war, the demand

is often for reparations in the form of money, as well as return of land and property. In fact, this has been a focus of attention for a number of survivors, particularly those with strong political affiliation with the Dashnak Party. Although reparations cannot resurrect the dead, they do help heal the emotional wounds of the afflicted. Indeed, their symbolic value is more important than the actual monetary compensation.

Several survivors showed us property deeds to land in their hometowns. At the minimum, they felt that territory formerly owned by Armenians should be returned to them. More radical Armenians believe that the area of historical Armenia currently situated in Turkey should be united with the Republic of Armenia; in addition, they seek monetary compensation for the suffering. Many survivors felt that the deaths of more than a million Armenians were but one manifestation of the genocide; an equally tragic loss is what they called the "white genocide": the loss of Armenian culture and language resulting from assimilation into a host culture. Hence, a homeland is essential as both the wellspring and the reservoir of a culture. To eliminate a homeland is to destroy the culture of a people.

Reparations often involve protracted negotiations and are at least one layer removed from the actual injustice for which one seeks compensation. Immediate revenge is a more primal response to injustice, and as was noted in a previous chapter, several leaders of the Young Turk government were assassinated by survivors: Talaat Pasha, the former Ottoman Minister of the Interior, was killed by Soghomon Tehlirian; Said Halim, the former Ottoman foreign minister, was assassinated by Arshavir Shiragian (who also gunned down two other collaborators who had organized and inspired the deportations); Jemal Pasha, military governor of Constantinople, and subsequently Minister of the Marine, was killed next; while Enver Pasha, Minister of War, died in an ambush and was rumored to have been killed by an Armenian.

One of the first survivors we interviewed pointed to a cluttered bulletin board on the wall in his one-room apartment. In the center of the board was a picture of Soghomon Tehlirian. This survivor said not once, but several times, "I would have done it myself, believe me. . . . I look at this picture each day for inspiration." Another survivor stated, "I remember that when Enver Pasha was killed, I said, 'Good!' " Several elderly male survivors we interviewed told us that, even now, they were willing to fight for their homeland. A seventy-three-year-old man exemplified these sentiments by saying that he was ready to join an Armenian army to fight for the return of the homeland. He stated emphatically, "Let the Turks feel it!"—adding parenthetically, "But they don't have feelings."

After approximately fifty years of relatively low-level political demands for recognition of the genocide, the pursuit of justice by survivors took on a new dimension. On January 28, 1973, Gourgen M. Yanikian, a seventy-eight-year-old survivor who had lost most of his family in the genocide, invited two Turkish consular officials to a Santa Barbara cafe and shot them at point-blank range. Between 1973 and 1985, Turkish officials claim that eighty-six separate terrorist incidents resulted in the deaths of forty-seven Turks, including thirty-one diplomats and officials.[6] Most of these assassinations appeared to have been carried out by a younger generation of Armenians (primarily the grandsons of survivors).[7]

We often asked survivors what they thought of these assassinations, and we received a range of responses in return. Although some survivors disagreed with the assassinations on various grounds, for example, that such actions were giving Armenians a bad name or that they were politically ineffective, we did not find many survivors who condemned them on moral grounds. In fact, a more typical reaction was that the deaths of a few Turks are nothing when compared with the mass destruction of the Armenian people. For example, a survivor stated, "I don't think these kids should be found guilty, even if they have killed some Turkish officials. Why should they be considered guilty when the Turks have killed one and a half million of us?" Another survivor discussed the assassinations in quantitative terms, stating that even if a few Armenian young men have to go to prison, their sacrifice is insignificant compared to that which occurred in the genocide: "If the boys are doing it [i.e., assassinating Turks], they do well! We've given thousands of sacrifices—died in deportations, in hangings, in prisons—let a few more go to jail. It doesn't make a bit of difference [if justice can be served]." Another survivor qualified his approval by saying, "I don't get happy [over the deaths of Turkish officials], but they are reaping their punishment."

Some survivors affirmed even more radical responses to the violence of the genocide, for example: "Is there not one *fedayee* [freedom fighter] who could drop a huge bomb on Turkey now? Is it a sin to say that? Isn't there one Armenian who could do that? This would be for revenge." Another survivor qualified his comments with a comparable religious reservation, but was equally strong in expressing his feelings: "Dear God, forgive me, but let there not be a single Armenian in Turkey, and then give them an earthquake. . . . I am sinful God, forgive me."

Other survivors, however, believed that God should be the one to take vengeance on the Turks. One man told us that he cannot reconcile himself to the fact that completely innocent people were massacred, and he affirmed his faith that God will surely punish the unjust: "My father, for example, he was a very kind and apolitical person, busy with his work. They took a man of forty like that, with seven children, and killed him. I cannot reconcile to that. I think God will avenge, and he will punish them for their sins and wrongs." This theme was repeated in many forms, but the following statement is representative: "I think God will avenge, and avenge really well. I am sure that even if I don't see it, God will punish them."

For some survivors, revenge taken by humans is wrong, but only because God is responsible for balancing the scales of justice: "God will give them their due punishment. God's word tells us that vengeance is his. God is going to give them their due verdict. There is no question about that. But what the Armenians are doing here is not right [i.e., the assassination of Turks]."

A number of other voices opposed the assassinations on various grounds. We have already alluded to the view held by some survivors that assassinations are wrong because the Turkish officials being killed are not the ones who perpetrated the genocide. But other reasons were also offered against assassinations. For example, a survivor cited the futility of the assassinations: "It is too bad that the youth are being killed because of revenge. That does no good. If you kill them by the thousands, their ears will not hear." Another survivor objected that the assassinations polarize the situation, making communication with the Turks impossible. Still another said that, though the assassinations bring attention to the genocide, there must be an alternative way of "telling the story," especially given the bad reputation that Armenians receive because of the killings. One woman expressed fear that the assassinations will cause the Turks to harm the few Armenians remaining in Turkey. Similarly, a survivor presented a vivid image of the assassinations provoking further violence against the Armenians: "I think it is harming more than helping. When you stick something in the beehive, the bees go wild! By killing one Turk, do you eliminate all the Turks? No, instead they become more vicious and do more damage. That is what worries me." This statement is a pragmatic, rather than a moral, argument against assassinations. However, there were also survivors who rejected terrorism not on strategic grounds but as a violation against the Christian ethic of forgiving one's enemies.

RECONCILIATION AND FORGIVENESS

We found virtually no survivors who were reconciled to the genocide—if reconciliation implies accepting the horrors that occurred. What we did find, especially among Protestant Evangelicals in our sample, was a perceived religious obligation to forgive the Turks. However, as we carefully examined the tone and statements regarding reconciliation, we found a great deal of ambivalence, even among Evangelicals, about the possibility of forgiveness when neither acknowledgement of the crime nor reparations have been offered. A pervasive attitude among survivors is that reconciliation exists as a logical possibility, and even a desirable goal, but that it cannot occur without, at the minimum, official acknowledgement of the genocide.

Forgiving the Turks as a matter of moral principle and Christian duty is quite different from the "feeling" of being reconciled. The emotional difficulty of reconciliation is poignantly expressed in the statements of survivors who recognize forgiveness as a moral ideal, but who nevertheless cannot reconcile themselves to the suffering they endured. When we asked a survivor from Severeg if she felt reconciled, she replied with a somewhat embarrassed laugh:

> I don't think I am reconciled. When I think of how my baby sister was left behind on the mountain, I just cannot get reconciled. What sin or fault did that poor baby have? I never saw or heard from my sister or from my brother. . . . To this day, when I recall or think about the stoning of those two young women, I get chills, and in the same way that I screamed when I witnessed it, I feel the same now. That fear is often with me.

At the end of nearly every interview, we asked survivors if they were reconciled, and their answers very frequently included vivid images that helped explain their difficulty in forgiving the Turks. One survivor, recalling deportees high on a mountain pass being beheaded and their bodies thrown into a valley below, said, "How can you be reconciled to that?" He then offered an additional image, of orphans he had observed: "All those starving, naked children, sitting and rocking. When those things come before my eyes, I feel like I am going to go crazy."

Another survivor was more pragmatic in asking, "If I forgive the Turks, will that bring my mother and father back? It won't! When you look at it, [the genocide] is something that cannot be forgiven." Indeed, the phrase—"the genocide cannot be forgiven"—echoed in a variety of other statements by survivors. Sometimes, in fact, our question about reconciliation was greeted with a rather emotional response, such as in the case of the survivor who said, "Are you crazy? Could I forgive the

Turks?" After this exclamation, she began to cry, saying, "I am left all alone in this world. I don't have anyone left. I have no one, no one, and no children." As with this individual, the sense of loss overpowered some survivors' ability to forgive. Thus, on occasion, survivors answered our question about forgiveness with a litany of relatives who had died: "How can I forgive them? It cannot be forgiven. Just think, my father's sister had five children. One was married [and apparently survived], but all the rest, she and her husband, were killed by the Turks." Another survivor responded to our question with a dismissive retort signaling the limits of human forgiveness by stating, "Let God forgive them!"

As previously stated, the survivors who talked about forgiveness were often Evangelicals, and when they commented on reconciling with the Turks, it was usually in the spirit that this was their Christian duty, as opposed to their personal inclination. A minister we interviewed made a clear distinction between his feelings as a human being and his obligations as a Christian: "I am glad I am a Christian. If not, with these feelings, I would have delighted to kill as many Turks as I could; especially, for example, when I think of my grandchildren. How could the Turks have killed children before their mother's very eyes? Believe me, it is unbearable!"

The model for forgiveness that more than one survivor mentioned was Jesus on the cross, saying of his persecutors, "Forgive them, Father, for they know not what they do." In citing this example, survivors emphasized again that forgiveness is a duty, not something that is natural to them as human beings. Indeed, one survivor stated: "We forgive because God *commands* us to forgive." This survivor, however, immediately followed his statement by saying, "I don't excuse them, though. They are guilty, and I would never say they were not."

As discussed in the previous section, survivors sometimes also talked about the obligation to forgive based on the theological conviction that revenge is God's responsiblity, not their own. In the words of one survivor, "I just say that God is going to judge. He should and he will. Blood does not stay on the ground." However, this view is certainly not shared by all; as another interviewee cynically remarked, "There is a Turkish saying which says that if you leave it up to God, it doesn't get done."

On occasion we felt that reconciliation and forgiveness were endorsed almost as being the only alternative. For example, a survivor stated: "As far as reconciliation, this has been our situation: we have no choice but to accept it. What else can we do? But I am not reconciled with the Turks. No!" Another survivor echoed this same sentiment in almost identical words: "We almost have no choice. We have to forgive, whether we want to or not." And several survivors framed the option of reconciliation in pragmatic, rather than philosophical or religious terms. For example, a survivor said that it does no good to "cry over spilled milk," commenting matter-of-factly: "Worrying and crying over something doesn't help you in any way." A similarly pragmatic attitude was reflected by another interviewee: "I have to be reconciled. Whether you want it or not, you have to be reconciled with your life—even though I cannot 'digest' what the Turks did."

On the other hand, a few survivors in our sample seemed to be genuinely reconciled, although their reconciliation came after a protracted struggle. For example, a survivor told us how she had gone to an April 24 commemoration of the genocide: "That night I found myself in tears, agonizing with God as to how and why do you allow the Turks to go on when they wiped out our people. I actually felt God standing next to me and talking with me, saying, 'If I have not revenged the death of my own son, then you need to be patient.' " She reported that from that day forward she felt a sense of peace about the genocide that was qualitatively different from the anger and outrage that had previously tormented her.

Another survivor situated her reconciliation within the framework of a conversion experience in which she became convinced of the reality of life after death: "Before I had my conversion, I used to always cry about my brothers—in their youth and their young widowed wives. But after my conversion, God wiped off my tears. Praise the Lord! I am comforted, and someday we will see them in heaven."

Other survivors seemed to achieve a degree of reconciliation by making a clear distinction between Turks who perpetrated the genocide and those who had nothing to do with it. For example, a survivor told us of her experience of living next door to a Turkish woman in Egypt. As she got to know her Turkish neighbor, she realized that this woman had nothing to do with the sufferings of the Armenians: "I felt like she was one of my homeland people. My heart truly went to her, and I was friendly to her."

When we asked survivors about being reconciled, some responded by telling us what would be required in order for them to forgive the Turks. It is apparent from their responses that denial of the genocide is the most important impediment to reconciliation. Of course, healing is a slow process, and even admission of the genocide will not result in an instantaneous cure. Nevertheless, acknowledgement of the genocide is, for many survivors, a precondition of reconciliation.

RESIGNATION AND DESPAIR

Among the survivors we interviewed were some who appeared melancholic and despairing over the genocide, not even showing any overt signs of an internal struggle with the event. Their passivity was not the result of being reconciled to the genocide; rather, these survivors seemed consumed by what Armenians call *houzom*—a deep feeling of sorrow and sadness. Some of these individuals appeared almost affectless as they told their story. Although they were not uninterested in the genocide, they seemed to lack any active sense of confrontation with the tragedy they had experienced. The spirit of their conversation was that these things had happened, they were in the past, and nothing could be done about them in the present. These interviewees did not avoid talking about their childhood experiences, but they did so without either reconciliation or outrage.

Throughout the interview, a survivor from Marash continually asked about his parents and family: "Why did they die? Who killed them? Why did they kill them?" Yet he offered no answers to these questions, beyond referring repeatedly to his fatalistic conviction that life is a struggle. He remembered being melancholic in the orphanage, and although he had raised four children of his own, he said that his later years had been filled with thoughts of the genocide: "I have come to this age and the question 'Why should this have happened?' presses on my soul. And I think that the life that I live is empty." He stated that the only "rest," or relief, that he gets from the pain of his life is when he is reading about the genocide. He referred to books about the genocide as his "nourishment," stating that he reads whatever he can find that relates to the genocide. In his words: "I want to do nothing but to live with those sufferings." He commented that many people were able to move beyond the pain of their childhood and get on with life, but, in his case, "This *is* life." At one point in the interview he stated:

> My spirit is blinded. I truly believe that no one will do anything good to me. That is the point I have come to. I have been like that in my work, too. I have lost and lost and lost. I have worked so very hard, and lost. I have never been able to get ahead because my spirit inside of me is so impressed with pessimism. . . . Nothing will come out of me, because I have been defeated by life.

Some survivors portrayed the genocide as a matter of fate. What chance did they have? Armenians were a minority people; their young had been drafted; their leaders imprisoned; their weapons confiscated. How could they resist? But, also, how could they have known what was to come? These sentiments were reflected in comments of a survivor who said: "What could the Armenians have done when those against them were so much stronger? It is an issue of six hundred years. They were too strong for us. Just two gendarmes used to control a whole group of people. Of course, the men were tied. They could not do anything, and what could the women do?"

Yet other survivors lamented the fact that they had not engaged in some form of civil disobedience and resisted deportation: "If the Armenians had known that they were going to be massacred, starve in the deserts, and suffer so much, they would have never left the cities. They could have fought, even though they know that they would have lost. But they would have died there! I am convinced that the poor women really did not know that the purpose of their deportation was a slow death." Hence, one source of the resignation felt by these survivors is their perception of the inevitability of the genocide: Armenians did not comprehend what was happening and were therefore helpless to prevent it.

This spirit of resignation and powerlessness carried over into the present circumstances of survivors and was expressed in the opinion that Armenians are helpless now, as they were in the past. Specifically, these survivors believed that Armenians cannot obtain justice so long as they lack a nation that can exert political pressure at an international level;[8] there was a widely held view that the United States will do nothing because of Turkey's strategic importance in the Middle East. Some survivors also stated that Turkey will never pay reparations or return land and territory owned by Armenians; the Turkish character has not changed since 1915, they argued, as demonstrated by continuing human and civil rights abuses in Turkey and the ongoing denial of the genocide. For example, after complaining about the futility of resisting the Turks during the genocide, one survivor stated: "You know, now it is useless again. The Turks will never admit to it. They'll never admit it, no matter what we do. It is impossible. It is futile for the Armenians to gain anything today. It is foolish. They want revenge, but they'll not succeed."

Another survivor expressed similar feelings: "I have no hope that the Turks will ever admit what they did to us. They never will. Never. They won't give our lands back, either. Are we going to shed blood for them [referring to the legal consequences of assassinating Turks]? Haven't they done enough to us? Have we not suffered enough at their hands? No! No! We won't get our land back. I have no hope."

The theme of powerlessness and lack of political strength was restated frequently by those who seemed resigned. One survivor employed the image that you need fingernails in order to scratch your head. Armenians are powerless, he said, and expressing anger without the strength to back it up is counterproductive. "Anger does not get you anywhere. You only hurt yourself." Another survivor was more pointed in her analysis: "If there was a war between the Armenians and the Turks, our young people would fight. That's how it seems. But you well know that, again, we are going to be the ones to suffer." Hence, survivors who appear resigned often draw parallels between the impossibility of resistance in 1915 and the unlikeliness of political reparations in the present.

It is possible that these feelings of resignation are rooted in the degradation, humiliation, and dehumanization that survivors experienced during the deportations. For example, one of our interviewees stated: "We had become like animals, without much feeling. We had reconciled to crying, being hungry, walking. We knew this was our fate. After a while I was no longer afraid because no feelings remained in me. We were concerned only about where we were walking and where we could get food and water." Obviously, some survivors were able to overcome such feelings of impotence and dehumanization in the orphanages, but others seemed to be marked permanently by their childhood experiences.

In summary, these survivors appeared to be depressed and melancholic, having lost all sense of hope—concerning both their own lives and the future of the Armenian nation. Their spirits seemed broken, lacking the resources to struggle with their memories. For this group, hope might have been the final victim of the genocide.

EXPLANATION AND RATIONALIZATION

Any breach in the moral order invites explanations that rationalize, or attempt to make sense of, occurrences which violate our sense of what is humanly reasonable. Genocide is, perhaps, the ultimate breakdown of the assumed structures of human civility. Indeed, genocide threatens us at the deepest level of our being, and one way in which people attempt to deal with this threat is to explain it away, or to justify it. In our interviews, it was apparent that some survivors were deeply troubled at a cognitive level by the genocide and had spent a lifetime seeking explanations for this event.

A variety of explanations were given by survivors for the occurrence of the genocide. Obviously, these were the theories of ordinary citizens—not historians or political scientists—attempting to make sense of an event whose rupture of the moral order cried out for interpretation. In citing the following three explanations, we are not representing them as necessarily valid interpretations of the origins of the genocide (see chapter 2 for our views on this subject), but rather as opinions frequently stated by survivors.

First, a number of survivors blamed the Germans for the genocide.[9] Historically, the Armenians had been repeatedly massacred by the Turks, but it was the Germans, they said, who suggested a systematic means of exterminating the Armenians through the pretense of deportation: "The Germans gave the Turks the idea that one easy way to kill all the Armenians was to have them deported away from their homes and towns under the pretense that they were in the war zone, and let them die slowly due to exposure, hunger, thirst, and disease. This was the Germans' idea."

This thought was repeated in a variety of expressions: "I think that the Germans were on the Turks' back. They opened up their eyes and warned them against us. I don't think that, if Germany had not backed them, they could have pulled this off."

In fact, one survivor implied that the Turks were not capable of having conceived of the idea of genocide: "I still say that the Turks are not smart enough to have come up with the idea of the genocide. The idea came from others, from European intellectuals. This is because they wanted to use Turkey for their benefit [i.e., specifically, building a railway through Turkey to the oil fields of Iraq]."

We heard conflicting views as to whether the Germans intended the deportations to result in a genocide or merely the relocation of the Armenians. On one hand, a survivor stated: "The Germans only said for them to relocate the Armenians, not to kill them." But other survivors argued that the German idea of deportation fit perfectly with the fact that the Turks had joined the war against the British and French: "They listened to and understood what the Europeans were saying. They couldn't just go to each Armenian home and kill them. Other nations would have for sure intervened if that were the case. But by deporting them, it was less obvious to other nations what was happening in the interior." Whatever the actual facts regarding the German role, a number of survivors saw them as having played a major part in conceiving of the deportations.

Second, numerous survivors cited jealousy as the motive for the genocide. Armenians were industrious, they said, while the Turks were backward and lazy. The Turks resented Armenian wealth, and the deportations presented an opportunity to confiscate their goods and remove them from positions of privilege and power. The following three quotations from our interviews all attribute the genocide to either fear of Armenian progress or jealousy over Armenian accomplishments:

> The reason [for the genocide] was that all the business and all the commerce and all the wealth were in the hands of the Armenians. Just like in Germany, everything was in the hands of the Jews, and Hitler came and cleaned them out. They [the Turks] were jealous.

> The Armenians were very progressive, building schools, getting educated, and overall moving ahead, while the Muslims were behind in all these areas. There were very few among them who were educated. But wherever the Armenians would go, they would start a school.

> Too many of the wealthy in Turkey were Armenians. They [Turks] were jealous and wanted the wealth for themselves. All the trades belonged to the Armenians. Many of the government officials were Armenians. The doctors were, too. All the businessmen were Armenian.

In citing jealousy as a cause of the genocide, a number of survivors stated that "when the Armenians left Turkey, so did the blessings."

Third, religious differences were often cited as contributing to the genocide. Survivors stated that Islam justifies coercive violence against non-Muslims. Negative comments were sometimes made about the fanatical character of Islam as practiced at the local level: "It is to their benefit or reward to torture and trouble a non-Muslim." Another survivor said, "They wanted all of us to become Muslims. They knew that we would not become Muslims, so they massacred us. Those who did convert to Islam were not killed."

In addition to offering explanations for the genocide, survivors sometimes even struggled to find positive by-products of the genocide. For example, several survivors said that at least the Armenians are no longer under Turkish rule, and one stated: "If it had not been for the genocide, we would have still been there with a massacre to face every fifteen years or so." Other survivors pointed to how well Armenians are doing in the diaspora, establishing businesses and succeeding in their professions. These explanations were not offered as justifications for the genocide;

rather, they were efforts to search for some consolation in the terrible reality of the genocide.

Another kind of after-the-fact rationalization was offered by a few survivors who said that the genocide must have been God's punishment of the Armenians. These respondents were Protestant survivors whose theological convictions compelled them to explain all historical events with reference to some divine plan. These survivors did not excuse the Turks for their actions; but because their view of God's sovereignty was clearly threatened by the genocide, they were committed to finding evidence of God's hand at work in every event. For example, a survivor said, "As a Christian nation, we lived as atheists." In her view, the genocide was God's way of bringing the Armenians back to a religious commitment. Also, several survivors said that they became "true" Christians in the orphanages, thus indirectly attributing their salvation to the genocide. Having offered these few examples, we hasten to say, however, that not all Protestants viewed the genocide in this manner, and, furthermore, in our opinion these statements appeared to be an attempt by survivors to declare that God is still in charge of this world—affirming the existence of a moral order—in spite of the evil that we see.

THE PROBLEM OF THEODICY

For many survivors, the fact that Armenia was historically a Christian nation raised the ancient question of how a good God could allow the destruction of his people. Stated philosophically, the problem of theodicy is this: How can a God who is all-powerful, loving, and just allow evil to occur? This is perhaps the most difficult question that religionists face, whether attempting to explain mass injustice, such as occurs in a genocide, or the death of an innocent child.

After listening to survivors talk about their faith and the genocide, we have become convinced that several layers of meaning are operating. On one level, survivors are involved in the task of theological debate and reconciliation, and their innovations in theological discourse should not be ignored. We also believe, however, that the "God issue" represents a deeper attempt to deal with injustice in the world. That is to say, whatever metaphysical status God may have, the debate about God's justice is, for survivors, an internal struggle with the issue of whether the universe is trustworthy.

Survivors' responses included a variety of alternative answers to this question: (1) Because of God's sovereignty and inscrutability, even if a stable moral order cannot be discerned using human standards of reason, nevertheless, there is some ultimate purpose in the chaos that man sees; (2) God eventually punishes transgressors, and the scales of justice are balanced through the fall of the wicked; and, in contrast, (3) if evil is ever to be conquered, it will be through human, not divine, effort.

A number of survivors told us that they might have been able to reconcile themselves to the deaths of the men, but they could not accept the deaths of women and children. For example, a woman recounted how a group of children was burned to death by the Turks, and then, distancing her emotions from her theological convictions, she said: "*Some people say* that there is no God . . . [but] If there is a God, how could he watch this activity without cutting off the hands of the Turks?" This survivor refused to say that she, herself, did not believe in God, instead stating that "some people" say there is no God. It is clear, however, that she was unable to reconcile herself to the idea that God stood by passively while Armenian children were slaughtered.

Other survivors wondered aloud how God could allow righteous people to be massacred. Several made an analogy between the situation of the Armenians and God's treatment of the wicked people in the Old Testament story of Sodom and Gomorrah. One survivor asked, "How did God destroy a whole nation, including their children and even the animals? What sense does this make when God says that not one ant can be hurt without his knowing it?" Raising his voice in frustration, this survivor asked why God would create a Christian people, the Armenians, only to destroy them: "You think of Sodom and Gomorrah and how God said that even if there were fifty faithful people he would not destroy them. Were there not fifty or five hundred righteous people [Armenians] so that God could not spare them?" He answered his own rhetorical question, stating: "I think that God should have intervened." He then offered two examples where, in his view, a just God would not have been silent. He recalled seeing pregnant women's stomachs being cut open by gendarmes, in sport, to determine whether the fetus was male or female, and, second, he witnessed children being thrown into an empty well and killed. In his view, a loving God who is all-powerful would not have allowed these two events to occur.

Another survivor said that the Turks would tell the Armenians to call on their God before shooting them. After saying this, he asked searchingly, "Where was God at this time?" If only one or two had died, he mused, it might be understandable. But thousands upon thousands dying made no theological sense. He went on to confess: "I am a Christian, but there are times that I lose my faith—especially when these things come before my eyes. I ask, why did God not help us? What had we done?"

A survivor recounted the process that he went through in attempting to reconcile the genocide with the existence of God, stating that he frequently asked: "Why should those things have happened to the Armenians . . . if there was a Lord and God? Where were they? This is a question, and I would like to know [the answer]. If he is a mighty God, and he knows everything, [then] he should have turned the swords and the guns against them [the Turks]."

Describing his own pilgrimage to disbelief, this survivor said that one day he declared: "God and Jesus Christ, from now on, *you* go your way, and *I* am going my way. Don't you ever bother me anymore." He then directed his commentary to us: "So since then, I have changed. And if you want to go to church, you go. But don't tell me that I am wrong, that I am a 'this' and 'that,' that I am a lost soul. If there is a heaven and a hell, I tell you, I will go to hell."

From the accounts we heard, it was not uncommon for deportees to lose their faith during the long marches. For example, a survivor quoted his mother as having cried out to God during the deportations, "Are you blind? Have you gone blind?" Another survivor told us how her father rebuked her for praying for help during the deportations, having himself lost faith in God's intervention.

While we encountered survivors who became outright atheists as the result of the genocide, we also found a great deal of ambivalence about God among survivors. Believers were troubled by God's silence, and those who felt that God had deserted them had difficulty reconciling that abandonment with the Christian heritage of the Armenians. A survivor illustrated this ambivalence when he told us that he used to tease religious Armenians, saying, "Where is God?" But he quickly followed by saying, "When they were gone, I crossed myself and said, 'In the name of the Father, Son, and Holy Ghost.' And then I would say, 'Praise be to God that you granted us another day.' " In reflecting on his own conflict, he said: "It is in our blood [referring to Christianity], and it is not possible to kick it altogether."

We also observed another pattern among survivors: they struggled to comprehend not only the deaths of their fellow Armenians but also their own survival. There is a deep human need to attribute good as well as evil to powers outside of oneself. Thus, in attempting to explain why they had survived, it was not uncommon for respondents to refer to

God's intervention in their lives: "We were with fear all the time, but my mother used to always encourage us. Walking over the dead bodies was a very bad thing. We have been hungry; we used to eat only once a day. But we survived. It is God's grace. The Lord is merciful. . . . Not a single Arab or Turk laid hands on us. This is God's work."

Some survivors were even more pointed in attributing survival to God's will rather than personal effort: "I think about those things and I see God's protection in it. I see his grace in it. Because there were many others who were both braver than me and also healthier than me. But many of them died. But why is it that I survived? . . . It was God's grace."

To some individuals, the very fact that they survived implies that God must have preserved them for a reason. An elderly survivor said that she often wakes up at night and prays, "Lord, you have saved me and brought me this far, but what is your purpose?" Although her question indicates some doubt whether her life currently has meaning, nevertheless she clings to the idea that unless her life served a divine purpose she would not have been spared. Another survivor said that "if God does not make you die, no one dies."

Contrary to research that remarks on the guilt that survivors feel for having lived while others around them died, we seldom encountered such feelings, at least at an explicit or a conscious level. Instead, we found survivors pondering the meaning of their survival rather than feeling guilty about it. When we did encounter guilt among our survivors, it was related to the tragic moral choices that were required of them—as described in chapter 5—and not to their own survival.

Occasionally, survivors told us of profound experiences, usually interpreted as religious revelations, that changed their perspective on the genocide. For example, one woman said that after she and her family had been deported, many of her surviving relatives contracted typhus and died. In despair she cried out in prayer, "Jesus, Jesus. Why is it that you used to heal the sick before and don't now?" Then, "All of a sudden, I noticed that the sky filled with clouds and Jesus descended into my room. He said to me, 'Let all the sick be healed.' He then put his hand on my head and blessed me. Then he put all of us in a line and gave each of us bulgur [wheat]." Although only a few survivors reported such dramatic experiences, many struggled to explain, in more ordinary ways, the seeming contradiction between God's mercy and his silence.

Members of the Apostolic Church, in particular, appeared to solve the theodicy problem by implying that evil is strictly a product of human intentionality. According to one survivor: "There are always wars. The

Bible is filled with them. God has nothing to do with them. It is people who fight with people." Another survivor reiterated the same argument rather tersely, saying: "This is not from God. It is due to man and his evil hand." But other survivors felt that such a distinction is too simplistic, for it does not explain why God *allows* evil to occur—if he has the power to stop it.[10]

Searching for other explanations, a few survivors resolved the dilemma by declaring that there is an unbridgeable gap between human understanding and God's intentions: "We do not understand God's works." Another survivor appealed to the scriptural reference, "My thoughts are not your thoughts." Amplifying this statement, another said: "We do not understand God's works. He says that as far as the skies are from earth, so are his thoughts from ours." Still other survivors held in tension both the irreconcilable theological problem and their own survival; for example, an interviewee said: "We have remained alive! We don't understand God's ways. At times you have certain feelings against God, especially when you are in pain. But we still do not forget God."

An alternative to declaring that God's ways are inscrutable is to avoid the question of why God allowed the genocide and instead to hold out the hope that God will punish evildoers. We found a range of survivor opinions of this nature. For example, a survivor told us that God will punish the Turks because he is a righteous judge. But when we asked whether God had already punished the Turks, she said, "Well, maybe. Sometimes the Lord does it right away, and sometimes he waits." In contrast, another woman offered these examples: "Among the Turks an epidemic broke out, where if one person got it in a family, the whole family died. It was typhus and many died. They [Turks] used to say after this, 'We killed those who were our brothers in our town [i.e., Armenians], and now God is punishing us.' " This survivor said that a Turk asked her why she didn't get sick and then replied that it was because she was a *gâvur* (infidel).

Other survivors maintained that not only did God punish the Turks immediately after the genocide, but he is also continuing to punish them. We were told, for example, "A couple of days ago we heard that there was an earthquake there [in Turkey] and about a thousand people died. These are all punishments." An even more radical notion of God's sovereignty was expressed by a survivor who proclaimed that God is behind the political assassination of Turks. Referring to the killing of Talaat by Tehlirian, this survivor said, "without God's permission, not a single hair falls."

CHAPTER 9

Moral Reflections on the Genocide

Genocide creates the occasion for profound religious and moral reflections, and in this concluding chapter, we will focus on three issues. First, scattered throughout our interviews is commentary about Turks and Turkish character, and here we wish to offer some examples of "righteous Turks"—individuals who disagreed with their government's policies toward the Armenians and/or who showed a generous spirit toward Armenian children. Second, in the context of discussing morally exemplary behavior, we will describe some instances of selfless actions by parents and relatives on behalf of survivor-children we interviewed. And, finally, we will conclude with some reflections on the emergence of the Republic of Armenia as an independent nation, a symbol of resurrection for the survivor generation.

THE GOOD TURK

When an overwhelming event, such as genocide, cries out for interpretation, there is a human tendency to imply that *all* members of the perpetrator group were guilty. Hence, Armenians may direct their anger against "the Turks," broadly defined, without qualifying that there were Turks who both assisted the Armenians and resisted the policies of their government. A careful examination of our interviews reveals that survivors, in fact, quite frequently mentioned Turks who had helped them or shown them kindness, even though some of these references are touched on only briefly in their narrative of the genocide.[1]

For example, one respondent told us how he had survived an attack on his caravan, despite being wounded by a dagger: "After the massacre, the Turks and Kurds were looking for loot among the dead. So a man came and searched all over me and saw that I was alive. He took me to his home without anyone knowing. He changed my name and gave me a Turkish name, Ahmad. He taught me how to pray in Turkish. I became a Turk and lived there for five years." When we asked him how he was treated, he replied that he was a servant, but this man was good to him, as well as to two other orphan children whose lives he had saved. He then stated: "During the massacre, there were a lot of good Turks who cursed their own government. They were crying [when Armenians were deported]. I remember that. They used to come out of their houses as we went to villages, and cry and curse their government. There are good and bad among all people."

Survivors also told us about Arabs who had treated them kindly during the deportations. A survivor who ended up in Der-Zor said that she had gone blind from starvation. When she was adopted, she was unable to see even the sun: "These Arabs turned out to be very nice. With home-type 'medication,' or actually 'cures,' they treated my eyes. They dug a ditch in the ground, stuck my head in it, and made me sweat. And when I was thoroughly wet, they took me out. Then I saw the sun. Once I came out, I saw the sun. They washed and cleaned me and changed my clothes." She was treated like a daughter during the year she stayed with them, but she decided nevertheless to run away, saying: "I reasoned that no matter what, I was Armenian and they were Arabs. If I remained there, I too would become an Arab and lose my Armenian identity. I thought that if I ran away, some Armenians, someplace, would take care of me."

Many survivors indicated that they were on friendly terms with neighboring Turks before the deportation orders were issued. Typical of the comments we heard was this statement:

> Our Turkish neighbors were very good people. They cried so much at our departure. We had no problem getting along with them. We were peaceful and friendly with each other. We had no fear of Turks. We visited each other and played with their children. When the orders came for us to leave, our Turkish neighbors could not face us. They felt so ashamed. And they did try

to keep some of us. They warned us not to leave. They especially wanted to keep us girls. But would my mom leave us behind?

Sometimes Turks confronted their fellow citizens and demanded that Armenians be treated humanely. A survivor remembered being taken with six other boys to one of the officials of their town. All the other Armenians had already been deported, and the question was what should be done with these boys:

> In the *mukhtar*'s [official's] house, there were about forty people gathered together discussing. The men [who had brought the boys there] asked him what they were to do with us boys, since we were crying day and night. "They want their parents," [the men said]. There was a middle-aged man there in old military clothes. He said to the rest, "Why are you worried about them? Give them to me, and I'll take them to a certain valley, butcher them, and throw them down." When this fellow said this, the wife of the *mukhtar* got up and slapped the man in the face, saying: "For shame that you would speak that way. God has not killed these children, and you are going to?" She turned to her husband and said to him, "Listen, I have seven brothers. If any harm is done to even the hair of any of these boys, I'll both divorce you and have each of my brothers fire a bullet in you."

Because of the *mukhtar*'s wife's intervention, the lives of all of the boys were spared. During our interviews, another account was offered of a Turkish woman's intervention on behalf of an Armenian youth.

A survivor told us that all of the men were being gathered in her town of Yozgat. In fact, the Turks had burned the vineyards to flush out any Armenians who might have been hiding there. The women were all crying over the loss of their husbands, but this survivor—who was a child at the time—was out playing when a Turkish man came bragging that they had killed all of the men. He was wearing her uncle's belt, and he demanded to see her fourteen-year-old brother, in order to take him, also. "While they were searching, our Turkish woman neighbor came out and said that Garo [the brother] was not there, that she had seen him go to the vineyard, but not return. She said, 'Why bother that old woman'; my mother was quite elderly, apparently. It turns out that she had taken him [the brother] to her house, hiding him. Since she was a Turk, these people believed her and left." Although this survivor's brother escaped through the Turkish woman's intervention, three of her sisters' husbands were killed.

Another survivor said that his father had been extremely helpful to the Turks who lived near Sivas. As a result, when all of the men were rounded up to be killed, a Turkish friend went to the guards, saying that his father should not be taken because of the assistance he had given to the local Turks. In response, one of the guards apparently said, "Well, then, I'll give him to you as a gift." The Turk who had intervened went and untied the hands of her father, and at the same time undid the ropes of several other Armenian men. We heard a similar story of intervention from a survivor from Urfa: there was a Turkish man who had saved Armenians by hiding them during the 1895 massacres, and when this survivor and her family were already walking out of their town as part of the deportation process, the man maneuvered them into a stable where they were able to hide.

Throughout our interviews, there were also incidental references to Turks who did not perform particularly dramatic acts on behalf of Armenians but, nevertheless, demonstrated genuine human kindness. For example, a number of references were made to gendarmes who seemed to take pity on the deportees and sometimes let children ride on their horse, or even gave money to mothers to buy food for their children. One survivor told us how his attitude toward Turks changed as the result of his relationship with a Turkish man who cared for him: "The first night when I was sleeping on the hay in the barn, I heard him coming and was so afraid that I was shaking. I thought for sure he was going to butcher me. But he came and covered me so gently. I was barely five years old, but I do remember." After this event, he would go running to this Turkish "father" whenever he saw him. As their relationship developed, he learned that this man had many Armenian friends: "He had no hatred in him toward the Armenians. They [the man and his wife] took care of me like their child."

Some Turks risked punishment by helping to feed Armenians. A survivor recalled a Turkish man who told a small group of Armenians to come to him during the night with bags filled with sand: "When they [the Armenians] did that after midnight, he made them dump their sand and fill up their bags with wheat. We did that for two or three days. We were so hungry, starving, there was no food or bread. But with that wheat, they lived for months." This survivor's husband (who was also a survivor and was present during the interview) said, "If I saw that man today, I would kiss his hands and feet."

Survivors who had directly experienced acts of kindness from Turks were careful to qualify their generalizations about Turkish character. Several survivors stated outright that if there had been no good Turks, no Armenians would have survived. And quite a number of survivors implied that the majority of Turks were not to blame for the genocide;

rather, the tragedy was caused by the government in Constantinople. A survivor from Adana reflected this view when he said: "We were like brothers. Our Turks said later, 'Whoever was the cause of this geno-cide, may God blind his eyes.' They did not wish our death. In fact, if it weren't for these good Turks, we all would have been killed, too. All of the orders came from Istanbul." Thus, while Armenians, espe-cially of the second and third generations, sometimes generalize about "the Turks" as if they were a monolithic entity, the survivors them-selves are often more careful to distinguish between "good" and "bad" Turks.

MORAL HEROISM

In addition to describing intervention by Turks, our interviewees also gave numerous accounts of heroism on the part of parents, relatives, or strangers who performed acts of self-sacrifice that were instrumental to their survival. Many of these stories have already been told in previous chapters. However, the point deserves to be made explicit that survival was not simply a matter of luck or personal initiative; many children survived or had their lives positively reoriented through direct inter-vention. Some acts of intervention took place during the deportations, but the children's destiny was also frequently altered by mediation that occurred in the orphanages or while families were struggling for eco-nomic survival.

For example, a survivor told us that her mother worked all day grind-ing wheat at a mill, receiving a portion of bread for herself and each family member as pay. The survivor's grandmother, however, refused to eat her portion, and gave it to the children instead, saying that she was ready to die, but the children should live. Another survivor offered a similar account of her own grandmother's selflessness:

> I had an old grandmother. She used to make socks and mend them for the soldiers, earn a few pennies, and then buy bread with it and bring it to us to eat so that we would not die. She used to say, "I am old and I don't care if I die, but I want you to be free." So most of the [children] who had someone like that lived. But the ones who did not have anybody and wanted bread, but couldn't get any, would eat the grass, swell up and die.

It is impossible to know how many grandparents, as well as parents, sac-rificed their lives for their children, but we suspect that it might have been a frequent occurrence.

Children, too, demonstrated deep compassion in attempting to feed siblings and even parents. For example, in an earlier chapter we cited the case of a survivor who lived in a Turkish home secretly giving food to a brother who regularly came to beg at their door. Another survivor, who lived with a baker, said that she used to give bread to an aunt, with the instructions that she should take it to her brother, who was living on the streets. Still another survivor remembered smuggling food out of the orphanage where he lived to give to his mother, who was sick. Family bonds were strong, and children tried to do their part in contributing to their family's welfare.

Even children who were not related sometimes helped one another. For example, a survivor told us how her mother, who had not been deported because of her job in a factory, used to rent houses close to her children's school so that they could help her make a living:

> We had to go home during our lunch hour everyday to clean cotton from plants. We had to separate the cotton from the hull. The hulls were used for fire for us. We cooked the food on it. We boiled the water for the wash with that. It was useful for us, and we would get paid for doing that. My mother used to give us a certain amount in bags that we had to finish "today." This was during recess hours. Sometimes our friends would come with us, saying that if they helped us, it would get done faster and then we could go back to school and play together.

In our interviews, we also found many examples of Armenians sharing their resources with the poor after the deportations ended. A survivor told us about a wealthy Armenian who gave her mother money, saying, "Buy some bread for the children so they don't die." Another survivor said: "The richer ones helped the poor ones . . . my mother would fill up a whole plate and send it to certain families or neighbors who did not have food."

When survivors were struggling to reestablish themselves financially after the deportations, the children whose parents had survived were aware that they were more privileged than the orphans. A woman recalled that when they went to church on Sunday, her grandmother would give her money for the offering during the service. She said that as they walked to church, she would often lag behind and give her offering money to children who were begging on the streets. After telling us this story, she said reflectively, "It used to affect me. These people looked like bones. Sometimes now, when we see pictures of kids from Cambodia or Ethiopia, I go back and remember those Armenians who looked just like that—the children bloated, lying on the ground, dying."

There are many instances in our interviews of individual acts of kindness that made a substantial difference in the circumstances of survivors. Sometimes these charitable acts were as simple as offering someone a meal or a place to sleep for a few nights. For example, a survivor told us that after being deported, his mother had become very ill and couldn't walk anymore, but they encountered a German worker who noticed their plight:

> [She] took pity on us and said she would bring something to eat. So she brought white bread, which at the time in that place was like finding gold, and some beans and other things. We were so hungry. My mother said for us to pray for her. The young woman who brought the food asked us if there was something else we needed. My mother asked for bekmez [a syrupy punch]. She went and brought us some of that, too.

This same woman then arranged for them to travel by train, rather than walking, and bought them free tickets.

In the chapter on emigration, we mentioned that survivors who came to the United States often sent part of their earnings back to relatives in the "old country." Although most of these immigrants were very poor themselves, they felt a strong commitment to bringing family members to "the land of freedom and opportunity." As a result, they often lived very simple lives in order to send money to relatives waiting to emigrate.

We were also impressed by stories of parents who worked and saved so that their children could go to the United States—while they often stayed behind. And we have many accounts of survivors and their parents and relatives making heroic sacrifices to educate their children. For example, in a nearly off-handed manner, a survivor mentioned that her husband's uncle used to eat only one meal a day so that he could contribute money toward his nephew's college education at the American University of Beirut. The stories are seldom told, yet these sacrifices were the foundation on which new lives were built in the diaspora.

THE REPUBLIC OF ARMENIA

The account of the Armenian Genocide does not end with the deportation of Armenians from Turkey and the creation of diaspora communities around the world. As mentioned in chapter 2, between 1918 and 1920 the Republic of Armenia existed as a fragile political entity comprising both Armenian refugees from Turkey and Armenians who had lived in Russian territory for many generations. When the republic came under Soviet rule in 1920, many Armenians despaired of ever regaining a homeland. For more than seventy years, Armenians struggled to preserve their culture and institutions against the corrupting influence of communist ideology and economic structures. Then on September 23, 1991, the unexpected occurred: Armenia declared its independence from the Soviet Union, and the Republic of Armenia was reborn. We will conclude this book with a few personal reflections on the current threats and promises surrounding the survival of the Armenians.

On the occasion of the seventy-fifth anniversary of the genocide, we had the privilege of visiting Yerevan to present a paper at an International Congress sponsored by the Academy of Sciences of the Armenian SSR. Even though the Soviet Union had not yet begun the dramatic disintegration for which the year 1991 will long be remembered, there were nevertheless unmistakable signs of a powerful spirit of nationalism emerging within Armenia. In the year before our visit, Armenians had been demonstrating for the return of the disputed region of Nagorno-Karabagh, which Stalin gave to Azerbaijan in 1923,[2] with as many as a million people filling the streets of Yerevan. And during our visit to Armenia, we continued to see strong expressions of nationalism: for example, we saw the red, blue, and orange flag of the Republic of Armenia displayed in public buildings; we witnessed the singing of the national anthem of the republic at a concert in the Opera House in Yerevan; and we heard children performing nationalistic songs in private homes.

In the course of our brief visit, we sensed that the issue of the Armenian people's survival was being redefined: the memory of the genocide was still strong, but there were more pressing problems, such as the massive trauma of the deaths of at least twenty-five thousand people in the earthquake that struck Armenia on December 7, 1988. They were struggling with the task of feeding orphans and rebuilding homes and lives that had been destroyed. But they were also feeling politically threatened: Armenians had been brutally massacred by Azerbaijanis in Sumgait and Baku, and shipments of fuel and earthquake relief supplies were being blockaded by Azerbaijan, seemingly with the approval of President Mikhail Gorbachev.

Our visit to Armenia included several formative experiences that directed our attention to the future of the Armenians rather than their past and, in some ways, placed the sufferings of 1915 in a new perspective. Simply stated, with the survivor generation having nearly all passed away, we have become convinced that the best monument to their memory is the resurrection of the Republic of Armenia as a politically free and economically viable nation. In these concluding pages, therefore, we want to share several images from our experience in Armenia that broaden the theme of survival to include the future of the Republic of Armenia.

FINAL REFLECTIONS

Near the end of our visit, an Armenian couple offered to take us to Spitak, Leninakan, and Kirovakan, three of the cities hit hardest by the earthquake. Because of the blockade, our first task was to find enough fuel for an all-day trip. Failing to buy petrol on the black market, we eventually switched cars and headed out through a countryside filled with rolling hills that are covered with snow in winter and dusty and hot in summer. The highlands on which we traveled were surrounded by beautiful mountains, including the majestic Mount Ararat, or Masis, as the local population calls it.

As we neared Spitak, we began to see the results of the 1988 earthquake. The stone houses in the outlying villages had collapsed, and the rubble had not yet been cleared. Makeshift structures and tents had been erected as survivors continued to carry on their lives. As we reached the city center of Spitak, we saw many barren areas, and our hosts told us that high-rise apartments and office buildings had previously occupied these vacant lots. Standing in their place were scattered temporary dwellings made of tin. We were struck by the somber mood of people on the streets, even though this was a year and a half after the earthquake.

Having brought candy and other small items to give to children, we went in search of a school in Spitak. The school we found, located in temporary quarters that appeared to be former military barracks, was meeting in double session. The principal told us that he had been buried under his desk for more than a day after the earthquake. In this school, which presently had 450 students, 13 teachers and 140 students had been killed. It was difficult to check our emotions as we visited with these bright-eyed Armenian children and imagined that the survivors we had interviewed must have resembled these youngsters as they attended their orphanage schools.

From Spitak we journeyed to Kirovakan. It is a large industrial city, and although the factories were not yet operating, there did not appear to be nearly as much structural damage to buildings as we had observed in Spitak. As we left Kirovakan and reached the outskirts of Leninakan, however, we were sobered by the sight of a newly constructed cemetery that extended for many acres. Marking thousands of graves were up-right stones with the etched photographic likeness of the deceased. In one plot, we saw the image of two children and a father; a neighboring gravestone depicted a teenage boy. We saw families visiting their loved ones' resting places, with fresh flowers decorating the ground. Viewing this scene, we were once again transported in our imagination to the genocide, although as we stared at these neatly arranged rows of grave markers, we realized that those who had died three-quarters of a century earlier had seldom enjoyed the dignity of a family burial; rather, they were left to rot on the deportation routes, were burned alive in their churches, or were forced to dig their own graves before being shot or bayoneted.

Once inside the city limits of Leninakan, we were greeted by more vacant lots and temporary houses, but we also saw the skeletons of many buildings; their walls were gone, leaving only the frames. In one of the central squares, we ventured into an ancient church that had received only superficial damage, like many of the older structures built before Soviet control. There, a gray-haired priest sat in a back pew, comforting a middle-aged man. We could overhear enough of the conversation to realize that this priest was struggling to find vocabulary from the Christian tradition to deal with the ancient problem of theodicy, a seemingly perennial issue in Armenian history, as we knew from our interviews.

Yet even within this landscape of despair, we also encountered images of hope. On the eve of our first night in Yerevan, the man who had driven us to the earthquake region offered to show us one of his favorite places on the outskirts of Yerevan. We drove for perhaps an hour and finally wound our way up the side of a rather deserted hill that over-looked the city, arriving at a thirteenth-century Armenian church. It was almost dark, but we parked the car and slogged down a muddy road to this stone structure. Our friend found a box of candles on the altar, and we lit several of them, illuminating a rather primitive altar that, surprisingly, contained a handful of freshly picked flowers.

As we were leaving the church, an Armenian peasant appeared and introduced himself as Megerdich, the caretaker of the church. We asked if we could take his picture; he graciously agreed and then asked us to his home to eat *madzoon* (yogurt). Somewhat hesitantly, we accepted his invitation and followed him to his house, a single room measuring about fourteen by sixteen feet. In the middle of the room was a wood-fueled stove, and in one corner was a bed that served as his seating area. One of us sat on the bed, while the others joined him in sitting on several stools in front of a small table at the foot of the bed. As soon as we were seated, his wife served us the promised *madzoon,* which was followed with a stack of thinly rolled *lavash* bread that she had baked. Soon the table was also filled with cheese and herbs to roll inside the bread. And, at last, Megerdich brought out a bottle of very inexpensive vodka.

As Megerdich raised his glass in toasts to us, and we to him, he told the story of how he had become caretaker of the church. As a young man, he had been a musician, but he also loved to visit old churches. In one of these churches he dozed off to sleep and had a vision in which two angels came to him and said, "Megerdich, you must take care of this church." And since that dream thirty-three years ago, he has been daily lighting candles and bringing fresh flowers to the altar of the church we had just visited, even though for many of these years there was scarcely a worshipper.

In reflecting on our meal with Megerdich, and especially the vodka and *lavash* bread, we could not help but see this earthy celebration of the Christian eucharist as a powerful reminder of the role the Armenian church has played in maintaining the heritage of an ancient people. Indeed, Megerdich's stewardship of this thirteenth-century church was a symbol of hope for the continuing role of the church in the preservation of Armenian culture.

On April 24, a few days before leaving Yerevan, we joined approximately one million people who had made their way to the Martyrs' Monument to commemorate the seventy-fifth anniversary of the genocide. In silent procession, we inched our way toward the eternal flame, which is surrounded by imposing granite pillars rising solemnly to the heavens. Each person carried a single carnation in his or her hand, and as we walked around the perimeter of the flame, we each gently laid our flower on a pile that grew to more than five meters high by the end of the day. As we stared into the flame over this wall of carnations, the image of Vahram's family and a million other victims of the genocide bade us farewell. Descending the hill from the monument, we could not have imagined that in just seventeen months the Republic of Armenia would declare its independence, fulfilling the dream of so many of the survivors we interviewed.

Methodology

In the initial stage of the research for this book, we interviewed survivors with whom we were personally acquainted. Some of these were family friends and others were neighbors and individuals who were introduced to us once it became known that we were interested in interviewing survivors. The older generation of Armenians is very communal, and survivors regularly told us that we should interview "so and so," that he or she has an interesting story. Hence, the first thirty interviews were with people we knew or who were referred to us by friends within the Pasadena area. The remaining seventy interviews took us beyond the boundaries of Pasadena. Fifteen of these interviews were conducted with elderly Armenians who lived in a retirement/nursing home for Armenians in a neighboring city. Six interviews were carried out on a visit to the San Francisco Bay Area. Also, occasionally we interviewed survivors from Lebanon or South America who were traveling through California. In addition, we interviewed two distant relatives in Evanston, Illinois. The rest of the interviews were all done in the greater Los Angeles area.

The criteria for selecting individuals to interview were (1) that they had gone through the genocide, (2) they remembered significant details about what they had experienced, and (3) they were willing to be interviewed. The median age of survivors at the time of the genocide was between eleven and twelve years old (two survivors were four years old in 1915, and at the other extreme, one respondent was twenty-seven and another was above thirty in 1915). Sixty-two of the survivors were women and forty-one were men. (Although we have consistently referred to "one hundred" interviews throughout the text, in fact we did 103 interviews.) They were born in a wide range of areas throughout Turkey, and we believe the sample is relatively representative of Armenians who survived the genocide.

Most survivors were first contacted by telephone to see if they were interested in being interviewed. In the initial conversation, we determined if they were suitable candidates according to the above criteria and, at the same time, explained to them that the interview would be tape-recorded. Individuals declined to be interviewed for a variety of reasons; for example, some felt that the interview would evoke painful memories that might be emotionally disturbing. In addition, we were sometimes told by sons or daughters that their father or mother used to talk continually about their past, but in recent years their memory of events had declined substantially because of old age.

Interviews typically lasted at least two hours. In sixteen cases we returned for a second, or even a third, interview. In almost all instances, interviews took place in the survivor's residence (those living in the retirement home were interviewed in their rooms). Frequently, other family members were present, observing the interview and sometimes adding their own comments or interpretations. In four cases, survivors asked that their names not be used; otherwise, survivors did not desire anonymity. In fact, we have one serious regret: that we could not include in this book the full story of each survivor we interviewed.

Many emotions were expressed during the interviews. It was not unusual for survivors—both men and women—to cry at some point, typically, when talking about the death of a parent or sibling. We made a point of not rushing away from interviews. Survivors often served coffee after the interview (always "Armenian," not "Turkish," coffee), and we often lingered and talked informally for a while. On a few occasions, survivors called several days after the interview to recount additional things that they had remembered. We believe that survivors enjoyed the interviews, even though emotionally painful issues were discussed.

In addition to answering our questions, survivors would sometimes read poetry they had written, or sing songs from their childhood. A few showed us land deeds from Turkey. Occasionally, interviewees brought out family albums and told us about their children and grandchildren. In several instances, it was only after the tape recorder had been turned off that survivors revealed highly personal memories. We valued these moments following the formal interview, because family members would often enter into the discussion of the genocide and the interviewee's experiences.

Very frequently, survivors or family members asked for a copy of the interview cassette tapes. We were always happy to oblige, and as survivors began to pass away, we discovered that our interview was frequently the only record of their life story. After each interview, we made a copy of the cassette tapes and stored them in a separate location from the originals. In a few instances, we noticed serious deterioration in the tape quality after the interview, but generally the tapes are in good condition. Each cassette is labeled with the survivor's name, the interviewer's name, the date and place of the interview, the language spoken during the interview, the length of the interview, and the hometown in Turkey of the interviewee.

We went through several stages in analyzing the interviews. At first, we did not realize the importance of transcribing the interviews and, instead, filled out a detailed form summarizing the interview. As the project developed, however, we recognized that it was imperative to have a full transcript of each interview. Hence, we went back and laboriously transcribed the first thirty interviews on a portable typewriter. This primitive technology was replaced thanks to the Faculty Research and Innovation Fund at USC, which provided us with a computer. Currently, each interview exists as a file in WordPerfect 5.1 format, and it is from these text files that the interviews were coded.

In terms of actual analysis, we went through thousands of pages of transcripts and copied appropriate portions of the text from each interview into 142 different topical files on the hard disk of our computer. These files were arranged into directories that corresponded roughly to what eventually emerged as chapter headings for this book—although at the time, we were simply attempting to identify specific themes and issues from the data. Thus, we had directories dealing with "predeportation" memories, "deportation" experiences, "orphanage" recollections, "emigration" experiences, and so on. In addition, we had two rather diffuse categories, one of which dealt with "psychological" reflections of survivors, while the other was simply called "interpretations," for lack of better nomenclature. The "psychological" directory included files on anger, forgiveness, guilt, revenge, and so on. The "interpretation" directory was a hodgepodge of files as diverse as "theodicy," "altruism," and "good Turks."

Every quotation that was copied into one of these files was first flagged with a reference, so that it was possible to find the context in which a particular statement was made. Page breaks were made after each entry, and eventually every quote was printed on a separate sheet of paper and placed in file folders, in much the same way that one might arrange file cards. The computer simplified the process of copying quotes and also eliminated the possibility of errors in copying.

Given the number of interviews and the very limited budget, we eliminated one step in the translation process used by some oral history projects. Rather than typing out a verbatim transcript of the interview in Armenian, we listened to each tape and translated the interview directly into English, simultaneously typing the translation. In this process, not every cough, pause, and "uh, huh" are included, although we tried to be faithful to the content, intent, and tone of the interviewees' responses to our questions. The transcription and translation process was extraordinarily laborious, taking at least three to four times longer than the actual interview. Eight of the interviews were conducted in English, two in Turkish (with a relative of the survivor translating during the interview), and all of the rest in Armenian (even though many of the survivors spoke at least limited English).

We used the questions and topics listed in Appendix B to guide our interviews with survivors. In constructing this interview guide, we drew on schedules of questions that had been designed as part of oral history projects at UCLA, the Armenian Assembly, and the Zoryan Institute. The principal difference between our interview guide and those of other oral history projects is that we included a number of questions related to survivors' personal attitudes, as well as their interpretation of the meaning of the genocide. Whenever possible, questions were asked in the order listed below. However, survivors were frequently anxious to begin by telling their story of the deportations, and in those instances we altered the order of the questions. There were no interviews in which we had time to ask every question in the interview guide. Nevertheless, answers to many of these questions emerged informally during the course of the interview.

Interview Guide

Section I: City/Village Life

1. City/Town/Village

   - Population: size, ethnic groups, ratio of Armenians to Turks/Kurds?
   - Occupational structure: What occupations were specific to Armenians/Turks/Kurds?
   - Physical layout: types of buildings, location of marketplace? (What was available? Who did the shopping? Who sold what?)

2. Neighborhood

   - Specific name? Boundaries? Who lived where (ethnic, religious, class groups)?
   - Physical layout: types of buildings, transportation, vendors?

3. Home

   - Physical description: floor plan, number of rooms, function of each room, furnishings, yard, heating, lighting, water supply, animals, pets?
   - What furnishings do you remember in each room?

4. Family

   - For each family member (e.g., great-grandparents, grandparents, parents, uncles, aunts, siblings), what was his or her name, age, sex, relationship to you, occupation, educational level?
   - Who lived in your house? Did non-family members live with you?
   - Who made family decisions? What was the division of responsibilities in your family?

- Where did your relatives live, and how often—and in what contexts—did you see them?
- What was the relationship between your family and other relatives?

5. Childhood

- Describe some of the happiest moments during your childhood.
- Do you remember specific songs, rhymes, or stories from your childhood?
- With whom did you play and where?
- What games did you play? What toys did you have?
- What responsibilities and expectations did your parents have for you, and at what ages?
- Do you remember being punished? If so, for what offenses? And by whom?

6. School

- Who attended school?
- Who ran the school?
- Do you remember names of teachers?
- What subjects did you study?
- How many years did you attend school?
- Do any incidents stand out in your mind?
- Were there other schools in your town/village/city?

7. Occupational Preparation

- Were there apprenticeships for specific jobs?
- What job or vocation did your parents want you to pursue?

8. Household Management

- How did you obtain, store, and prepare food?
- How were children bathed? Clothes washed?
- Describe a typical day in the life of an Armenian housewife.
- How was money used within the household? What were typical expenses?
- Who made decisions on household matters?

9. Health Care

- Was there a hospital in your town? Were there doctors? Midwives? Nurses?
- What happened when someone became sick in your house?
- Were there home remedies? Medicines?
- How did mothers give birth? What customs surrounded the birth of a child?
- How were the elderly cared for? The mentally retarded? The physically handicapped?

10. Leisure Pastimes

- What did you do during the summer? After school?
- What books and newspapers were read in your home? By whom?
- Did you have a summer house? Describe it.
- Did your family go on vacations? Trips?
- Describe patterns of visitation with others in your household.
- How was leisure time spent by men? Women? Boys? Girls?

11. Church

- What churches were in your city? Names? Who went?
- To what church did you belong? What activities do you remember?
- Was there an Evangelical church in your city? What was the relationship between its members and those who belonged to the Apostolic Church?
- Were there missionaries from abroad? Names? Denomination?
- Did religious leaders play an active role in your community? Politics?

12. Religious Observances

- How did you celebrate Christmas, Lent, Easter, various saints' days?
- How religious were people in your household? How often did you attend services? How often did most people in your community attend church? For what specific occasions?
- Was religious commitment higher among Apostolics? Catholics? Protestants?

13. Folk Heritage

- Do you remember any proverbs? Songs? Legends? Tales? Turkish sayings?
- Do you remember any superstitions?

14. Manners and Customs

- What customs existed relating to birth? Death? Health? Illness? Engagement? Marriage?
- Rituals associated with entry into manhood/womanhood?
- At what age did marriage occur? Who could marry whom? How was marriage permission secured? Could the girl refuse?
- Was there divorce? Remarriage?
- How were girls treated? How were wives treated?

15. Armenians and Turks/Kurds

- Were there Turks in your city? Kurds?
- How did Armenians and Turks/Kurds get along with each other?
- Did you or your family have Turkish/Kurdish friends?
- Did Armenians have any different rights from Turks?

- Did you know any Armenians who became Muslims at the time of the deportations? Why did they convert? How were they treated by other Armenians?

16. Clubs, Organizations, Political Groups

   - Were there revolutionary parties in your area? How many members did they have? How active were they?
   - Outside of church, what clubs and organizations were there? To which did you or your family belong? Who belonged to these groups?
   - Were there charitable organizations in your community? What did they do?

17. Community Organization

   - Who were the Armenian leaders in your area? What were their responsibilities? How did they relate to the Turks in your area?
   - Were Armenians free to govern their community?
   - Were Armenians in complete control of their churches? Schools?

18. Social Control by Turks

   - In your community, what do you remember about courts? Prisons? Taxes? Drafting of Armenian men/boys?
   - Did Armenians ever try to defend themselves against attacks by Turks/ Kurds? How?
   - How did Armenian leaders maintain control in your community?

19. Military Service

   - Did you or anyone else in your family serve in the military?
   - Who was drafted? Were men able to avoid the draft? How?

Section II: Massacre and Deportation

1. Before 1915

   - Did anyone in your extended family die in the 1894–96 massacres? The 1909 massacres? Who? How?
   - What were relationships like between Turks and Armenians immediately before the deportations of 1915? Were there any indications of growing political tensions?

2. Imprisonment and Torture

   - Were Armenians arrested or tortured in your area before the deportations?
   - Were guns or other weapons gathered from Armenians by Turkish officials in your area?

- Did you observe any brutalities toward Armenians before the deportations?

3. Resistance

   - Was there any resistance by Armenians against Turkish orders or brutalities?
   - Did any Turks/Kurds come to the rescue of Armenians? Did any Turks/Kurds shelter families? Children?

4. Deportation

   - Were Armenians deported from your area?
   - How were deportation orders given?
   - How many days did Armenians have to prepare for deportation?
   - How did Armenians prepare for deportation? What did you take with you?
   - Did you have transportation during the deportation?
   - Who was deported from your extended family?
   - Describe the first day or two of your deportation journey.

5. Deportation Marches

   - Where were you deported? Specific towns/villages?
   - Describe specific events that occurred during the deportation marches.
   - What role did gendarmes or soldiers play during the deportations?
   - Were you attacked at any point during the deportations?
   - Did you observe any incidents of rape? Abduction of children? Women?
   - Where did you sleep?
   - How did you secure food? Water?
   - How long were you deported? Days? Weeks? Months?
   - Did you observe people who died from attack? Dehydration? Starvation? Disease? Describe specific instances.
   - Did any of your family members die during the deportation marches? Were any abducted? Did any family members become separated?

6. Deportation Caravan

   - How many were deported from your area?
   - How many arrived at the destination point of your caravan?
   - Was there any resistance to being deported? Why or why not?
   - Did you observe other deportation caravans? What was their condition?

III. *Orphanage Life* (if survivor lived in an orphanage)

1. Admission

   - When did you first become aware that there were orphanages for survivors?

- In what orphanage(s) did you live? Name? Place? How long did you live there? Who was in charge? Names of people?
- How did you enter the orphanage? What procedures were followed in admitting you?

2. Orphanage Life

- Describe a typical day in the orphanage.
- Describe the facilities. How was the orphanage organized?
- How was the food? Clothing?
- Did you go to school? Or receive vocational training?
- What did you do for recreation?
- What are your favorite memories and worst memories of orphanage life?

3. Armenian Identity

- Did you have to relearn the Armenian language?
- Were there efforts to instill a nationalistic spirit in the orphans?
- What was the role of religious education within your orphanage?
- Do you remember specific songs or other things that you learned in the orphanage?

4. Leaving the Orphanage

- When did your orphanage leave Turkey? Describe the process.
- Where were you resettled after leaving Turkey? Describe the new setting.
- At what age did children finally leave the orphanages? Were there engagements and marriages in the orphanages?

5. Reunions

- How did you become reunited with family? Relatives? Friends?
- After leaving the orphanage, did you return to Turkey? If so, describe the process of going home and what you found in your hometown.

IV. Emigration and Marriage

1. Marriage

- Where did you meet your spouse? Describe courtship/marriage.
- Where did you live? In how many different places/countries did you live? What years? Why did you move?
- What job(s) did you and your spouse have? Describe your economic circumstances.
- How many children do you have? Where were they born? When?

2. United States

- When did you immigrate to the United States? Why?

- Did children, relatives, or friends immigrate before you?
- Did you encounter any problems in entering the United States?
- What were your first impressions of the United States?
- How did you make a living after coming to the United States? Describe your job history.
- Where in the United States have you lived?

3. Adjustment

- Were there any Armenian organizations, churches, or other groups that were particularly helpful to you?
- How did your children adjust to the United States? Your spouse?
- Have you experienced any discrimination in the United States?
- What have been your hardest times since coming to the United States?
- Did you ever regret moving to the United States?

4. Children/Grandchildren

- Describe your children. Did they marry Armenians? How many grandchildren do you have? Where are your grandchildren going to school? What type of work do your children do? Where do they live?
- Did you name any of your children after siblings or relatives who died in the genocide?
- Do your grandchildren speak Armenian? Can they write Armenian? Do they know your story? Are they proud to be Armenian?
- What churches do your children/grandchildren attend?
- Do your children/grandchildren belong to any Armenian organizations?
- Do they subscribe to any Armenian newspapers?

5. Armenian Identity

- Do you have many non-Armenian friends? What percentage of your closest friends are Armenian?
- To what Armenian organizations do you currently belong? How active are you?
- Do you speak Armenian in your home? With your spouse? Children? Grandchildren?
- Do you attend an Armenian church? Name? How regularly?
- Are you worried about the future of Armenians in the United States? Why? In what ways?
- What advice do you have for Armenian young people?
- What does it mean to be a good Armenian?

V. Attitudes and Interpretations

1. Causes of the Genocide

- In your view, why did the genocide occur?

- Were the Armenians in any way to blame for the genocide?
- What role did the revolutionary groups play?

2. Attitude Toward Turks

- What was your attitude toward Turks before the genocide?
- Did you observe Turks who were helpful to Armenians—both during the deportations and afterward?
- Do you think the average Turk approved of the actions of the government against the Armenians?
- After you left Turkey, did you have any contact with Turks? What was your experience with these individuals?
- How would you describe Turkish character?

3. Childhood Feelings

- What specific events from your childhood stand out most clearly in your mind? What were your most painful experiences? Joyful moments? Do you think most often of the good or bad times from your childhood?
- As a child, were you able to understand why the deportations were occurring? Or why there was hostility toward the Armenians?
- As a child, particularly in the orphanage, did you talk with others about the genocide (i.e., sharing stories of what you had experienced and witnessed)?
- If orphaned during the genocide, how sad, depressed, or lonely do you remember being? How did you cope with these feelings as a child? What sources of comfort did you have?

4. Adult Feelings

- How much did you think about the genocide as an adult, and how did your feelings change over time?
- In the last few years, how preoccupied have you been with the genocide? Is it something that you think about every day?
- Have you ever had, or do you currently have, dreams about events you experienced during the genocide?
- Do you attend special events on April 24 to commemorate the Armenians who died in 1915? How do you feel on that day?
- Do you feel that your "wound" from the genocide has healed, or does it still occupy a lot of your thinking?

5. Guilt

- Have you ever felt guilty that you survived when so many Armenians perished?
- Are there any specific events from the deportations about which you feel bad—where you failed, or perhaps your mother or father failed or compromised?

- Did you observe Armenian women abandoning children or infants? How do you feel about such decisions?

6. Shame and Humiliation

   - In what ways were Armenians shamed and humiliated during the deportations?
   - Did you ever feel that you had become less than human during the deportations?

7. Talking About the Genocide

   - Do you talk with fellow survivors about the genocide? Is this a regular or infrequent topic of conversation?
   - Do you frequently talk with non-Armenians about the genocide?
   - Have you told your story to your children? To your grandchildren? In how much detail? What have been their reactions? How interested have they been in your story?
   - What attitudes about the genocide do you think you have communicated to your children and grandchildren?

8. Effects of the Genocide

   - How do you think the genocide has affected you? Physically? Emotionally? Educationally and vocationally?
   - Has anything positive resulted from the genocide for Armenians? For you personally?

9. Religious Practice and Attitudes

   - What was your religious background as a child?
   - How would you describe your religious commitment and beliefs as an adult?
   - As a child, did you wonder why God was allowing the Armenians to be deported?
   - As an adult, have you wondered about God's "silence" during the genocide?
   - Has it troubled you how a God who is good and all-powerful could have allowed the destruction of the Armenians?
   - Do you think God had anything to do with your own survival?
   - Do you think God will punish the Turks for what they did to the Armenians?

10. Responses to the Genocide

   - To what extent do you try *not* to think about the genocide?
   - Do you feel that you have a satisfactory explanation for why the genocide occurred?
   - Do you think any good resulted from the genocide?
   - Should the Armenians seek reparations or return of their lands from the Turks?

- Do you think Armenians would be better off if they abandoned any hope of regaining their homeland?
- What do you think about the assassination of Turkish officials as a way of pursuing recognition of Armenian claims?
- How reconciled are you toward the genocide?
- How angry are you toward the Turks? What would have to happen in order to reduce your anger? Would acknowledgement of the genocide by Turkey be sufficient?
- When someone asks you why Armenians continue to talk about an event that happened so many years ago, what is your answer?

Survivors Interviewed

Following is an alphabetical listing of the survivors we interviewed, including their year and place of birth. In some instances, the year of birth is an estimate; many survivors who were orphaned assumed a birthdate based on estimates made by relatives or orphanage personnel.

Sione Abajian (1909, Marash)

Geulania Afsharian (1900, Hadjin)

Mardiros Afsharian (1895, Hadjin)

Sarkis Agojian (1906, Chemeshgezak)

Elizabeth Agopian (1901, Konia)

Albert Ailanjian (1906, Yozgat)

Martha Ailanjian (1911, Kharpert)

Mary Apkarian Almoyan (1903, Aintab)

Anonymous (1900, Kaiseri)

Anonymous (1901, Kaiseri)

Anonymous (1904, Palu)

Anonymous (1907, Kessab)

Anaguel Ajemian (1909, Mezre)

Garabed Amiralian (1901, Marash)

Esther Apelian (1900, Kessab)

Astor Arakelian (1880, Hoghe)

Araxie Arslanian (1903, Konia)

Mariam Babagochian (1893, Aintab)

Bedros Bahadourian (1903, Gurin)

Annalin Basmajian (1898, Aintab)

Levon Beshgaturian (unknown, Gurin)

Hagop Boyajian (1910, Aintab)

Ghevont Chorbajian (1896, Marash)

Mary Coumarian (1897, Constantinople)

Arousiag Dakessian (1906, Mitaserif)

Krikor Derderian (1896, Hadjin)

Zarouhi Derderian (1905, Osmanie; moved to Hadjin ca. 1908)

Manoug Dergazarian (1908, Adana)

Lousaper Der Ghevondian (1902, Marash)

Mary Dulgerian (1893, Amasia)

Eflaton Elmajian (1889, Marash)

Hagop Elmassian (1896, Sivas)

Dzaghig Yessaian Etoian (1904, Mezre)

Sharon Eurejian (1909, Hadjin)

Repega Tashjian Garabedian (1908, Severeg)

Rebecca Gedikian (1892, Hadjin)

Yacoub Giroyan (1910, Aintab)

Helen Koundakjian Hadidian (1891, Hassanbeyli)

Mariam Halajian (1901, Silifkee)

Araxie Haleblian (1907, Marash)

Megerdich Haroutunian (1908, Garmouch)

Parantzem Haroutunian (1902, Adana)

Souren Haroutunian (1911, Kharpert)

Mary Haytaian (1902, Dort Yol)

Baydzar Kerebian Idris (1894, Keghi)

Verzhine Toulahian Iskenderian (1908, Eskishehir)

Hovsep Janjikian (1905, Arabkir)

Mary Janjikian (1911, Aintab; was living in Aleppo in 1915)

Setrag Keshishian (1898, Hadjin)

Selver Ketchedjian (1907, Behesni)

Yulia Ketenjian (1911, Adana)

Sarkis Konsulian (1900, Kharpert)

Takouhi Levonian (1900, Keghi)

Yeghisapet Manjikian (1912, Afion Karahissar)

Khatoun Marashlian (1908, Tarsus)

Satenig Marashlian (1902, Belikesir)

Araxie Sangigian Marganian (1907, Zeitun)

Dikran Matossian (1900, Marash)

Aghavni Mazmanian (1895, Sivas)

Khoren Megerdichan (1909, Jibin)

Dikranouhi Parseghian Mereshian (1906, Misis)

Iskender Mereshian (1892, Misis)

Ephtim Topalian Merjanian (1906, Dikranagerd)

Garabed Merjanian (1904, Marash)

Hanna Mesrlian (1903, Kessab)

Ohannes Mesrlian (1897, Kessab)

Minas Minasian (1907, Baghche)

Mariam Moursalian (1907, Shivilgi)

Sarkis Manoug Moursalian (1899, Shibidia)

Marie Movsesian (1900, Sivrihissar)

Michael Narinian (1898, Hadjin)

Ashkhen Ohannesian (1899, Van)

Mariam Paloian (1889, Sivas)

Dikran Paloulian (1910, Bor)

Mary Panosian (1905, Marash)

Catherine Petrosian (1910, Trebizond)

Simon Piranian (1903, Aksaray)

Edward Racoubian (1906, Sivas)

Mardiros Ruzgerian (1907, Erzinjan)

Hagop Sanjian (1912, Marash)

Missak Sarian (1906, Hromkla)

Nazeli Sarkissian (1907, Darman)

Souren Sarkissian (1900, Darman)

Azniv Shahbaghlian (1904, Kharpert)

Levon Shahbaghlian (1888, Van)

Mayreni Shahinian (1910, Yozgat)

Perus Shahoian (1910, Chanakkale)

Isabel Sulahian (1905, Aleppo)

Ardem Svadjian (1909, Biledjik)

Haig Tashjian (1908; born in U.S. but lived in Sivas)

Lousaper Tashjian (1907, Aintab)

Hovagim Tatoulian (1893, Adana)

Sara Taylor (1896, Kharpert)

Hayastan Maghakian Terzian
(1905, Kharpert)

Shavarsh Topazian (1904, Van)

Adelina Touryan (1907,
Marash)

Vahram Sarkis Touryan (1907,
Darman)

Henry Vartanian (1906, Sivas)

Kevork Voskeritchian (1904, Urfa)

Sara Voskeritchian (1910, Sivas)

Yeghisapet Voskeritchian (1910,
Urfa)

Elmast Yeghoian (1892, Marash)

Azniv Yousoufian (1910, Urfa)

Notes

INTRODUCTION

1. Donald E. Miller and Lorna Touryan Miller, "Armenian Survivors: A Typological Analysis of Victim Responses," *Oral History Review* 10 (1982): 47–72.

2. See Kevork B. Bardakjian, *Hitler and the Armenian Genocide* (Cambridge, Mass.: Zoryan Institute, 1985).

3. Roger W. Smith, "Human Destructiveness and Politics: The Twentieth Century as an Age of Genocide," in *Genocide and the Modern Age: Etiology and Case Studies of Mass Death,* ed. Isidor Walliman and Michael N. Doblowski (New York: Greenwood Press, 1987), 21.

4. Lawrence J. LeBlanc gives the following litany of genocides: "Since World War II, genocide is alleged to have occurred in various regions of the world: in Africa, against tribal groups in various countries, including Burundi, Rwanda, and Uganda; in Latin America, against primitive Indian tribes in Paraguay and Brazil; in Asia, during the breakup of India in the late 1940s, the creation of Bangladesh in the early 1970s, the struggle for control of Cambodia (formerly Democratic Kampuchea) by the Khmer Rouge in the 1970s, and the suppression of Tamil separatists in Sri Lanka during the 1980s" (*The United States and the Genocide Convention* [Durham, N.C.: Duke University Press, 1991], 2–3).

5. See Richard G. Hovannisian, "Genocide and Denial: The Armenian Case," in *Toward the Understanding and Prevention of Genocide: Proceedings of the International Conference on the Holocaust and Genocide,* ed. Israel W. Charny (Boulder: Westview Press, 1984), 84–99; see also Marjorie Housepian-Dobkin, "What Genocide? What Holocaust? News from Turkey, 1915–23: A Case Study," in Charny, 100–12.

6. See Roger W. Smith, "Genocide and Denial: The Armenian Case and Its Implications," *Armenian Review* 42, no. 1 (Spring 1989): 1–38.

CHAPTER 1

1. Richard G. Hovannisian, *The Armenian Holocaust: A Bibliography Relating to the Deportations, Massacres, and Dispersion of the Armenian People, 1915–1923* (Cambridge, Mass.: Armenian Heritage Press, 1980).

2. U. S. National Archives, Record Group 59, 867.4016/373; a selection of these documents was reprinted in the *Armenian Review* 37, no. 1 (Spring 1984): 60–145, and it is from this publication that the following citations are drawn.

3. Ibid., 131–32.

4. Ibid., 132–33.

5. Ibid., 133.

6. Ibid., 133.

7. Ibid., 135–36.

8. Ibid., 136.

9. Ibid., 118.

10. Ibid., 111–12.

11. Ibid., 95–97.

12. Ibid., 97.

13. Great Britain, Parliament, *Treatment of Armenians in the Ottoman Empire: Documents Presented to Viscount Grey of Fallodon, Secretary of State for Foreign Affairs,* preface by Viscount Bryce (London: Sir Joseph Causton & Sons, 1916); hereafter referred to as Bryce/Toynbee. In the preface to this volume, Viscount Bryce states: "These accounts [referring to the testimony that had been collected from survivors and observers of the deportations] described what seemed to be an effort to exterminate a whole nation, without distinction of age or sex, whose misfortune it was to be the subjects of a Government devoid of scruples and of pity, and the policy they disclosed was one without precedent even in the blood-stained annals of the East" (Bryce/Toynbee, xxi).

14. The charge has been made that the blue book compiled by Toynbee was intended as a propagandistic tool. However, in several autobiographical reflections, Toynbee reasserted the integrity of his research on the genocide. For example, in *Acquaintances* (London: Oxford University Press, 1967), he states on p. 149: "At the time, I was unaware of the politics that lay behind this move of H.M.G.'s, and I believe Lord Bryce was as innocent as I was. Perhaps this was fortunate. For, if our eyes had been opened, I hardly think that either Lord Bryce or I would have been able to do the job that H.M.G. had assigned to us in the complete good faith in which we did, in fact, carry it out. Lord Bryce's concern, and mine, was to establish the facts and to make them public, in the hope that eventually some action might be taken in the light of them. The dead—and the deportees had been dying in their thousands—could not be brought back to life, but we hoped (vain hope) that at least something might be done to ensure, for the survivors, that there should never be a repetition of the barbarities that had been the death of so many of their kinsmen."

15. Bryce/Toynbee, Account 9, p. 20.

16. Ibid., Account 12, p. 25.

17. Ibid., Account 12, p. 26.

18. Ibid., Account 12, p. 27.

19. Ibid., Account 22, p. 85.

20. Ibid., Account 22, p. 86.

21. Ibid., Account 23, p. 89.

22. Ibid., Account 23, p. 90.

23. Ibid., Account 23, p. 90.

24. Henry Morgenthau, *Ambassador Morgenthau's Story* (Garden City, N. Y.: Doubleday, Page, 1918).

25. Johannes Lepsius, *Bericht über die Lage des armenischen Volkes in der Türkei* (Potsdam: Tempelverlag, 1916).

26. Johannes Lepsius, *Der Todesgang des armenischen Volkes: Bericht über das Schicksal des Armenischen Volkes in der Türkei während des Weltkrieges* (Potsdam: Tempelverlag, 1919).

27. See the commentary on German sources, including the Lepsius reports, by Tessa Hofmann, "German Eyewitness Reports of the Genocide of the Armenians, 1915–16," in *A Crime of Silence: The Armenian Genocide* (London: Zed Books, 1985).

28. Johannes Lepsius, *Deutschland und Armenien, 1914–1918: Sammlung diplomatischer Aktenstücke* (Potsdam: Tempelverlag, 1919).

29. Martin Niepage, *The Horrors of Aleppo, Seen by a German Eye-Witness* (London: T. Fisher Unwin, 1917), 6.

30. Ibid., 12.

31. Armin T. Wegner, *Offener Brief an den Präsidenten der Vereinigten Staaten von Nord-Amerika, Herrn Woodrow Wilson, über die Austreibung des armenischen Volkes in die Wüste* (Berlin: O. Fleck, 1919).

32. Marjorie Housepian-Dobkin, "What Genocide? What Holocaust? News From Turkey, 1915–23: A Case Study," in *Toward the Understanding and Prevention of Genocide: Proceedings of the International Conference on the Holocaust and Genocide*, ed. Israel W. Charney (Boulder: Westview Press, 1984), 101.

33. Articles from the *New York Times, New Republic, Current History,* and other publications from the period have been reprinted by Richard D. Kloian, ed., *The Armenian Genocide: News Accounts from the American Press, 1915–1922,* 3d ed. (Berkeley, Calif.: AAC Books, 1985).

34. See *The Armenian Genocide as Reported in the Australian Press* (Sydney: Armenian National Committee, 1983).

35. Clarence D. Ussher and Grace H. Knapp, *An American Physician in Turkey: A Narrative of Adventures in Peace and in War* (Boston: Houghton Mifflin, 1917).

36. Jacob Künzler, *Im Lande des Blutes und der Tränen: Erlebnisse in Mesopotamien während des Weltkrieges* (Potsdam, 1921) and Ida Alamuddin, *Papa Kuenzler and the Armenians* (London: Heinemann, 1970).

37. Stanley E. Kerr, *The Lions of Marash: Personal Experiences with American Near East Relief, 1919–1922* (Albany: State University of New York Press, 1973).

38. See, for example, Joseph L. Grabill, *Protestant Diplomacy and the Near East: Missionary Influence on American Policy, 1810–1927* (Minneapolis: University of Minnesota Press, 1971).

39. Abraham H. Hartunian, *Neither to Laugh nor to Weep: A Memoir of the Armenian Genocide* (Boston: Beacon Press, 1968).

40. Representative examples of survivor autobiographies include: Ephraim K. Jernazian, *Judgement unto Truth: Witnessing the Armenian Genocide,* trans. Alice Haig (New Brunswick, N. J.: Transaction Publishers, 1990); Haig Baronian, *Barefoot Boy from Anatolia* (Los Angeles: Abril Printing Company, 1983); Dirouhi Kouymjian Highgas, *Refugee Girl* (Watertown, Mass.: Baikar Publications, 1985); Kerop Bedoukian, *Some of Us Survived: The Story of an Armenian Boy* (New York: Farrar Straus Giroux, 1978); Bertha Nakshian Ketchian, *In the Shadow of the Fortress: The Genocide Remembered,* ed. Sonia I. Ketchian (Cambridge, Mass.: Zoryan Institute, 1988); John Yervant, *Needle, Thread and Button* (Cambridge, Mass.: Zoryan Institute, 1988).

41. The fiftieth anniversary of the genocide brought a widespread awakening of Armenian consciousness regarding the genocide. The new awareness was manifested in at least two ways: one was the emergence of a terrorist movement that sought to reverse years of denial of the genocide by the Turkish government; the other was a commitment to document eyewitness accounts of the genocide before the remaining survivors died.

One of the earliest oral history projects was initiated in 1967 by V. L. Parsegian of Troy, New York, in connection with the Armenian Educational Council. Another early project was done by young people who were members of the Armenian Youth Federation in Boston. The first large-scale project of more than a hundred interviews was directed by Bethel Charkoudian and was undertaken in 1973 by the Armenian Library and Museum of America (ALMA) in Boston. This project served as an important prototype for a major project carried out in 1979 by the Armenian Assembly, which was the first project to receive major funding (National Endowment for the Humanities). Richard Hovannisian (UCLA) originated a course in Armenian Oral History in 1977, and he has provided important intellectual leadership in a number of projects.

42. In 1986, in collaboration with the Zoryan Institute, we made a survey of all universities, individuals, and organizations that we were aware of having been involved in interviewing survivors. In spring of 1990, we made a modest attempt to update statistics that had been given in 1986. Although this was not a definitive survey of Armenian oral history, it does represent most of the major projects, and subsequent statistics draw on this survey. It should be noted that our estimate of the number of oral histories is somewhat lower than the estimate of four thousand interviews offered by Samuel Totten, *First-Person Accounts of Genocidal Acts Committed in the Twentieth Century: An Annotated Bibliography* (New York: Greenwood Press, 1991), xliv–xlv.

43. Film, photography, and musicology projects utilizing oral history research methods include the following:

- Project SAVE (a photographic archive of Armenian culture based in Watertown, Massachusetts)—64 interviews;
- Armenian Film Foundation (documentary films, Los Angeles)—300 interviews;
- Armenian Day (documentary videos for television)—35 interviews;
- Bedros Alahaidoyan (ethnomusicology)—450 interviews.

44. Major institutionally affiliated oral history projects that have been recorded on audiotape include the following:

- UCLA (Richard Hovannisian)—700 interviews;
- Armenian Assembly of America (Washington, D.C.)—217 interviews; duplicate copies of the 200 interviews done by the Armenian Library and Museum of America are also in this collection, making a total of 417 interviews;
- Armenian Student Association (Syria)—130 interviews;
- Armenian Educational Council (V. L. Parsegian, New York)—80 interviews (includes 44 interviews done by Nor Hyke);
- Multicultural History Society (Ontario)—38 interviews;
- Armenian Youth Federation (Boston)—30 interviews;
- Greek Orthodox Church (Greece)—10 interviews;
- Armenian Youth Association (Greece)—7 interviews.

Projects not affiliated with institutions include the following:

- Donald and Lorna Miller (Pasadena)—100 interviews;
- Florence Mazian (Michigan)—75 interviews;
- Isabel Kaprielian (Ontario)—60 interviews;
- Zarouhi Sarkisian (New England)—25 interviews;
- Rouben Adalian (Washington, D.C.)—24 interviews.

Institutional and individual oral history projects on audiotape total 1,696, although many of these figures are estimates.

45. Institutionally based oral history projects on videotape include the following:

- Zoryan Institute (Boston)—600 interviews;
- Zoryan Institute (Canada)—16 interviews;
- Armenian National Committee (Montreal)—90 interviews;
- Armenian Audio Visual Association (Paris)—40 interviews;
- Academy of Sciences (Armenia)—35 interviews;
- Armenian Testimonial Research (Argentina)—35 interviews.

Videotape projects not institutionally affiliated include the following:

- Alvin D. Bedrosian—15 interviews;
- Rouben Adalian—3 interviews.

The total number of videotape interviews is 934, although, as with the audiotape interviews, many of the figures are estimates.

46. Published studies that draw on oral history interviews include: Florence Mazian, "Armenian Wedding Customs 1914: From Sacred to Profane," *Armenian Review* 37, no. 4 (Winter 1984), 1–13; Susie Hoogasian Villa and Mary Kilbourne Matossian, *Armenian Village Life Before 1914* (Detroit: Wayne State University Press, 1982); Zarouhi Sarkisian, "Coping with Massive Stressful Life Events: The Impact of the Armenian Genocide of 1915 on the Present Day Health and Morale of a Group of Women Survivors," *Armenian Review* 37, no. 3 (Autumn 1984), 33–44; Richard Hovannisian, "Intervention and Shades of Altruism during the Armenian Genocide," in *The Armenian Genocide:*

History, Politics, Ethics, ed. Richard G. Hovannisian (New York: St. Martin's Press, 1992), 173–207.

47. "Setting the Record Straight," published by the Assembly of Turkish American Associations, P.O. Box 13012, Washington, D.C. 20009. The statement quoted is from the last page of the text, which is not numbered.

48. See the interesting analysis of Holocaust survivor memories by Lawrence L. Langer, *Holocaust Testimonies: The Ruins of Memory* (New Haven: Yale University Press, 1991).

CHAPTER 2

1. For introductions to Armenian history, see David Marshall Lang, *Armenia: Cradle of Civilization* (London: George Allen & Unwin, 1970); Arnold Toynbee, "A Summary of Armenian History up to and Including the Year 1915," in Great Britain, Parliament, *Treatment of Armenians in the Ottoman Empire: Documents Presented to Viscount Grey of Fallodon, Secretary of State for Foreign Affairs,* preface by Viscount Bryce (London: Sir Joseph Causton & Sons, 1916), 591–653 (hereafter referred to as Bryce/Toynbee); Christopher J. Walker, *Armenia: The Survival of a Nation* (London: Croom Helm, 1980); Ara Baliozian, *The Armenians: Their History and Culture* (Saddle Brook, N. J.: AGBU Press, 1980); Michael J. Arlen, *Passage to Ararat* (New York: Farrar, Straus & Giroux, 1975). A fascinating archaeological overview of Urartu civilization is found in the book written by Boris B. Piotrovsky, *The Ancient Civilization of Urartu,* trans. James Hogarth (New York; Cowles Book Company, Inc., 1969).

2. See the calculations of David Marshall Lang and Christopher J. Walker in *The Armenians,* Report No. 32 (London: Minority Rights Group, 1981), 3.

3. Bryce/Toynbee, p. 604, notes that the Armenian nation's first contact with modern Western Europe resulted from Lesser Armenia's taking the side of the Crusaders.

4. See Dickran Kouymjian, "The Destruction of Armenian Historical Monuments as a Continuation of the Turkish Policy of Genocide," in *A Crime of Silence: The Armenian Genocide* (London: Zed Books, 1985), 173–85.

5. Arnold Toynbee's summary of Armenian history at the end of the Bryce/Toynbee Blue Book states the following regarding the Armenian language: "The modern Armenian language . . . is an Indo-European tongue. There is a large non–Indo-European element in it—larger than in most known branches of the Indo-European family—and this has modified its syntax as well as its vocabulary. It has also borrowed freely and intimately from the Persian language in all its phases—a natural consequence of the political supremacy which Iran asserted over Armenia again and again, from the sixth century B.C. to the nineteenth century A.D. But when all these accretions have been analysed and discarded, the philologists pronounce the basis of modern Armenian to be a genuine Indo-European idiom—either a dialect of the Iranian branch or an independent variant, holding an intermediate position between Iranian and Slavonic" (Bryce/Toynbee, 597).

6. In many areas west of the Euphrates, Armenians spoke Turkish rather than their mother tongue. Some children learned Armenian in the orphanages, and a few survivors never learned Armenian, even after emigrating to the United States.

7. For a brief overview of religious practice of Armenians, see Robert Mirak's article on the "Armenians," in the *Harvard Encyclopedia of American Ethnic Groups*, ed. Stephan Thernstrom (Cambridge, Mass.: Harvard University Press, 1980), 138.

8. An important center of Armenian Catholic scholarship is the Mekhitarist monastery on the island of San Lazzaro in Venice, which possesses a fine library and has many valuable Armenian manuscripts.

9. Writing in 1916, Toynbee makes the following assessment of the role of Protestant missionaries: "Four generations of mission work have produced a strong Protestant Armenian community, but proselytism has not been the deliberate object of the missionaries. They have set themselves to revive and not to convert the national Armenian Church, and their schools and hospitals have been open to all who would attend them, without distinction of creed. Their wide and well-planned educational activity has always been the distinctive feature of these American Missions in the Ottoman Empire. Besides the famous Robert College and the College for Women on the Bosporus, they have established schools and other institutions in many of the chief provincial towns, with fine buildings and full staffs of well-trained American and Armenian teachers. Due acknowledgement must also be given to the educational work of the Swiss Protestants and of the Jesuits; but it can hardly compare with the work of the Americans in scale, and will scarcely play the same part in Armenian history" (Bryce/Toynbee, 609).

10. In 1831, there were only three *millets:* the Greek Orthodox, Jewish, and Armenian Gregorian. By 1914, 17 *millets* had been recognized. For further discussion of the *millet* system, see Joseph L. Grabill, *Protestant Diplomacy and the Near East: Missionary Influence on American Policy, 1810–1927* (Minneapolis: University of Minnesota Press, 1971), 50.

11. Toynbee states the following about the *millet* system of the Ottoman Empire: "These Christian Millets [which included the Armenians, Greeks, and other groups] were instituted by Sultan Mohammed II, after he had conquered Constantinople in 1453 and set himself to reorganise the Ottoman State as the conscious heir of the East Roman Empire. They are national corporations with written charters, often of an elaborate kind. Each of them is presided over by a Patriarch, who holds office at the discretion of the Government, but is elected by the community and is the recognized intermediary between the two, combining in his own person the headship of a voluntary "Rayah" association and the status of an Ottoman official. The special function thus assigned to the Patriarchates gives the Millets, as an institution, an ecclesiastical character [the word *millet* means simply "religious sect" in the Arabic language, from which it was borrowed by the Turks]; but in the Near East a church is merely the foremost aspect of a nationality, and the authority of the Patriarchates extends to the control of schools, and even to the administration of certain branches of civil

law. The Millets, in fact, are practically autonomous bodies in all that concerns religion, culture, and social life; but it is a maimed autonomy, for it is jealously barred from any political expression" (Bryce/Toynbee, 617–18).

Richard Hovannisian notes that the *millet* system offered certain advantages to minorities within the empire: "The millet system, while useful in managing the sultan's second class citizens, was not without advantages for the affected groups. Most Armenian laymen, for example, were shielded from direct contact with the central government by the official hierarchy of their millet, and the Armenian church, though losing much of its spiritual and intellectual vitality, found it possible to maintain the separate identity of the nation. While the Ottoman Empire was still mighty and expanding, the Armenians enjoyed more peace and security than at any other time since the fall of their medieval kingdoms" ("The Armenian Question in the Ottoman Empire," *East European Quarterly* 6, no. 1 [March 1972]: 3).

12. Toynbee notes that the Armenians were financially well established in many areas of Turkey: "A traveller entering Turkey by the Oriental Railway from Central Europe would have begun to encounter Armenians at Philippopolis in Bulgaria, and then at Adrianople, the first Ottoman city across the frontier. Had he visited any of the lesser towns of Thrace, he would have found much of the local trade and business in Armenian hands, and when he arrived at Constantinople he would have become aware that the Armenians were one of the most important elements in the Ottoman Empire. He would have seen them as financiers, as export and import merchants, as organisers of wholesale stores; and when he crossed the Bosphorus and explored the suburban districts on the Asiatic side, he might even have fancied that the Armenian population in the Empire was numerically equal to the Turkish" (Bryce/Toynbee, 611).

Summarizing the economic influence of the Armenians in Turkey, Toynbee states: "Wherever an opportunity presented itself, wherever the Government omitted to intervene, the Armenians were making indefatigable progress towards a better civilization. They were raising the pastoral and agricultural prosperity of their barren highlands and harassed plains; they were deepening and extending their education at the American schools; they were laying the foundation of local industries in the Vilayet of Sivas; they were building up Ottoman banking and shipping and finance at Trebizond and Adana and Constantinople. They were kindling the essential spark of energy in the Ottoman Empire, and anyone acquainted with Near Eastern history will inevitably compare their promise with the promise of the Greeks a century before" (Bryce/Toynbee, 616).

13. See the excellent historical discussion of Armenian and Kurdish interactions by Tessa Hofmann and Gerayer Koutcharian, "The History of Armenian-Kurdish Relations in the Ottoman Empire," *Armenian Review* 39, no. 4 (Winter 1986): 1–45.

14. Hoffman and Koutcharian argue this point, also quoting Garo Sasuni, who states that "the Armenians were ground between the Kurdish and Turkish millstone and did not know to which side they should lean." Ibid., 7.

15. The feudal relationship between Armenians and their Turkish beys is aptly described by H. F. B. Lynch: "Serfdom is an institution which is not unknown in the country, though its existence is softened over by the Turkish au-

thorities, who shrink from dispensing a purely nominal sovereignty. The serfs, who are Armenians, are known as *zer kurri*, signifying bought with gold. In fact they are bought and sold in the same manner as sheep and cattle by the Kurdish beys and aghas. The only difference is that they cannot be disposed of individually; they are transferred with the lands which they cultivate. The chief appropriates as much as he wishes from their yearly earnings, capital or goods; and in return he provides them with protection against other Kurdish tribes" (*Armenia. Travels and Studies*, vol. 2 [London, 1901 (reprinted in Beirut: Khayats Bookseller and Publishers, 1965)], 430–31).

16. Toynbee states that Kurds began entering Armenia during the tenth century A.D. Because of the difference in culture and lifestyle, Kurds and Armenians existed in an uneasy state of tension, according to Toynbee: "The juxtaposition of nomad and cultivator, dominant Moslem and subject Giaour, was henceforth an ever-present irritant in the social and political conditions of the land; but it did not assume a fatal and sinister importance until after the year 1878, when it was fiendishly exploited by the Sultan Abd-ul-Hamid" (Bryce/Toynbee, 610).

Later in his historical overview, Toynbee states: "The Kurd and the Armenian are not merely different nationalities; they are also antagonistic economic classes, and this antagonism existed in the country before ever the Kurdish encroachments began" (p. 613).

Toynbee argues that Abdul-Hamid, exploiting this antagonism, used the Kurds to subjugate the Armenians in the 1880s and 1890s: "His Armenian subjects must be deprived of their formidable vitality, and he decided to crush them by resuscitating the Kurds. From 1878 onwards he encouraged their lawlessness, and in 1891 he deliberately undid the work of his predecessor, Mahmoud. The Kurdish chieftains were taken again into favour and decorated with Ottoman military rank; their tribes were enrolled as squadrons of territorial cavalry; regimental badges and modern rifles were served out to them from the Government stores, and their retaining fee was a free hand to use their official status and their official weapons as they pleased against their Armenian neighbors" (p. 624).

17. According to Anaide Ter Minassian, the Kurds often plundered Armenian goods, and this was an important stimulus to the Armenian self-defense movement that developed in the late nineteenth century: "With the approval of the Turkish authorities, the area allotted to the movement of the nomadic southern Kurds was extended further and further north and northeastward. The Kurds, nomads or semi-nomads, would winter in the regions of Mush, Van, and around Ararat, occupying the towns and villages of sedentarized peoples, demanding upkeep and tribute from the Armenian peasants, forcing them to purchase their protection (*hafir*), pillaging with impunity, and carrying off women and flocks" (*Nationalism and Socialism in the Armenian Revolutionary Movement* [Cambridge, Mass.: The Zoryan Institute, 1983], 4).

18. Instances of Turks hiding Armenians will be discussed in chapter 9, but it is important to note that Kurds also intervened on behalf of Armenians. According to Hofmann and Koutcharian: "For the sake of historical justice, one must also mention the large numbers of cases where Kurds helped Armenians survive. For example, Mutullah-Bey from Shatakh was against the Armenian

massacres and prevented the Kurdish mob from going overboard. The district of Dersim, colonized by the Kurds, was a major area of refuge, in which 20,000 Armenians hid themselves. A certain Sheko from the village of Khut-Motgan and Sasun protected the neighboring Armenians. In 1916, when Mush was occupied by the Russians, there were still 12,000 Armenians alive, many of whom had been hidden by Ashiret Kurds. Armenian refugees in Syria reported similar stories" (Hofmann and Koutcharian, 25–26).

19. Ronald Suny argues that Armenians and Turks modernized at very different rates during the nineteenth century, which increased the alienation between the two peoples: "The Armenian national awakening of the first two-thirds of the nineteenth century created a sense of secular nationality among Armenians, a feeling of kinship with Christian Europe, and a growing alienation from the Muslim peoples among whom they lived. Armenian education, publishing and upward mobility in the urban economy was significantly more developed than that of the Muslims. And as the Turks themselves strove to imitate the ways of the West, it seemed as if many Armenians were already halfway there. The attractiveness of European models gradually undermined the traditional hierarchical, Muslim-dominated political and social order in which Christians were at a legal disadvantage" (Ronald Suny, "Rethinking the Unthinkable: An Historian's Reading of the Armenian Genocide," unpublished manuscript, 18).

20. Grabill, 41.

21. Ronald Suny states that a four-sided struggle for power developed in the nineteenth century: "When one looks at the social structure and history of eastern Anatolia in the late nineteenth century, it seems clear that an intense four-sided struggle for power, position, and survival was going on in that area between the centralizing Ottoman government, the semi-autonomous Turkish notables of the towns, Kurdish nomadic leaders, and the Armenians" (Ibid., 20).

22. Grabill, 27.

23. See Louise Nalbandian, *The Armenian Revolutionary Movement: The Development of Armenian Political Parties Through the Nineteenth Century* (Berkeley and Los Angeles: University of California Press, 1963).

24. Richard Hovannisian summarizes the political awakening of the Armenians: "Feeling abandoned and betrayed, a growing number of Armenians began to espouse extralegal means to achieve what they now regarded as the natural rights of man. They came to believe that, like the Balkan Christians, the Armenian people would have to organize, perhaps even take arms. Thus, by the 1890s, formally structured and broadly based secret societies were supplanting the earlier local self-defense groups. Still, few among the membership of these organizations were prepared to expound national independence as a goal. Rather, Armenian cultural freedom and regional autonomy were the stated aims of those who called themselves revolutionaries" (Hovannisian, "The Armenian Question in the Ottoman Empire," 12).

25. *Fedayee* is a Persian term meaning "he who is committed" or "he who is sacrificed." See Anaide Ter Minassian, *Nationalism and Socialism in the Armenian Revolutionary Movement* (Cambridge, Mass.: Zoryan Institute, 1983), 19ff.

26. Although it is disputed by Armenian scholars, see the discussion of Armenians in the Ottoman Empire by Justin McCarthy, *Muslims and Minorities: The Population of Ottoman Anatolia and the End of the Empire* (New York: New York University Press, 1983), 47–88. McCarthy's analysis has been challenged by Levon Marashlian, "Population Statistics on Ottoman Armenians in the Context of Turkish Historiography," *Armenian Review* 40, no. 4 (Winter 1987): 1–59.

27. Bryce/Toynbee, 621.

28. Richard Hovannisian summarizes the result of Article 61 of the Treaty of Berlin: "Article 61 of the Treaty of Berlin transformed the Armenian question into an international issue, but the Armenians gained no advantage from that status. On the contrary, Kurdish tribesmen, organized and armed by the government as the irregular 'Hamidiye' cavalry corps, spread havoc over the eastern provinces, particularly in the districts from which the Russian army had recently withdrawn. Neither the petitions of the patriarch nor the establishment of more European consular posts in Turkish Armenia served to alter the situation. The consuls at Kharput, Erzerum, Van, and other interior centers could do little more than relay daily dispatches describing the rapacious acts to which the Armenians were subjected. For two years the European powers, outwardly cooperating under the joint responsibility of Article 61, issued collective and identic notes reminding the Sublime Porte of its treaty obligations, but in 1881 Austria-Hungary declared that there was no necessity for any further communiques and Imperial Germany added that a solution to the Greco-Turkish boundary dispute and other critical issues should take precedence over the complex Armenian question. It was at that junction that the powers, already engaged in the scramble for empire, shelved the Armenian problem for nearly fifteen years" (Hovannisian, "The Armenian Question in the Ottoman Empire," 10).

29. Hofmann and Koutcharian, 18.

30. See James J. Reid, "Total War, the Annihilation Ethic, and the Armenian Genocide, 1870–1918," in *The Armenian Genocide: History, Politics, Ethics,* ed. Richard Hovannisian (New York: St. Martin's Press, 1992), 37.

31. There is some indication that the sultan was aware that the bank would be attacked even before it was occupied. Apparently, the former military attaché saw the police distribute sticks and truncheons studded with nails to Turks and Kurds on the eve of the occupation of the Ottoman Bank. See Stephan H. Astourian, "Genocidal Process: Reflections on the Armeno-Turkish Polarization," in *The Armenian Genocide: History, Politics, Ethics,* 59.

32. For discussion of the Young Turks, see Ernest E. Ramsaur, Jr., *The Young Turks* (Princeton: Princeton University Press, 1957), as well as Feroz Ahmad, *The Young Turks* (Oxford: Clarendon Press, 1969). For an overview of modern Turkey, see the classic work by Bernard Lewis, *The Emergence of Modern Turkey* (London: Oxford University Press, 1968).

33. Hofmann and Koutcharian state on p. 23 that some classes of Kurds were displeased that the constitution was being restored, because they had enjoyed considerable advantage at the expense of the Armenians.

34. See Urid Heyd, *Foundations of Turkish Nationalism: The Life and Teachings of Ziya Gökalp* (London: Luzac and Co. Ltd. and the Harvill Press,

Ltd., 1950); see also the brief discussion of Gökalp by Stanford J. Shaw and Ezel Kural Shaw, *History of the Ottoman Empire and Modern Turkey,* vol. 2 (Cambridge: Cambridge University Press, 1977), 301–4.

35. The Young Turk movement was divided between two factions: those with liberal notions favoring full equality for non-Turks and those with nationalistic and centralist views. The rise to power of the triumvirate of Enver, Talaat, and Jemal represented the defeat of a political agenda that would have been much more sympathetic to Armenian aspirations, and was, in fact, clearly articulated in Article 17 of the Ottoman Constitution of 1876: "All the Ottomans are equal before the law. They have the same rights and same duties toward the country, without prejudice to religion" (Astourian, 63).

36. Stephan Astourian maintains that the 1909 massacres were in response to Armenians practicing the liberties guaranteed by the Ottoman Constitution: "The freer public behavior which the Turks considered a provocation consisted of religious processions, of communal meetings, and of theater plays during which references were made to the history of the medieval Armenian kingdom of Cilicia. As a result of such remembrances of times past rumors circulated to the effect that Armenians wanted to recreate such a kingdom. Under the Constitution, the behavior of the Armenians was legal and certainly not subversive. What counts, however, in this case as in previous ones, is the Turkish perception of it. From their perspective, Armenians had lost the sense of modesty and discretion that befitted a *dhimmi,* especially in religious matters. Turkish outrage stemmed from the fact that the regulation and ritualization of interaction between the Turks and the Armenians, which had lasted for centuries, were undergoing radical change under the new constitutional regime" (Ibid., 64).

37. See the excellent description by Vahakn N. Dadrian of the factors leading to the 1909 Adana massacres. He demonstrates how rumors developed that the Armenians were going to attack and destroy the Turks of Adana, and how this fear was mobilized to whip the Turkish population into a hysterical mood of revenge. "The Circumstances Surrounding the 1909 Adana Holocaust," *The Armenian Review* 41, no. 4 (Winter 1988), 1–16.

38. Grabill, 50.

39. For historical overviews focusing on the nineteenth and early twentieth centuries and emphasizing the event of the Armenian Genocide, see Richard G. Hovannisian, "The Historical Dimensions of the Armenian Question, 1878–1923," in *The Armenian Genocide in Perspective,* ed. Richard G. Hovannisian (New Brunswick: Transaction Books, 1986); Vahakn N. Dadrian, "Genocide as a Problem of National and International Law: The World War I Armenian Case and Its Contemporary Legal Ramifications," *Yale Journal of International Law* 14, no. 2 (1989): 221–334; Dickran H. Boyajian, *Armenia: The Case for a Forgotten Genocide* (Westwood, N. J.: Educational Book Crafters, 1972); Gerard Chaliand and Yves Ternon, *The Armenians: From Genocide to Resistance,* trans. Tony Berret (London: Zed Books, 1983). For a bibliography of documents related to the genocide, see Richard G. Hovannisian, *The Armenian Holocaust: A Bibliography Relating to the Deportations, Massacres, and Dispersion of the Armenian People, 1915–1923* (Cambridge, Mass.: Armenian Heritage Press, 1978).

40. Often overlooked is the fact that in the winter of 1916 some 300,000 Kurds were also deported. Hofmann and Koutcharian quote Jacob Kuenzler's description: "The Young Turks did not want these Kurdish elements to ever return to their ancestral homeland. They should be absorbed gradually into the Turkish way of life in inner Anatolia. The treatment of these Kurds during their deportation expedition differed drastically from that of the Armenians. They came to no harm on their journey and no one was allowed to torment them. The worst part, however, was that the deportation took place in the middle of the winter. When such a Kurdish procession arrived in a Turkish village in the evening, the inhabitants quickly locked their doors out of fear. Thus the poor people had to spend the winter night out in the cold and snow. The next morning the villagers had to dig mass graves for those who were frozen to death" (Hofmann and Koutcharian, 26–27).

41. For a discussion of the role of Greeks in saving Armenian children, as well as of the persecution of Greeks during this period, see Ioannis K. Hassiotis, "The Armenian Genocide and the Greeks: Response and Records (1915–23)," in *The Armenian Genocide: History, Politics, Ethics*, 129–51.

42. The escape of the Armenians was fictionalized in the novel by Franz Werfel, *The Forty Days of Musa Dagh* (New York: Viking Press, 1934).

43. See Vahakn N. Dadrian, "The Role of Turkish Physicians in the World War I Genocide of the Ottoman Armenians," *Holocaust and Genocide Studies* 1, no. 2 (1986): 169–92.

44. Writing in 1916, and thus not including later massacres, Toynbee makes the following assessment of the death toll: "There is no dispute as to what happened in 1915. The Armenian inhabitants of the Ottoman Empire were everywhere uprooted from their homes, and deported to the most remote and unhealthy districts that the Government could select for them. Some were murdered at the outset, some perished on the way, and some died after reaching their destination. The death toll amounts to upwards of six hundred thousand; perhaps six hundred thousand more are still alive in their places of exile; and the remaining six hundred thousand or so have either been converted forcibly to Islam, gone into hiding in the mountains, or escaped beyond the Ottoman frontier" (Bryce/Toynbee, 627).

45. For a brief discussion of the controversy over the number of Armenians who died, see Robert Melson, "Provocation or Nationalism: A Critical Inquiry into the Armenian Genocide of 1915," in Hovannisian, ed., *The Armenian Genocide in Perspective*, 64–66.

46. Raphael Lemkin coined the term "genocide," combining the Greek word *genos* (race or tribe) with the Latin word *cide* (killing). In his view, genocide referred to killing individuals not for reasons of individual culpability, but because they are a member of a particular group. For a bibliographical overview of research and commentary on genocide, see Israel W. Charny, ed., *Genocide: A Critical Bibliographic Review* (New York: Facts on File Publications, 1988–91). For various definitions and theoretical statements on genocide, see Helen Fein, *Accounting for Genocide: National Responses and Jewish Victimization During the Holocaust* (New York: Free Press, 1979); Norman Cohn, *Warrant for Genocide* (New York: Harper & Row, 1966); Ervin Staub, *The Roots of Evil: The*

Origins of Genocide and Other Group Violence (Cambridge: Cambridge University Press, 1989); Irving Louis Horowitz, *Taking Lives: Genocide and State Power* (New Brunswick: Transaction Books, 1980); Israel W. Charny, *How Can We Commit the Unthinkable? Genocide: The Human Cancer* (Boulder, Colo.: Westview Press, 1982); Richard L. Rubenstein, *The Age of Triage: Fear and Hope in an Over-Crowded World* (Boston: Beacon Press, 1983); Leo Kuper, *The Prevention of Genocide* (New Haven: Yale University Press, 1985). For case studies and a historical assessment of genocide, see Frank Chalk and Kurt Jonassohn, *The History and Sociology of Genocide: Analyses and Case Studies* (New Haven: Yale University Press, 1990).

47. For a discussion of the attitude of the United States toward the Genocide Convention, see Lawrence J. LeBlanc, *The United States and the Genocide Convention* (Durham: Duke University Press, 1991). On p. 17, LeBlanc refers to the Armenian Genocide and the Holocaust as the two modern historical paradigms of genocide.

48. The text of the Convention is cited in full in Appendix 1 of Leo Kuper, *Genocide: Its Political Use in the Twentieth Century* (New Haven: Yale University Press, 1982), 210–14.

49. See LeBlanc (89–115) for the debate that has surrounded each of these five expressions of genocide.

50. Melson, 72.

51. Robert Melson, "Revolution and Genocide: On the Causes of the Armenian Genocide and the Holocaust," in Hovannisian, ed., *The Armenian Genocide,* 92.

52. Regarding the change in leadership of the Committee of Union and Progress, Stephan Astourian states on p. 63: "The significance of these events is momentous. For one thing, the failure of Ottoman liberalism after the *coup d'état* of January 1913 sealed the fate of the only policies, enjoying support among the Turkish political circles themselves, that could have handled the deep problems of a plural society by means of reforms and not repression."

53. Astourian cites the following characteristics of Armenians as being responsible for their economic advancement. "Their cultural and psychological adaptability to foreigners, their facility in foreign languages, their past background in trade and the crafts, their migrating tendencies which entailed a broader cultural perspective and which facilitated the establishment of trading family networks, the nineteenth-century educational activities of the missionaries in their midst, as well as the fact that some of them could benefit from *berats* or certificates of protection from foreign diplomatic agents, helped the Armenians take better advantage of the slow integration of the Ottoman Empire into the world economy" (Ibid., 65).

54. Ibid., 59.

55. See Leo Kuper, "The Turkish Genocide of Armenians, 1915–17," in Hovannisian, ed., *The Armenian Genocide in Perspective,* 56.

56. Suny, 25.

57. Astourian, 66.

58. With regard to this proposition, Robert Melson states on p. 90: "The implication is that powerlessness, poverty, and humility are a small price to pay for life itself."

59. According to Stephan H. Astourian, p. 60, "From the reign of Abdul-Hamid II to 1915, anti-Armenianism was a formula for those who rejected the liberalism, the theoretical egalitarianism and the cultural and economic influences of nineteenth-century Europe, all of which the Armenians stood for."

60. The labeling of Armenians as a hostile threat has some parallels to the American internment of Japanese during World War II.

61. For a sample of articles from the American press, see Richard D. Kloian, *The Armenian Genocide: News Accounts from the American Press* (Walnut Creek, Calif.: AAC, 1980).

62. See the three volumes by Richard G. Hovannisian, *Armenia on the Road to Independence: 1918* (Berkeley and Los Angeles: University of California Press, 1967); *The Republic of Armenia. Vol. 1, The First Year, 1918–1919* (Berkeley and Los Angeles: University of California Press, 1971); *The Republic of Armenia. Vol. 2, From Versailles to London, 1919–1920* (Berkeley and Los Angeles: University of California Press, 1982).

63. Hoffman and Koutcharian state that Kurds were also involved in these attacks: "Both campaigns [1918 and 1920] were accompanied by looting and massacres wherein approximately another 130,000 Armenians were killed and over 200,000 Armenians starved to death. This time, numerous Kurds from the Armenian plateau again took part in the Turkish crimes of war and genocide. While the Kurds from Olti and Korb committed sabotage in the interior, the Ashiret Kurds from Kadaran (near Arjesh and Manazkert) dispatched a cavalry regiment under the leadership of Keor Hussein Pasha, which took part in the bloody battles of Kars and Alexandropol" (Hoffman and Koutcharian, 40).

64. For an account of the burning of Smyrna, see Marjorie Housepian Dobkin, *Smyrna 1922: The Destruction of a City* (Kent, Ohio: Kent State University Press, 1988).

CHAPTER 3

1. For ethnographic discussions of Armenian culture, see Susie Hoogasian Villa and Mary Kilbourne Matossian, *Armenian Village Life Before 1914* (Detroit: Wayne State University Press, 1982); this study is based on forty-eight interviews with survivors. See also the two-volume study by H. F. B. Lynch, *Armenia. Travels and Studies* (London: 1901 [reprinted Beirut: Khayats Booksellers and Publishers, 1965]). In addition, see the valuable article by Jennifer Gurahian, who argues from a postmodern perspective that survivors' memories of their lost culture inevitably reflect issues they are presently struggling with in considering the meaning of their lives. "In the Mind's Eye: Collective Memory and Armenian Village Ethnographies," *Armenian Review* 43, no. 1 (Spring 1990): 19–29.

2. The practice may have varied from place to place. The missionary Grace Knapp, for example, states the following: "In the early days the bride was the slave of the household. She was not supposed to speak aloud until the next son brought home his wife to the patriarchal roof, and the last bride whispered the rest of her life, at least in the presence of her father-in-law." Quoted by Barbara J. Merguerian, "Mt. Holyoke Seminary in Bitlis: Providing an American Education for Armenian Women," *Armenian Review* 43, no. 1 (Spring 1990): 61.

3. Villa and Matossian, 24.

4. Drawing from missionary records, Barbara J. Merguerian gives the following description of houses and their surrounding yards in Bitlis: "The flat-roofed houses are built of blocks of hewn stone, broken by a layer or two of thick beams, to equalize the shock in case of earthquake. The stone, of volcanic origin and mined nearby, hardens to a warm grey. The climate, temperate with very cold winters (and heavy snows) and hot summers, favors heavy vegetation, with willow and poplar trees growing along the river beds, and abundant walnut and elm trees. All of the terraced homes are surrounded by lush gardens" (Merguerian, 37).

5. Villa and Matossian, 35–36.

6. Quoted by Merguerian, 40.

7. Villa and Matossian, 56–57.

8. Ibid., 59–60.

9. Ibid., 61.

10. In her research on Bitlis, Barbara J. Merguerian describes women as having extremely difficult lives: "Given these local attitudes, there was a great deal of resistance to the education of women. In 1875 a father in one of the villages agreed to place his daughter in the school even though he was ridiculed by his friends: Was he incapable of taking care of his own daughter? Why place her in the care of strangers? Wasn't it a shame to give her up to others in this way? In many cases it was a hardship to give up a daughter who, if at home, could help out with the housework and farming. 'Who will bring our bread and water, if we send our girls to school?' the men of one village once asked the Rev. Knapp at the end of the day, as they watched a group of women slowly making their way down the mountain paths with heavy loads strapped to their backs; the women had spent the day digging up roots to be used as fuel" (Merguerian, 49).

11. Although our accounts are from survivors who were children at the time, the Bryce/Toynbee Blue Book offers numerous descriptions of torture, such as the following summary of the practice of beating the underside of the foot: "The prisoner is put in a room (just as was done in the time of the Romans), and gendarmes standing in twos at both sides and two at the end of the room administer bastinadoes, each in their turn, as long as they have enough force in them. In Roman times forty strokes were administered at the very most; in this place, however, 200, 300, 500, even 800 strokes are administered. The foot swells up and then bursts open, owing to the number of the blows, and thus the blood spurts out" (Bryce/Toynbee, Account 91, p. 367).

Bryce/Toynbee also documented many other sadistic procedures, as in this account of events at Marsovan: "It was the 29th April that the Turkish Government began to arrest the leading Armenians at X [Marsovan].

"Mr. OO., Professor of Armenian, was sent to Z [Sivas] with sixteen other Professors; they suffered fiendish atrocities. Their hair was plucked out by the roots; they were burned with red hot irons; they were sprinkled with boiling water; they were flogged daily; some of them died in prison. Mr. OO. himself had his eyes gouged out, and was then hanged" (Bryce/Toynbee, Account 94, p. 378).

12. An informant in the Bryce/Toynbee Blue Book reports: "The Young Turk Government has published, as an excuse or perhaps as a means of exciting

greater hatred against the Armenians, a book entitled *The Armenian Separatist Movement*, which is as ridiculous as it is criminal. The reader finds in it not only copies of entirely fictitious publications, but actually pictures of enormous depots of arms and munitions purporting to be Armenian" (Bryce/Toynbee, Account 11, p. 23).

13. One of the informants in the Bryce/Toynbee Blue Book reports: "The Armenians said that they could not give up their arms while the Kurds were left armed to the teeth and went about unmolested" (Bryce/Toynbee, Account 22, p. 83).

14. The Bryce/Toynbee Blue Book reports that a few Armenians resisted briefly at Bitlis and then took their own lives: "On the 25th June, the Turks surrounded the town of Bitlis and cut its communications with the neighbouring Armenian villages; then most of the able-bodied men were taken away from their family by domiciliary visits. During the following few days, all the men under arrest were shot outside the town and buried in deep trenches dug by the victims themselves. The young women and children were distributed among the rabble, and the remainder, the 'useless' lot, were driven to the south and are believed to have been drowned in the Tigris. Any attempts at resistance, however brave, were easily quelled by the regular troops. The recalcitrant, after firing their last cartridges, either took poison by whole families or destroyed themselves in their homes, in order not to fall into the hands of Turks" (Bryce/Toynbee, Account 22, p. 84).

15. See Christopher J. Walker, *Armenia: The Survival of a Nation* (London: Croom Helm, 1980), 205–9.

16. Franz Werfel, *The Forty Days of Musa Dagh* (New York: Viking Press, 1934).

17. See the excellent discussion of the provocation thesis by Robert Melson, "Provocation or Nationalism: A Critical Inquiry into the Armenian Genocide of 1915," in *The Armenian Genocide in Perspective,* ed. Richard G. Hovannisian (New Brunswick: Transaction Books, 1986), 61–84.

18. See the attempt to discredit Morgenthau by Heath Lowry, *The Story beyond Ambassador Morgenthau's Story* (Istanbul: The Isis Press, 1990) and Roger W. Smith's review and rebuttal of Lowry's argument ("Was Morgenthau a Liar?" *Ararat: A Quarterly* 32, no. 128 [Autumn 1991]: 51–52).

19. See the informative account by Clarence D. Ussher and Grace H. Knapp, *An American Physician in Turkey: A Narrative of Adventures in Peace and in War* (Boston: Houghton Mifflin, 1917).

20. Henry Morgenthau, *Ambassador Morgenthau's Story* (Garden City, N.Y.: Doubleday, Page, 1918), 297.

21. Ibid., 298–99.

22. Ibid., 300. Morgenthau is not alone in countering the provocation thesis. Arnold Toynbee also addresses this issue in his summary of the deportations. Referring to the charge that Armenians took up arms and joined with Russian forces in areas near the Turkish border, Toynbee states: "The standard case its champions cite [i.e., of the provocation argument] is the 'Revolt of Van.' The deportations, they maintain, were only ordered after this outbreak to forestall the danger of its repetition elsewhere. This contention is

easily rebutted. In the first place, there was no Armenian revolt at Van. The Armenians merely defended the quarter of the city in which they lived, after it had been beleaguered and attacked by Turkish troops, and the outlying villages visited with massacre by Turkish patrols. The outbreak was on the Turkish side, and the responsibility lies with the Turkish governor, Djevdet Bey. The ferocious, uncontrollable character of this official was the true cause of the catastrophe. . . . And, in the second place, the deportations had already begun in Cilicia before the fighting at Van broke out. The Turks fired the first shot at Van on the 20th April, 1915; the first Armenians were deported from Zeitoun on the 8th April, and there is a record of their arrival in Syria as early as the 19th" (Bryce/Toynbee, 627).

CHAPTER 4

1. Toynbee offers the following extended summary of events on the deportation routes: "From the moment they left the outskirts of the towns they were never safe from outrage. The Moslem peasants mobbed and plundered them as they passed through the cultivated lands, and the gendarmes connived at the peasants' brutality, as they had connived at the desertion of the drivers with their carts. When they arrived at a village they were exhibited like slaves in a public place, often before the windows of the Government Building itself, and every Moslem inhabitant was allowed to view them and take his choice of them for his harem; the gendarmes themselves began to make free with the rest, and compelled them to sleep with them at night. There were still more horrible outrages when they came to the mountains, for here they were met by bands of 'chettis' and Kurds. The 'chettis' were brigands, recruited from the public prisons; they had been deliberately released by the authorities on a consideration which may have been tacit but which both parties clearly understood. As for the Kurds, they had not changed since 1896, for they had always retained their arms, which Abd-ul-Hamid had served out and the Young Turks could not or would not take away; and they had now been restored to official favour upon the proclamation of the Holy War, so that their position was as secure again as it had been before 1908. They knew well what they were allowed and what they were intended to do. When these Kurds and chettis waylaid the convoys, the gendarmes always fraternized with them and followed their lead, and it would be hard to say which took the most active part in the ensuing massacre—for this was the work which the brigands came to do. The first to be butchered were the old men and boys— all the males that were to be found in the convoy except the infants in arms—but the women were massacred also. It depended on the whim of the moment whether a Kurd cut a woman down or carried her away into the hills. When they were carried away their babies were left on the ground or dashed against the stones. But while the convoy dwindled, the remnant had always to march on. The cruelty of the gendarmes towards the victims grew greater as their physical sufferings grew more intense; the gendarmes seemed impatient to make a hasty end of their task. Women who lagged behind were bayoneted on the road or pushed over precipices, or over bridges. The passage of rivers, and especially of the Euphrates, was always an occasion of wholesale murder. Women and children were driven into the water, and were shot as they struggled, if they seemed

likely to reach the further bank. The lust and covetousness of their tormentors had no limit. The last survivors often staggered into Aleppo naked; every shred of their clothing had been torn from them on the way. Witnesses who saw their arrival remarked that there was not one young or pretty face to be seen among them, and there was assuredly none surviving that was truly old—except in so far as it had been aged by suffering. The only chance to survive was to be plain enough to escape their torturers' lust, and vigorous enough to bear the fatigues of the road." (Great Britain, Parliament, *Treatment of Armenians in the Ottoman Empire: Documents Presented to Viscount Grey of Fallodon, Secretary of State for Foreign Affairs*, preface by Viscount Bryce [London: Sir Joseph Causton & Sons, 1916], 643–44.)

2. An observer's report recorded in the Bryce/Toynbee Blue Book summarized the fate of the men at Kharpert: "The system that is being followed seems to be to have bands of Kurds awaiting them on the road, to kill the men especially, and, incidentally, some of the others. The entire movement seems to be the most thoroughly organized and effective massacre this country has ever seen" (Bryce/Toynbee, Account 65, p. 263).

3. For a transcript of Soghomon Tehlirian's trial, see *The Case of Soghomon Tehlirian*, trans. Vartkes Yeghiayan (Los Angeles: A. R. F. Varantian Gomideh, 1985). For commentary on the motives surrounding Tehlirian's assassination of Talaat, see Jacques Derogy, *Resistance and Revenge: The Armenian Assassination of the Turkish Leaders Responsible for the 1915 Massacres and Deportations* (New Brunswick: Transaction Publishers, 1990) and Edward Alexander, *A Crime of Vengeance: An Armenian Struggle for Justice* (New York: Free Press, 1991).

4. Talaat Pasha, "Posthumous Memoirs of Talaat Pasha," *Current History* 15, no. 1 (October 1921): 295.

5. Ibid., 295.

6. Ibid., 295.

7. Henry Morgenthau, *Ambassador Morgenthau's Story* (Garden City, N.Y.: Doubleday, Page, 1918), 333.

8. Ibid., 336–37.

9. Ibid., 337.

10. Ibid., 322.

11. Ibid., 386.

12. Ibid., 342.

CHAPTER 5

1. The Bryce/Toynbee Blue Book records numerous instances where women were unable to continue carrying their children. For example, a survivor from Kharpert noted: "Everywhere one passes corpses lying unburied in the open. On my journey I saw heartrending incidents—women in their last agony lying on the ground with their sucklings, already dead, beside them" (Great Britain, Parliament, *Treatment of Armenians in the Ottoman Empire: Documents Presented to Viscount Grey of Fallodon, Secretary of State for Foreign Affairs*, preface by Viscount Bryce [London: Sir Joseph Causton & Sons, 1916], Account 67, p. 270).

2. Accounts of rape also fill the Bryce/Toynbee Blue Book. For example, an informant from Moush stated: "All the old women and the weak who were unable to walk were killed. There were about one hundred Kurdish guards over us, and our lives depended on their pleasure. It was a very common thing for them to rape our girls in our presence. Very often they violated eight- or ten-year-old girls, and as a consequence many would be unable to walk, and were shot" (Bryce/Toynbee, Account 24, p. 92).

3. Extracts from a report made by the Board of Foreign Missions of the Presbyterian Church in the U.S.A. illustrate the prevalence of rape: "A sad case was that of the mother of a girl of twelve who was being taken away to a life of slavery. The mother protested and tried to save her child, who was ruthlessly torn from her. As the daughter was being dragged away the mother made so much trouble for her oppressors, and clung to them so tenaciously, that they stabbed her twelve times before she fell, helpless to save her little girl from her fate. . . ."

"After the massacre in the village of ——, almost all the women and girls were outraged, and two little girls, aged eight and ten, died in the hands of Moslem villains. A mother said that not a woman or girl above twelve (and some younger) in the village of —— escaped violation. This is the usual report from the villages. One man, who exercised a great deal of authority in the northern part of the Urmia plain, openly boasted of having ruined eleven Christian girls, two of them under seven years of age, and he is now permitted to return to his home in peace and no questions are asked. Several women from eighty to eighty-five years old have suffered with the younger women" (Bryce/Toynbee, Account 35, p. 161).

4. Although there were no instances of mercy killing in our interviews, some accounts are offered in the Bryce/Toynbee Blue Book. This example involved Armenians fleeing across the Russian border: "One of our Christian workers from Urmia told me that with his own eyes he saw a man go up to his mother, who had sunk exhausted in the mud, and shoot her through the head, rather than leave her to die by degrees or to be killed by wolves" (Bryce/Toynbee, Account 30, p. 115).

5. One of the informants in the Bryce/Toynbee Blue Book reports that women in Sassun elected suicide in a manner paralleling the account just cited: "Several young women, who were in danger of falling into the Turks' hands, threw themselves from the rocks, some of them with their infants in their arms" (Bryce/Toynbee, Account 22, p. 87).

6. Anaguel's embarrassment about accepting charity is similar to that in one of the accounts offered in the Bryce/Toynbee Blue Book: "The day after the flight from Geogtapa we went with a basket of bread to one of the larger rooms of the Press, which was filled with self-respecting people who had the day before been in comfortable circumstances, but who had fled with nothing, or had been robbed of whatever they had tried to bring with them. When they saw the bread for distribution, they began to cry and cover their faces, and we had to drop the bread into their laps—they didn't reach out for it. Of course, we assured them that under such circumstances, it was no shame to eat the bread of charity" (Bryce/Toynbee, Account 31, p. 123).

CHAPTER 6

1. See the interesting account of Leslie Davis's experience in Turkey, *The Slaughterhouse Province: An American Diplomat's Report on the Armenian Genocide, 1915–1917,* ed. and with an introduction and notes by Susan K. Blair (New Rochelle, N.Y.: Aristide D. Caratzas, Publisher, 1989).

2. Suzanne Elizabeth Moranian, "Bearing Witness: The Missionary Archives as Evidence of the Armenian Genocide," in *The Armenian Genocide: History, Politics, Ethics,* ed., Richard G. Hovannisian (New York: St. Martin's Press, 1992), 104.

3. The Bryce/Toynbee Blue Book contains many accounts of missionary relief efforts. The following excerpt from a report by the American Committee for Armenian and Syrian Relief offers a glimpse into the immense undertaking that was required to provide even minimal covering from the cold: "For bedding it was decided to issue large wool quilts, large enough to cover several persons. These we found could be made for three or three and a half tomans (12s.) per quilt. Under the efficient direction of Miss Lewis, and later of Miss Lamme, a quilt factory was started, which in time employed over a hundred needy women in carding wool and sewing the quilts. This factory during its three months' existence consumed over 84,000 yards of calico, 35,000 pounds of wool, and some 1,500 pounds of cotton, and expended over 18,000 tomans. . . . Our plan was to give only one quilt to four persons, families of over four to receive two or more according to the number of members; but after the issue of tickets we found that we could not possibly supply the need, and so regretfully we had to limit our giving to one quilt to a family" (Great Britain, Parliament, *Treatment of Armenians in the Ottoman Empire: Documents Presented to Viscount Grey of Fallodon, Secretary of State for Foreign Affairs,* preface by Viscount Bryce [London: Sir Joseph Causton & Sons, 1916], Account 44, p. 189).

4. See the highly informative narrative of fund-raising events by Joseph L. Grabill, *Protestant Diplomacy and the Near East: Missionary Influence on American Policy, 1810–1927* (Minneapolis: University of Minnesota Press, 1971), 70ff.

5. Near East Relief was the name used in 1919. Prior to that it was called the American Committee for Relief in the Near East (1918) and, even earlier, the American Committee for Armenian and Syrian Relief (ACASR), when it was founded on November 20, 1915. ACASR resulted from the merger of the Syrian-Palestine Relief Fund, the Persian War Relief Fund, and the Dodge Relief Committee.

6. Richard G. Hovannisian, *The Republic of Armenia.* Vol. 1, *The First Year, 1918–1919* (Berkeley and Los Angeles: University of California Press, 1971), 134.

7. Quoted by Grabill, 131–32. The second verse was as follows:

Then let us take our lighter Cross
With hearts and courage high,
And give until we fell the loss,—
Our faces to the sky!
Armenia! Armenia!
We share our best with thee
Our hearts and hands, our harvest-lands,
Our Christianity!

8. Ibid., 165.

9. Ibid., 165–66.

10. These statistics are cited by Bayard Dodge, Foreword to *The Lions of Marash*, by Stanley E. Kerr (Albany: State University of New York Press, 1973), x. The medical risks faced by missionaries are revealed in the diary of a missionary quoted in the Bryce/Toynbee Blue Book:

Thursday, 3rd June

Almost two months since I last wrote in my journal. On Sunday, the 11th April, I went to bed with typhoid or typhus, and three days later Miss Schoebel went down with it also. Rabi Elishua, a teacher of the Persian Girls'-School, came to nurse me at once. She kept up for three weeks and saw me through the worst of my sickness; then she took the disease. Three of the other Seminary teachers in succession came to care for Miss Schoebel, and each one went down with the disease in turn. Miss Bridges, of the American Orphanage, came to help us during the day, and in twelve days went to bed with typhus. She is just getting about again. All the teachers who helped to care for us have recovered, though one of the other teachers died (Bryce/Toynbee, Account 31, p. 149).

11. Dodge, Foreword to Kerr, xiii.

12. Grabill, 233.

13. In spite of the heroic efforts of relief workers, it is important to note the overwhelming conditions they faced and their inability, in many instances, to meet the needs they encountered, as is evident in a scene reported in the Bryce/Toynbee Blue Book: "At the Etchmiadzin Secondary School, 3,500 children who have lost their parents are huddled together. They sleep on the floor. Yesterday evening I visited the building; in the big hall I counted 110 babies lying on the floor absolutely naked; some of them were sleeping, others were crying. The effect was so harrowing that one could not restrain one's tears. The sight was too terrible for me to stand, and I fled from this hell" (Bryce/Toynbee, Account 46, p. 195).

14. A poignant description of orphanage life is contained in the autobiographical reflections of Andranik Zaroukian, *Men Without Childhood*, trans. Elise Bayizian and Marzbed Margossian (New York: Ashod Press, 1985).

15. See the biography by his daughter, Ida Alamuddin, *Papa Kuenzler and the Armenians* (London: Heinemann, 1970).

CHAPTER 7

1. See the description of Marash by Stanley E. Kerr, *The Lions of Marash: Personal Experiences with American Near East Relief, 1919–1922* (Albany: State University of New York Press, 1973).

2. Ibid., 254.

3. Ibid.

4. See Marjorie Housepian Dobkin, *Smyrna 1922: The Destruction of a City* (Kent, Ohio: Kent State University Press, 1988).

5. See Robert Mirak, *Torn Between Two Lands: Armenians in America, 1890 to World War I* (Cambridge, Mass.: Harvard University Press, 1983), 35–59; see also Gayané Hagopian, "The Immigration of Armenians to the United States," *Armenian Review* 41, no. 2 (Summer 1988): 67–76.

6. Hagopian, 71–72.

7. Mirak, 47.

8. Ibid., 55.

CHAPTER 8

1. Relatively little material using psychological categories of analysis has been written on Armenian survivors. One exception is the informative chapter by Levon Boyajian and Haigaz Grigorian, "Psychosocial Sequelae of the Armenian Genocide," in *The Armenian Genocide in Perspective*, ed. Richard G. Hovannisian (New Brunswick: Transaction Books, 1986), 177–86. However, there is considerable literature on survivors more generally. For example, see the important work of William G. Niederland: "The Problem of the Survivor," *Journal of the Hillside Hospital* 10 (1961): 233–47; "Psychiatric Disorder among Persecution Victims: A Contribution to the Understanding of Concentration Camp Pathology and Its After-effect," *Journal of Nervous and Mental Diseases* 139 (1964): 458–74; "Clinical Observations on the 'Survivor Syndrome': Symposium on Psychic Traumatization through Social Catastrophe," *International Journal of Psychoanalysis* 49 (1968): 313–15. For a bibliography on survivors and especially the impact on the second generation, see the extensive listing in *Generations of the Holocaust*, ed. Martin S. Bergmann and Milton E. Jucovy (New York: Basic Books, 1982), 317–26.

2. See Max Weber, *The Methodology of the Social Sciences* (New York: Free Press, 1949), 90ff.

3. For variations on this typology that we have published elsewhere, see: "Armenian Survivors: A Typological Analysis of Victim Response," *The Oral History Review* 10 (1982): 47–72; "Responses to the Armenian Genocide: An Oral History Perspective," *Ararat: A Quarterly* 25, no. 1 (Winter 1984): 2–7; "An Oral History Perspective on Responses to the Armenian Genocide," in *The Armenian Genocide in Perspective*, ed. Richard G. Hovannisian (New Brunswick: Transaction Books, 1986), 187–203; "Image and Memory: Armenian Survivors Remember Their Past," *Ararat: A Quarterly* 31, no. 122 (Spring 1990): 16–18.

4. In summarizing the impact of the genocide on survivors, we can identify three different types of suffering that characterize their experience: physical suffering, emotional suffering, and moral anguish. Within each of these general categories, it is also possible to distinguish a number of subtypes. Thus, *physical suffering* includes (1) hunger, (2) thirst, (3) exhaustion, (4) illness, (5) exposure, (6) physical attack, and (7) torture. *Emotional suffering* comprises at least five specific subtypes: (1) grief, (2) fear, (3) insecurity, (4) indignity, and (5) abandonment. And related to *moral anguish* are the following tragic moral choices faced by parents (and children): (1) abandoning children on the deportation routes, (2) suicide, (3) forced religious conversion, and (4) children leaving adopted families for orphanages (sometimes deeply disappointing the surrogate parents).

5. It is a peculiarly modern notion that self-revelation to others is virtuous. Perhaps this is a piece of the modern folklore advocated only by those whose life

experience has little tragic depth to reveal. This is not true of our survivors, however, and, in our view, there is substantial integrity in the struggle of those who seek sanity through denial.

6. These statistics were cited in an article published on December 21, 1991, in the *Los Angeles Times*, "Armenian Terrorist Group Tries to Kill Turkish Envoy," Section A, p. 18, and confirmed in a telephone conversation on December 30, 1991, with Turkish Vice-Consul Kerem Kiratti of the Los Angeles office. See also Michael Gunter, "The Armenian Terrorist Campaign Against Turkey," *Orbis: A Journal of World Affairs,* Summer 1983: 447–77; and *"Pursuing the Just Cause of Their People": A Study of Contemporary Armenian Terrorism* (New York: Greenwood Press, 1986).

7. See Donald E. Miller and Lorna Touryan Miller, "Memory and Identity Across the Generations: A Case Study of Armenian Survivors and Their Progeny," *Qualitative Sociology* 14, no. 1 (1991): 13–38.

8. Our interviews were done prior to the reestablishment of the Republic of Armenia and its recognition by the United States.

9. It is very likely that blaming the Germans for the genocide reflects the survivors' retrospective reading of their experience through the lens of the Nazi extermination of Jews in World War II. See Ulrich Trumpener's analysis of the German role in the Armenian Genocide in *Germany and the Ottoman Empire, 1914–1918* (Princeton, N. J.: Princeton University Press, 1968).

10. Vigen Guroian has written an interesting unpublished article, "Genocide and Christian Existence: Theology after the Armenocide."

CHAPTER 9

1. See Richard G. Hovannisian, "Intervention and Shades of Altruism During the Armenian Genocide," in *The Armenian Genocide: History, Politics, Ethics,* ed. Richard G. Hovannisian (New York: St. Martin's Press, 1992), 173–207.

2. For a history of the Nagorno-Karabagh issue, see *The Karabagh File,* ed. Gerard J. Libaridian (Cambridge, Mass.: Zoryan Institute, 1988).

Bibliography

Alamuddin, Ida. *Papa Kuenzler and the Armenians.* London: Heinemann, 1970.

Andonian, Aram, ed. *The Memoirs of Naim Bey.* London: Hodder & Stoughton, 1920.

Arlen, Michael J. *Passage to Ararat.* New York: Farrar, Straus & Giroux, 1975.

Armenian National Committee, *The Armenian Genocide as Reported in the Australian Press.* Sydney: Armenian National Committee, 1983.

Armenian Review. Genocide: Crime Against Humanity. Special issue of the *Armenian Review* 37 (1984).

Astourian, Stephan H. "Genocidal Process: Reflections on the Armeno-Turkish Polarization." In *The Armenian Genocide: History, Politics, Ethics,* edited by Richard G. Hovannisian, 53–79. New York: St. Martin's Press, 1992.

Bardakjian, Kevork B. *Hitler and the Armenian Genocide.* Cambridge, Mass.: Zoryan Institute, 1985.

Chaliand, Gerard, and Yves Ternon. *The Armenians: From Genocide to Resistance.* Translated by Tony Berret. London: Zed Press, 1983.

Chalk, Frank, and Kurt Jonassohn. *The History and Sociology of Genocide: Analyses and Case Studies.* New Haven: Yale University Press, 1990.

Charny, Israel. *How Can We Commit the Unthinkable? Genocide: The Human Cancer.* Boulder, Colo.: Westview Press, 1982.

————, ed. *Toward the Understanding and Prevention of Genocide: Proceedings of the International Conference on the Holocaust and Genocide.* Boulder, Colo.: Westview Press, 1984.

————, ed. *Genocide: A Critical Bibliographic Review.* 2 vols. New York: Facts on File, 1988–91.

Dadrian, Vahjakn N. "The Naim-Andonian Documents on the World War I Destruction of the Ottoman Armenians: The Anatomy of Genocide." *International Journal of Middle East Studies* 18 (1986): 311–60.

———. "The Role of Turkish Physicians in the World War I Genocide of Ottoman Armenians." *Holocaust and Genocide Studies* 1 (1986): 169–92.

———. "The Circumstances Surrounding the 1909 Adana Holocaust." *Armenian Review* 41 (1988): 1–16.

———. "Genocide as a Problem of National and International Law: The World War I Armenian Case and Its Contemporary Legal Ramifications." *Yale Journal of International Law* 14 (1989): 221–334.

———. "Ottoman Archives and Denial of the Armenian Genocide." In *The Armenian Genocide: History, Politics, Ethics*, edited by Richard G. Hovannisian, 280–310. New York: St. Martin's Press, 1992.

Davis, Leslie. *The Slaughterhouse Province: An American Diplomat's Report on the Armenian Genocide, 1915–1917*. Edited and with an introduction and notes by Susan K. Blair. New Rochelle, N.Y.: Aristide D. Caratzas, Publisher, 1989.

Dekmejian, R. Hrair. "Determinants of Genocide: Armenians and Jews as Case Studies." In *The Armenian Genocide in Perspective*, edited by Richard G. Hovannisian, 85–96. New Brunswick: Transaction Books, 1986.

Dobkin, Marjorie Housepian. "What Genocide? What Holocaust? News from Turkey, 1915–1923: A Case Study." In *The Armenian Genocide in Perspective*, edited by Richard G. Hovannisian, 97–110. New Brunswick: Transaction Books, 1986.

———. *Smyrna 1922: The Destruction of a City*. Kent, Ohio: Kent State University Press, 1988.

Fein, Helen. *Accounting for Genocide: National Responses and Jewish Victimization During the Holocaust*. New York: Free Press, 1979.

Gibbons, Herbert Adams. *The Blackest Page in Modern History: Events in Armenia in 1915: The Facts and the Responsibilities*. New York: G. P. Putnam's Sons, 1916.

Grabill, Joseph L. *Protestant Diplomacy and the Near East: Missionary Influence on American Policy, 1810–1927*. Minneapolis: University of Minnesota Press, 1971.

Guroian, Vigen. "Collective Responsibility and Official Excuse Making: The Case of the Turkish Genocide of the Armenians." In *The Armenian Genocide in Perspective*, edited by Richard G. Hovannisian, 135–52. New Brunswick: Transaction Books, 1986.

———. "The Politics and Morality of Genocide." In *The Armenian Genocide: History, Politics, Ethics*, edited by Richard G. Hovannisian, 311–40. New York: St. Martin's Press, 1992.

Great Britain. Parliament. *The Treatment of Armenians in the Ottoman Empire: Documents Presented to Viscount Grey of Fallodon, Secretary of State for Foreign Affairs*. Preface by Viscount Bryce. London: Sir Joseph Causton & Sons, 1916.

Hartunian, Abraham H. *Neither to Laugh nor to Weep: A Memoir of the Armenian Genocide*. Boston: Beacon Press, 1968.

Hofmann, Tessa. "German Eyewitness Reports of the Genocide of the Armenians, 1915–16." In *A Crime of Silence: The Armenian Genocide*, edited by the Permanent Peoples' Tribunal, 61–93. London: Zed Books, 1985.

Hofmann, Tessa, and Gerayer Koutcharian. "The History of Armenian-Kurdish Relations in the Ottoman Empire." *Armenian Review* 39 (1986): 1–45.

Horowitz, Irving Louis. *Taking Lives: Genocide and State Power*. New Brunswick: Transaction Books, 1980.

Hovannisian, Richard G. *Armenia on the Road to Independence: 1918*. Berkeley and Los Angeles: University of California Press, 1967.

———. *The Republic of Armenia*. Vol. 1. *The First Year, 1918–1919*. Berkeley and Los Angeles: University of California Press, 1971.

———. "The Armenian Question in the Ottoman Empire." *East European Quarterly* 6 (1972): 1–26.

———. *The Armenian Holocaust: A Bibliography Relating to the Deportations, Massacres, and Dispersion of the Armenian People, 1915–1923*. Cambridge, Mass.: Armenian Heritage Press, 1980.

———. *The Republic of Armenia*. Volume 2. *From Versailles to London, 1919–1920*. Berkeley and Los Angeles: University of California Press, 1982.

———. "The Armenian Question, 1878–1923." In *A Crime of Silence: The Armenian Genocide*, edited by the Permanent Peoples' Tribunal, 11–36. London: Zed Press, 1985.

———. "The Armenian Genocide." In *Genocide: A Critical Bibliographic Review*, edited by Israel Charny, 89–115. New York: Facts on File Publications, 1988.

———, ed. *The Armenian Genocide in Perspective*. New Brunswick: Transaction Books, 1986.

———, ed. *The Armenian Genocide: History, Politics, Ethics*. New York: St. Martin's Press, 1992.

Jernazian, Ephraim K. *Judgement Unto Truth: Witnessing the Armenian Genocide*. Translated by Alice Haig. New Brunswick, N. J.: Transaction Books, 1990.

Kerr, Stanley E. *The Lions of Marash: Personal Experiences with American Near East Relief, 1919–1922*. Albany: State University of New York Press, 1973.

Kloian, Richard D., ed. *The Armenian Genocide: News Accounts from the American Press, 1915–1922*. 3d ed. Berkeley, Calif.: AAC Books, 1985.

Kuper, Leo. *Genocide: Its Political Use in the Twentieth Century*. New Haven: Yale University Press, 1982.

———. *The Prevention of Genocide*. New Haven: Yale University Press, 1985.

Lang, David Marshall. *Armenia: Cradle of Civilization*. London: George Allen & Unwin, 1970.

Lang, David Marshall, and Christopher J. Walker. *The Armenians*. London: Minority Rights Group, Report no. 32 (revised), 1981.

Lewis, Bernard. *The Emergence of Modern Turkey*. London: Oxford University Press, 1968.

Libaridian, Gerard J. "The Ideology of the Young Turk Movement." In *A Crime of Silence: The Armenian Genocide*, edited by the Permanent Peoples' Tribunal, 37–52. London: Zed Press, 1985.

McCarthy, Justin. *Muslims and Minorities: The Population of Ottoman Anatolia and the End of the Empire*. New York: New York University Press, 1983.

Marashlian, Levon. "Population Statistics on Ottoman Armenians in the Context of Turkish Historiography." *Armenian Review* 40 (1987): 1–59.

Melson, Robert. "A Theoretical Inquiry into the Armenian Massacres of 1894–96." *Comparative Studies in Society and History* 24 (1982): 481–509.

———. "Provocation or Nationalism: A Critical Inquiry into the Armenian Genocide of 1915." In *The Armenian Genocide in Perspective*, edited by Richard G. Hovannisian, 61–84. New Brunswick: Transaction Books, 1986.

———. "Revolution and Genocide: On the Causes of the Armenian Genocide and the Holocaust." In *The Armenian Genocide: History, Politics, Ethics*, edited by Richard G. Hovannisian, 80–102. New York: St. Martin's Press, 1992.

Merguerian, Barbara J. "Mt. Holyoke Seminary in Bitlis: Providing an American Education for Armenian Women." *Armenian Review* 43 (1990): 31–65.

Miller, Donald E. and Lorna Touryan Miller. "Armenian Survivors: A Typological Analysis of Victim Response." *Oral History Review* 10 (1982): 47–72.

———. "Memory and Identity Across the Generations: A Case Study of Armenian Survivors and Their Progeny." *Qualitative Sociology* 14 (1991): 13–38.

Mirak, Robert. "Armenians." In *Harvard Encyclopedia of American Ethnic Groups*, edited by Stephan Thernstrom, 136–49. Cambridge: Harvard University Press, 1980.

———. *Torn Between Two Lands: Armenians in America 1890 to World War I*. Cambridge: Harvard University Press, 1983.

Moranian, Suzanne Elizabeth. "Bearing Witness: The Missionary Archives as Evidence of the Armenian Genocide." In *The Armenian Genocide: History, Politics, Ethics*, edited by Richard G. Hovannisian, 103–28. New York: St. Martin's Press, 1992.

Morgenthau, Henry. *Ambassador Morgenthau's Story*. Garden City, N.Y.: Doubleday, Page, 1918.

Nalbandian, Louise. *The Armenian Revolutionary Movement: The Development of Armenian Political Parties Through the Nineteenth Century*. Berkeley and Los Angeles: University of California Press, 1963.

Niepage, Martin. *The Horrors of Aleppo, Seen by a German Eye-Witness*. London: T. Fisher Unwin, 1917.

Nogales, Rafael de. *Four Years Beneath the Crescent*. New York: Charles Scribner's Sons, 1926.

Permanent Peoples' Tribunal. *A Crime of Silence: The Armenian Genocide*. Preface by Pierre Vidal-Naquet. London: Zed Books, 1985.

Reid, James J. "Total War, the Annihilation Ethic, and the Armenian Genocide, 1870–1918." In *The Armenian Genocide: History, Politics, Ethics*, edited by Richard G. Hovannisian, 21–52. New York: St. Martin's Press, 1992.

Smith, Roger W. "Human Destructiveness and Politics: The Twentieth Century as an Age of Genocide." In *Genocide and the Modern Age: Etiology and Case Studies of Mass Death*, edited by Isidor Walliman and Michael N. Doblowski. New York: Greenwood Press, 1987.

———. "Genocide and Denial: The Armenian Case and Its Implications." *Armenian Review* 42, no. 1 (Spring 1989): 1–38.

———. "The Armenian Genocide: Memory, Politics, and the Future." In *The Armenian Genocide: History, Politics, Ethics,* edited by Richard G. Hovannisian, 1–20. New York: St. Martin's Press, 1992.

Staub, Ervin. *The Roots of Evil: The Origins of Genocide and Other Group Violence.* Cambridge: Cambridge University Press, 1989.

Totten, Samuel. *First-Person Accounts of Genocidal Acts Committed in the Twentieth Century: An Annotated Bibliography.* New York: Greenwood Press, 1991.

Toynbee, Arnold. *Armenian Atrocities: The Murder of a Nation.* London: Hodder & Stoughton, 1915.

Ussher, Clarence D., and Grace H. Knapp. *An American Physician in Turkey: A Narrative of Adventures in Peace and in War.* Boston: Houghton Mifflin, 1917.

Villa, Susie Hoogasian and Mary Kilbourne Matossian. *Armenian Village Life Before 1914.* Detroit: Wayne State University Press, 1982.

Walker, Christopher J. *Armenia: The Survival of a Nation.* London: Croom Helm, 1980.

———. "British Sources on the Armenian Massacres, 1915–1916." In *A Crime of Silence: The Armenian Genocide.* Edited by the Permanent Peoples' Tribunal, 53–60. London: Zed Press, 1985.

Werfel, Franz. *The Forty Days of Musa Dagh.* New York: Viking Press, 1934.

Zaroukian, Antranik. *Men Without Childhood.* Translated by Elise Bayizian and Marzbed Margossian. New York: Ashod Press, 1985.

Index